22 JANUARY
- Karkare arranges for a lawyer for Madanlal in Delhi; leave

23 JANUARY
- Nathuram and Apte reach Bombay from Kanpur, via Jhansi.

24 JANUARY
- Nathuram and Apte check into Hotel Elphiston Annexe, Bombay; make a new plan; Nathuram decides to shoot Gandhi without anyone's help.

27 JANUARY
- Bombay: Nathuram and Apte take a flight to Delhi, under false names – D. Narain Rao and N. Vinayak Rao; Karkare decides to be with Nathuram and Apte in Delhi.
- From Delhi, Nathuram and Apte catch the Delhi-Bombay Express for Gwalior and meet Sadashiv Parchure, secretary of the Hindu Mahasabha, for a good dependable weapon.

28 JANUARY
- Parchure helps them get the weapon, the 9 mm Beretta.

29 JANUARY
- Nathuram and Apte return to Delhi; book a retiring-room at Old Delhi railway station.

30 JANUARY
- Nathuram, Apte and Karkare go to the woods behind the Birla Temple, Mandir Marg for target practice.
- 4.15 p.m.: Nathuram leaves for Birla House; Karkare and Apte leave minutes later.
- Birla House: At 5.10 p.m. Gandhi leaves room; walking briskly he reaches the prayer ground.
- Gandhi greets crowd; Nathuram folds his hands and says 'Namaste'; pushing aside one of the girls walking with Gandhi, he shoots the Mahatma; surrenders to the police; taken to Tughlak Road police station.

31 JANUARY
- Badge arrested in Poona, becomes approver.

2 FEBRUARY
- Apte and Karkare reach Bombay; stay at Sea Green Hotel (North).

5 FEBRUARY
- Gopal Godse arrested in Poona.

13 FEBRUARY
- Apte and Karkare arrested from Pyrke's Apollo Hotel, Bombay.

22 JUNE
- The trial commences in a Special Court at Red Fort, before Judge Atma Charan.

6 NOVEMBER
- Examination of the witnesses and recording of their evidence conclude.

10 FEBRUARY 1949
- Court pronounces its judgement: death sentence for Nathuram and Apte, life imprisonment for Karkare, Madanlal, Gopal, Shankar and Parchure; and pardon for Badge, the approver.

2 MAY
- The hearing begins in the appeal court of Justice G.D. Khosla, Justice Acchruram, and Justice Bhandari.

21 JUNE
- Appeal court confirms the judgement.

15 NOVEMBER 1949
- Nathuram Godse and Narayan Apte hanged till dead in Ambala prison.

Nathuram Vinayak Godse

OTHER LOTUS TITLES:

Amir Mir	*The True Face of Jehadis*
Bidyut Chakrabarty	*Mahatma Gandhi: A Biography*
Gyanendra Pandey and Yunas Samad	*Fault Lines of Nationhood*
HT Leadership Initiative	*India: The Next Global Superpower*
HT Leadership Initiative	*Building a Better Future*
HT Leadership Initiative	*The Peace Dividend: Progress for India and South Asia*
Humayun Khan and G Parthasarthy	*Diplomatic Divide*
Jawed Laid	*The Maverick Republic*
Khushwant Singh	*Train to Pakistan*
MJ Akbar	*The Shade of Sword*
MJ Akbar	*Riot after Riot*
MJ Akbar	*India: The Siege Within*
MJ Akbar	*Nehru: The Making of India*
Manoj Mitta & HS Phoolka	*When a Tree Shook Delhi: The 1984 Carnage and Its Aftermath*
Meghnad Desai and Aitzaz Ahsan	*Divided by Democracy*
Mushirul Hasan	*John Company to the Republic*
Mushirul Hasan	*India Partitioned. 2 Vols*
Nayantara Sahgal(ed)	*Before Freedom: Nehru's Letters to his Sisters*
Rohan Gunaratna	*Inside Al Qaeda: Global Network of Terror*
Sharmistha Gooptu and Boria Mazumdar (eds)	*Revisiting 1857: Myth, Memory, History*
Shashi Joshi	*The Last Durbar: A Dramatic Presentation of the Division of British India*
Sudarshan Bhutani	*A Clash of Political Cultures*
Sukeshi Kamra	*Bearing Witness: Partition, Independence, End of the Raj*
Thomas Weber	*Gandhi, Gandhism and the Gandhians*

FORTHCOMING TITLES:

Ajit Bhattacharjea	*Tragic Hero of Kashmir: Sheikh Mohammad Abdullah*
MB Naqvi	*Pakistan on the Edge*

ILLUSTRATED WITH RARE AND UNPUBLISHED DOCUMENTS AND PHOTOGRAPHS

THE MEN WHO KILLED GANDHI

Manohar Malgonkar

CONCEPT, RESEARCH & EDITING
Pramod Kapoor

LOTUS COLLECTION
ROLI BOOKS

Lotus Collection

Credits: Chirodeep Chaudhuri, Corbis, Deepak Rao, Delhi Police,
Getty Images, Hindustan Times Photo Archives, Magnum, Mrs Kilpady,
Mrs Himani Savarkar, National Archives of India, Nehru Memorial Library,
Romi Khosla, Shivay Bhandari

This edition published in 2008
The Lotus Collection
An imprint of Roli Books Pvt Ltd
M-75, G.K. II Market, New Delhi 110 048
Phones: ++91 (011) 2921 2271, 2921 2782
2921 0886, Fax: ++91 (011) 2921 7185
E-mail: roli@vsnl.com; Website: rolibooks.com

Also at
Varanasi, Agra, Jaipur, Mumbai, Bangalore, Chennai and the Netherlands

Cover design: Supriya Saran
Design: Naresh L Mondal
Production: Naresh Nigam, Kumar Raman

ISBN: 978-81-7436-617-7
Rs 395

Typeset in Fairfield LH Light by Roli Books Pvt Ltd.
Printed at Gopsons Papers Limited, NOIDA, India

AUTHOR'S NOTE TO THE FIRST EDITION

Throughout the period covered by this book – that is, from Lord Mountbatten's arrival as the Viceroy right up till the end of the Red Fort trial – I was living in New Delhi, only one bungalow away from Birla House where Gandhi was murdered. I can thus claim to have known the Delhi of those days as a citizen, an insider, and I also happen to be equally familiar with Poona (the place where the conspiracy was spawned), both as a city and as a state of mind.

Of the six men who were finally adjudged to have been implicated in the murder conspiracy, two were hanged. The other four – the approver Badge and the three who got life sentences, Karkare, Gopal and Madanlal – talked to me freely and at length. My ability to speak Marathi well was an immense advantage because two of them, Karkare and Badge, were at home only in that language.

All four gave me much information that they had never revealed beforehand. Gopal Godse and his wife Sindhu filled me in on details which could not have been known outside the Godse and Apte families. Gopal also kindly loaned me his personal papers among which were eight large volumes of printed records of the Red Fort trial which had been prepared for the High Court appeal. These volumes had been actually used by Nathuram Godse, the man who killed Gandhi, and were scribbled all over with his notes and comments.

The author wishes to thank Mr R.E. Hawkins – who, for many years, guided the affairs of the Indian branch of the Oxford University Press – for going through the manuscript of this book and suggesting many improvements.

Burbusa
28 April 1975

Manohar Malgonkar

A LOOK BACK IN GRATITUDE

The Men Who Killed Gandhi first came out in 1978, which means that it is now thirty years old. Then again this edition of it is the eleventh of its kind published in English with six in translations in other languages. Not many books do so well.

I began modestly enough a whole decade earlier. In the late 1960's I was well and truly launched as an author, a freelancer who made his living by the pen, and someone always on the lookout for stories to sell. At this time, the surviving members of the conspiracy to kill Mahatma Gandhi had served out their jail terms and were free to tell their stories. I thought I would find out from them why they had participated in the crime and what part they had played.

I could try to get my story published on the 20th Anniversary of the Mahatma's death.

I was lucky and things went off as I had planned. One of the most prestigious magazines of the times, *LIFE International*, agreed to publish my story and commissioned a well-known photographer, Jehangir Gazdar to visit the homes of the men in it and take photographs. It came out in the magazine's issue of February 1968. But by then I had realized that my story deserved a full book to itself. I broached the idea to my Agents in London and they agreed and found a publisher, Macmillan.

I was fully aware that what I was going to write was based on people's memories of events that had taken place more than twenty years earlier. Then again, those who had themselves participated in the murder plot were only going to tell me what they thought worth revealing. But my real problem was the lack of precision in their knowledge. Some details, which I regarded as vital, were beyond their comprehension. For instance, after close and painstaking questioning, all I had been able to find out about the murder weapon, was that it was a magazine pistol and not a revolver.

None of them knew.

That was when, almost as an answer to an unsaid prayer, a friend in Delhi who knew of my predicament, Mr Shankar Nayar of the Indian Police Service, sent me a copy of the Kapur Commission's published report.

In the mid 1960's, what with the revelations made by some of those involved in the crime, there were persistent allegations that several people in responsible positions in Mumbai had advance knowledge of the murder plot but had failed to report the information to the police. To determine the truth behind these allegations, the Government had appointed a one-man Commission headed by Justice K.L. Kapur. It was the report of the findings of this Commission that my friend had sent me.

Now I had a wide-ranging and penetrating report of the commission and all I had to do was to check out the authenticity of my own findings against those of Justice Kapur.

Sure I could still have written my book. But without the help of the Kapur Commission's report I doubt if *The Men Who Killed Gandhi* would have turned out to be so robust, or lived so long.

The book first came out when the country was in the grip of the 'Emergency', and books were subjected to a censorship of the utmost ruthlessness. This made it incumbent upon me to omit certain vital facts such as, for instance, Dr Bhimrao Ambedkar's secret assurance to Mr L.B. Bhopatkar, that his client, Mr V.D. Savarkar had been implicated as a murder-suspect on the flimsiest grounds. Then again, certain other pertinent details such as the 'doctering' of a confession by a magistrate whose duty it was only to record what was said only came out in later years.

With these and other bits and pieces fitted into their right places I feel confident that this book is now the complete single account of the plot to murder Mahatma Gandhi.

Barbusa
January 2008

Manohar Malgonkar

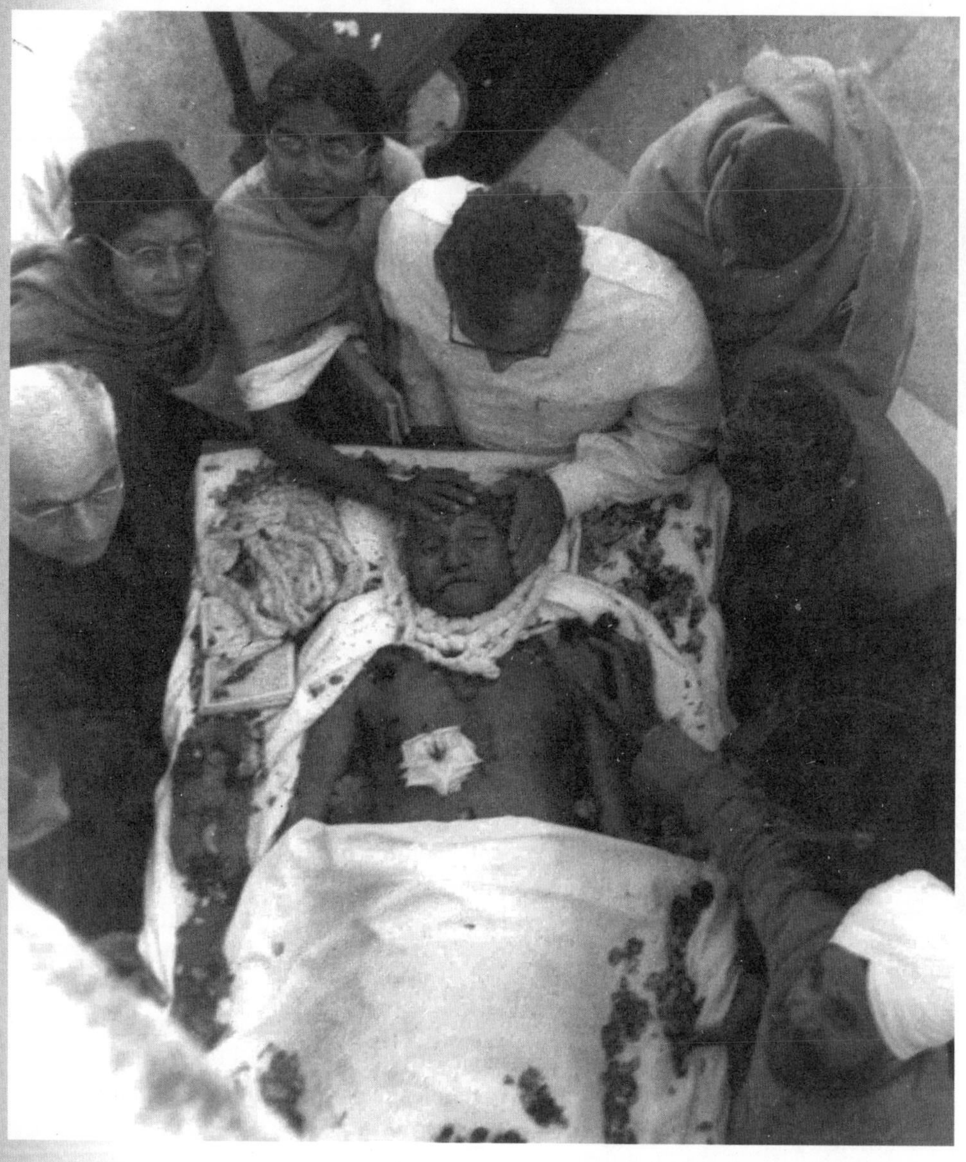

'I came alone in this world, I have walked alone in the valley of the shadow of death, and I shall quit alone when the time comes.'

—Mahatma Gandhi, 1869-1948

SKETCHING AN ASSASSINATION

In the early 1970s, when Manohar Malgonkar was researching this book, most of the protagonists involved with the story were alive. Their memories were fresh and their notes and papers intact. He was able to meet and talk to Gopal Godse, Vishnu Karkare, and Madanlal Pahwa, who had each served his life sentence, and approver Badge, who was pardoned. Each one of them gave his part of the story freely, perhaps spicing it with many more details that may not have figured in the trial.

Thirty-three years later, I took upon myself the task of putting faces, figures and graphics to his text when we decided to publish an illustrated edition of this incredibly well-researched book that reads like a thriller.

Unparalleled in recent history, this was no ordinary murder. This was an assassination that shook the world. Mahatma Gandhi, a messiah of peace, who fought and saw an end to an empire with his non-violence, was violently put to death by some of his own people. If he was to make a post-mortem statement, he would have done so with a sense of failure. After all he was unable to convert his very own people to his philosophy of peace and harmony.

On the other hand, Nathuram Godse and Narayan Apte, fiercely patriotic Hindu fanatics, who ironically held Gandhi in esteem, put their religious zeal above all and murdered a leader who, if he had survived, would have perhaps completely changed the shape of India's polity and society. The world may not have been as violent as it is today.

With all this and more, it was not an easy book to illustrate. The players had passed away. A majority of photographs had perished and a lot of documents had decayed beyond recognition. Whatever remained was difficult to locate.

However, through painstaking research, we found some very rare and unpublished photographs and documents. I would rate our discovery of trial pictures as the first among other equally important visuals. These images show Nathuram Godse, Narayan Apte, Gopal Godse and Vishnu Karkare, looking rather relaxed in the courtroom.

Group photographs of the killers with Veer Savarkar and Nathuram Godse's photo as martyr, hung proudly in Gopal Godse's daughter's home, make their own statements. Police investigator Haldipur was an amateur but an accomplished caricaturist. His daughter very generously gave us the sketches he made of Godse and Jaswant Singh, the investigating officer of Delhi Police.

At the National Archive we found the Bombay-Delhi air tickets used by Godse and Apte, and bills of the hotel used by Godse. There were many affidavits and other court records. I found the statement made by Nathuram Godse in his defence in the special court rather impressive. Despite having committed a heinous crime, he was convinced what he did was correct. These photographs and documents helped us greatly in attempting to re-construct the murder trial.

We were greatly helped by Nehru Memorial Library, *Hindustan Times*, Gopal Godse's family, and descendants of police inspector Mr Haldipur, Getty Images London, Corbis Worldwide, Justice G.D. Khosla's son Romi Khosla, Deepak Rao in Mumbai, and photographer Chirodeep Chaudhuri, who photographed the sites connected with the crime in Pune and Mumbai.

The personnel at the National Archive, the storehouse of Indian history, were helpful and facilitated the search with everything they had. They were helpless when it came to locating the material that was missing. This extremely important institution needs to be urgently rescued with manpower and money. If the government, the corporate sector and the citizens of India do not come forward soon, a great part of our documented past will soon become oral history and who knows, after a few hundred years, the assassination of Gandhi and many such defining moments may become part of Indian mythology.

On a more personal note I would like to thank my editorial colleague Neelam Narula, who worked tirelessly to collect material to ensure that this book comes out on the 60th anniversary of the Mahatma's assassination. Thanks also to my colleague Priya Kapoor, who persuaded Gopal Godse's daughter, Himani Savarkar, widow of Veer Savarkar's nephew, to share her memories and photographs. Thanks also to Supriya, Naresh Mondal, Kapil, Naresh Nigam and Raman for speedy and creative design and production.

Incidentally, this was the first manuscript I read as a publishing intern in 1975. That I was able to produce an illustrated edition thirty-three years later cements my belief that publishing is the most satisfying profession I could have pursued.

New Delhi
January 2008

PRAMOD KAPOOR

The world was stunned: Young women reading a newspaper among members of London's Indian and Pakistani population outside India House after hearing of the assassination of the Mahatma.

ONE

I shall see to it that
there is no bloodshed and riot.

— LORD LOUIS MOUNTBATTEN

Around six in the evening on 12 January 1948, Alan Campbell-Johnson, the Press Secretary to the Governor-General of India, Lord Louis Mountbatten, was returning to his bungalow in New Delhi's Government House estate after a hard game of squash when, passing the french windows of Mountbatten's study, he saw His Excellency in earnest talk with Mahatma Gandhi. Campbell-Johnson knew that the meeting had been arranged at short notice and at Gandhi's instance, but did not at the time attach any special importance to it.

The Raj had pulled out five months earlier in a ceremonial lowering of the Union Jack from public buildings, and India was now an independent country. But Mountbatten, who in his person represented Britannia's rule far more palpably than any flag could have done, had stayed on.

He had come to India almost straight from his glittering triumphs as the Supreme Allied Commander in South-East Asia, to be Britain's last Viceroy, charged by His Majesty's Government with the task of winding up the Empire as quickly and as cleanly as possible.

Lord Louis Mounbatten's success as the representative of the British Raj lay in persuading the Congress leaders to accept the inevitability of Partition. Gandhi, Nehru and Patel were the three stalwarts of Congress who consented to his formula, as Nehru expressed it, 'to the cutting off of the head to get rid of the headache'. **Facing page:** The last Viceroy of India, Lord Mountbatten stayed on after August 1947 as the designated Governor-General, on the request of the Indian leaders 'to see the interim phase through'. Like Gandhi, he too believed that peace in Delhi was the 'last hope of world peace'. Mahatma Gandhi is seen here with Mountbatten and his wife Edwina at the Governor-General's house in New Delhi.

Partition – also Jinnah's formula lead to the creation of a new country, Pakistan. Revered as 'Quaid-e-Azam', Jinnah insisted on a separate Muslim state and was sworn in as the first Governor-General of free Pakistan on 17 August 1947 in Karachi.

A noble birth, theatrical good looks, a personality nurtured on strong doses of the Royal Navy's 'Destroyer Spirit' and crackling with charisma, a reputation for efficiency combined with dynamic physical energy and abounding self-confidence – all these 'superman' attributes were now, at the age of forty-six, backed up by a row of resounding military victories. No man could have more fittingly been appointed to fill this epoch-making role or have assumed it with so overpowering a conviction of his fitness for it. Even as Viceroy, Mountbatten still remained very much the Supreme Commander, the man in absolute control, the final authority.

He was both a dazzling success and a colossal failure. The leaders of the Indian National Congress, notably Gandhi, Nehru and (to a lesser extent) Patel, immediately fell victim to his ebullience, sincerity and, above all, charm, which Nehru described as being 'dangerous'. But before the flinty obduracy of Mohammed Ali Jinnah, who headed the only other major political party, the Muslim League, it was Mountbatten who capitulated. Unable to get the two leading parties to agree upon a common formula for taking over power, he proceeded to impose on them his own formula, which was, virtually, Jinnah's formula: Partition. He agreed to the creation of a new country, Pakistan, by hacking away from India the areas which contained predominantly Muslim populations, and thus left for the Congress a truncated India that was mainly a Hindu land. As it happened, the Congress had never hankered for a purely, or even mainly, Hindu land. On the contrary, its declared creed and proud boast was that it was a wholly secular organization, embracing within its fold all the diverse religions of India: Sikhism, Buddhism, Jainism, Christianity and Zoroastrianism as well as Islam and Hinduism.

Mountbatten's success lay in persuading the Congress leaders to accept the inevitability of a truncated India to accommodate the intransigence of a minority group who wanted to secede, for something like this same offer had been made earlier by the British and had been flatly rejected by the Congress. It was as though the Congress now realized that, if Mountbatten could not make Jinnah give up his insistence on secession, no one else could, and that it was futile to hold out for an undivided India. So this time they consented, as Nehru expressed it, 'to the cutting off of the head to get rid of the headache'.

What was more, even though they had every right to feel dissatisfied with the verdict, they were so convinced about the uprightness of the judge that they continued to look upon him as a friend and well-wisher. As the talks progressed, a close friendship sprang up between Mountbatten and Nehru which continued to rile Jinnah even after he had got what he wanted, and provoked him to maintain towards Mountbatten a stance that varied between icy formality and insufferable waspishness. He seldom passed up an opportunity to demonstrate a cavalier disregard for Government House protocol, and once sent Mountbatten a letter so offensively worded that, upon reading it, Mountbatten's Chief of Staff, Lord Ismay, remarked to Campbell-Johnson: 'It was a letter which I would not take from my King, or send to a coolie.'

Gandhi, Nehru and Patel, on the other hand, even though they were on terms of easy familiarity with Mountbatten; were scrupulous about observing the proprieties. They would meticulously cede precedence to him on all official occasions and never went to see him without making an appointment in advance.

Having, perhaps to his own surprise, got the Congress leaders to swallow his plan, Mountbatten had proceeded to administer a further shock: he announced that he had advanced the expected date of transferring power into Indian (and Pakistani) hands from some time in June 1948 to 15 August 1947; from a whole year, to seventy-five days.

It was a shrewd move, calculated to throw the Congress leaders off balance and, at the same time, to bring home to those who so far had been no more than agitators for freedom the hard realities of the consequences of that freedom. They could no longer sit back and criticize whatever was done or not done by the British, but had to prepare for taking over the running of the government into their own hands.

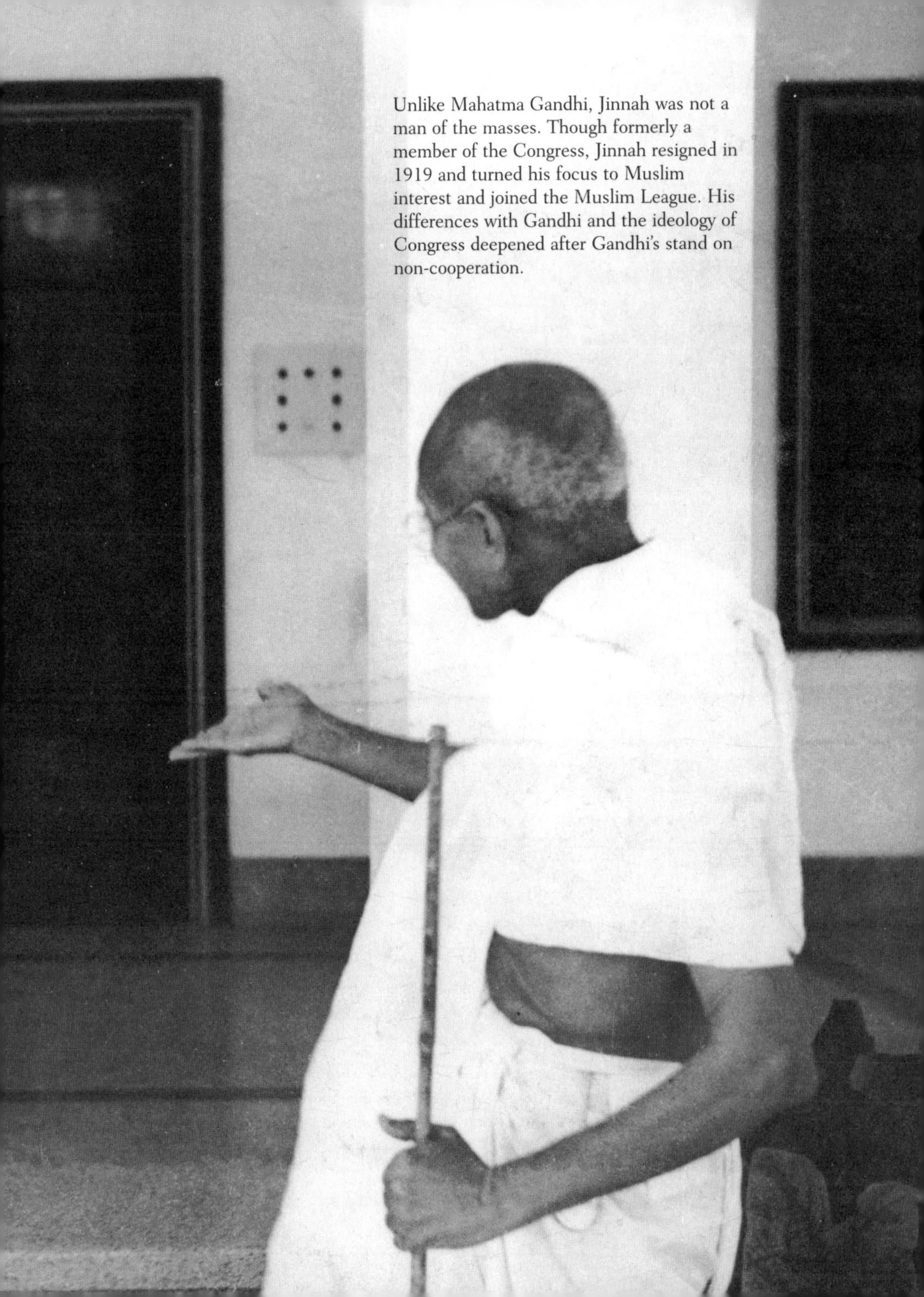

Unlike Mahatma Gandhi, Jinnah was not a man of the masses. Though formerly a member of the Congress, Jinnah resigned in 1919 and turned his focus to Muslim interest and joined the Muslim League. His differences with Gandhi and the ideology of Congress deepened after Gandhi's stand on non-cooperation.

A very controversial arrangement between the leaders and political parties lead to the complete breakdown of law and order. Riots and mass exodus of people resulted in millions of people losing their homes, their identity. Children and women were the

worst sufferers in these dark days before a new beginning. A child looks poignantly (on the facing page) at his surroundings – an abandoned ammunition dump – where the family took shelter after the communal riots broke out in Delhi.

Partition forced Hindus and Sikhs from Pakistan and Muslims from India to leave their homes over night. Innocent people took with them in this 'exchange of population', tales of unimaginable horrors – things that had happened to them or they had seen or heard. Reportedly around 14.5 million people crossed the border from either side.

Some of those who had been clamouring for years for the British to 'quit India' were now not so sure that the quitting should be got over quite so precipitately, particularly when they could see that freedom now not only meant that they would have to take over the business of the government which had, for the past century and a half, been run for them by others, but also meant facing the aftermath of their decision to accept Partition. One of the startled members of the Constituent Assembly asked His Excellency whether this desperate hurry to dismantle the framework that had held the country together, even if in subjugation, might not weaken the government's power to control the spreading violence in the country. This fear was altogether real for, while the proposal of dividing India between Muslims and the rest of the population was being discussed with the country's leaders, the northern and eastern parts of the country were experiencing a spate of race riots such as the Raj had never been called upon to tackle.

Mountbatten had grandly waved away such qualms. He told his questioner that, on this particular point, he could give him complete assurance: there would be no bloodshed. 'I speak as a soldier, and not a civilian,' His Excellency pointedly added.

How futile this pledge proved to be is a matter of history. There was bloodshed; carnage on a scale that even primitive conquerors had seldom indulged in. The Partition displaced vast populations, causing a two-way tide of migration that involved twelve million people. Hindus and Sikhs from Pakistan and Muslims from India poured out to become parts of refugee columns that resembled great rivers of humanity. They took with them tales of unimaginable horrors; things that had happened to themselves or they had seen and heard. Their sufferings generated a wave of hatred that left few among the subcontinent's millions untouched. Everyone talked of retaliation, of getting their own back.

In India, there were nearly forty million Muslims who had decided to stay on. In the towns and villages in which they lived, they became the natural, almost legitimate targets for the mob fury of the Hindus and the Sikhs.

And yet, at the time that Mountbatten gave his assurance that there would be no bloodshed, it was the one thing that the Congress leaders must have longed to hear. Brought up on a diet of non-violence, and unused to wielding authority, they were altogether overwhelmed by what was happening all around them. Clearly, this was a job for a professional; and if Mountbatten, speaking 'as a soldier', was telling them that there would be no bloodshed, why, they had nothing whatsoever to fear.

Provided, of course, that Mountbatten was on hand to make good his promise.

To ensure that he would remain, they had 'unconditionally' requested him to stay on in India even after the country became independent, 'to see the interim phase through'.

So Mountbatten had stayed on. He was now designated the Governor-General, but he was still what he had been as the Viceroy, the Supreme Commander, and, what was more, still regarded himself as a sort of umpire (or at least a balancing influence) between the two dominions; an outsider who would ensure fair play even though, to be sure, he no longer possessed any authority over Pakistan, since Jinnah had refused to have a British head of state even for the interim phase and had decided to make himself the Governor-General of Pakistan.

With Mountbatten had stayed on his personal friend and confidant, Alan Campbell-Johnson, who had been his Press Secretary since his South-East Asia Command days.

Working tirelessly to a specially printed calendar which, along with the date, also showed how many days were still left to the transfer of power, Mountbatten managed to wind up the Raj in the seventy-five days that he had allotted himself for the task. It was an altogether amazing performance, but the process could hardly have been messier, or more painful to those at the receiving end. Not that anyone can hold Mountbatten responsible for what happened, or accuse him of not having done everything in his power to prevent it. His miscalculation was that he had banked on the formidable Indian Army and the Air Force being at his disposal to put down communal disturbances. 'I shall adopt the severest methods,' he had declared. 'I will use tanks and aeroplanes to suppress anybody who wants to create trouble.' He had evidently lost sight of the fact that, with the partition of the country on a communal basis, it was inevitable that the armed forces of the country too would be shared between the two new nations on the same basis.

And this was what happened. Immediately upon Partition, the Muslim regiments of the army had gone over to Pakistan and so had all but a handful of the Muslim officers and other ranks in the remaining regiments and in the ancillary services; the Navy and Air Force followed much the same pattern. The Indian armed forces no longer comprised the efficient, integrated, well-disciplined fighting machine that the Supreme Allied Commander had been familiar with during the war. To be sure, there were in India a good many all-Hindu and all-Sikh regiments, and these were largely intact, but the communal hatred that Partition had unleashed had soon become so wide-ranging that military personnel too had become affected by it, or at least so it was generally believed. Hindu and Sikh soldiers could no longer be relied upon not to look the other way when the mobs on the rampage were their own brethren and the victims the Muslims, for had they not been fed on a daily diet of atrocities of the Pakistani soldiers against Hindu and Sikh refugees?

Nevertheless, there can be no doubt that, in the hands of a seasoned overall commander such as Mountbatten, even this eviscerated and supposedly partisan military force would have been perfectly adequate for the task of policing the country's main refugee routes and ensuring that any violent uprisings by the mobs were immediately put down.

Unfortunately, even this force was not long available to Mountbatten. Within two months of Britain's quitting, the two newly independent nations had embarked upon their first military conflict; most of the troops available to India had suddenly to be diverted to prevent Kashmir from being overrun by Pakistan. Virtually none could be spared for taking care of the communal violence that now raged like a prairie fire over most of northern and eastern India.

Under the Raj, Kashmir or, to give it its full name, Jammu and Kashmir was India's largest princely state, and it was ruled by a Maharaja. A landlocked principality of 84,000 square miles stretching from the parched plains of the Punjab to the icebound watershed of the Himalayas, it was as large as Great Britain. Because of its mountainous terrain, Kashmir had no railway line, and its principal outlets joining it with the outside world were three roads.

Whatever its geographical boundaries, the Kashmir the tourists know is confined to the Srinagar valley, which lies roughly in the centre of what, in British days, was the princely state of Jammu and Kashmir. This valley is all but inaccessible from three sides because of the formidable chains of mountains that guard it, and its open side faced the part of India that was to go to Pakistan. Both the major roads that joined the Srinagar valley with the outside world came from this side. The third road, which had begun life as a road privately owned by the maharaja to enable him to travel between his summer and winter capitals of Srinagar and Jammu without having to go through what was British territory, now gave the Srinagar valley direct access to India; but this was more like a makeshift mountain track than a proper road, and categorized in Ordnance Survey maps as being 'jeepable'. It had a treacherously crumbly surface; it was subjected to frequent landslides; it had dozens of terrifying blind bends with no room for oncoming vehicles and, in any case, for five months of the year, from December to April, it was completely cut off by a deep fall of snow. Admittedly, in 1947, work had already begun to transform this track into an all-weather road, but it was not till 1955 and after the Bannihal Tunnel which lies at an elevation of nearly 10,000 feet above sea-level was opened that it was completed.

Of Kashmir's population of 4.5 million, all but a million, or fully 77 per cent, were Muslims, the remainder being Hindus, Sikhs and Buddhists. The Maharaja was a Hindu.

In virtually all books written about the partition, the Maharaja of Kashmir, Lieutenant-General His Highness Sir Hari Singh, Indar Mahindar, Sipar-i-Saltanat, GCSI, GCIE and ADC to the King Emperor, is shown up as the man responsible for creating what has come to be known as 'The Kashmir problem', the principal culprit, the villain of the piece; in particular, the Indian press and political leaders have tended to outdo all others in maligning him. But, while from the point of view of Pakistan such criticism would be entirely justified it was difficult to see how India could have been served better by the maharaja. If anything, instead of denouncing Sir Hari Singh as a sinner, India has every reason to acclaim him as a benefactor.

Being a border state, Kashmir was, in theory, free to choose either dominion to merge itself in, and Mountbatten, the inflexibly-just outsider, had advised the maharaja to ascertain the will of the people and to act accordingly. This, since the population was overwhelmingly Muslim, was as good as telling him to join Pakistan. For a time the maharaja toyed with the idea of holding back from either dominion and continuing as an independent kingdom, an Asian Switzerland; but he was sternly warned by the Indian Government that it was 'not prepared to entertain the prospect of an independent Kashmir'. In the light of subsequent events, it seems difficult to believe that the Indian leaders were actually prepared to let Kashmir go over to Pakistan rather than remain as an independent state; but such, to all appearances, was the wisdom of the times.

Maharaja Sir Hari Singh, who was fifty-two years old and had spent most of those years in the pursuit of pleasure, looked what he was, a bumbling and ineffectual feudal lord – plump, soft, portly, indolent. Being a Hindu, his inclinations were heavily on the side of joining India, but he was shrewd enough to realize that the slightest hint on his part that he was about to do so would have provoked Pakistan into blocking off both of Kashmir's supply routes at a time when the road linking the Srinagar valley with India was altogether undependable. So Hari Singh did what he had habitually done when confronted with a crisis; he pretended that the crisis did not exist and carried on.

Jinnah fumed, and with good reason, but Nehru and the Indian leaders had no cause for complaint. They had as good as written off Kashmir and, indeed, had informed the maharaja that, if he were to accede to Pakistan, they would not take it amiss, Now it looked as though Kashmir, or a large part of it, was likely to fall into their laps. Neither Nehru nor Patel, nor even Savarkar, the firebrand chief of the Hindu Mahasabha, which was the one political organization in India which had stood firmly against the division of the country and had denounced the Congress for agreeing to it, could have written a neater scenario for manoeuvring Kashmir's accession to India.

If Jinnah had emulated Maharaja Hari Singh and done nothing, it is difficult to see how he could have lost Kashmir. But of late he had become a firm believer in what he called 'direct action'. If Gandhi's satyagraha was mass civil disobedience, Jinnah's direct action should be defined as mass violence, it had brought him results in the past and, indeed, had won him Pakistan. Jinnah now decided to employ these strong-arm methods against the Maharaja of Kashmir.

This time direct action turned out to be a costly blunder, for it provided India with valid grounds to send troops into Kashmir.

What Jinnah did was to seal off both the roads that led into Kashmir through Pakistani territory, and at the same time to unleash what were originally sought to be passed off as 'tribal raiders' to invade it. This barefaced aggression against his domain prompted the Maharaja to cry 'Foul!' and to run to India for military help to save his state from being plundered by tribal raiders.

Now it was India's turn to dither. For two whole days, Nehru and his cabinet colleagues dutifully sat and listened to Mountbatten who, true to his role of a moderator between the two dominions, harangued them about why it would be wrong to send troops into Kashmir. Incredible as it may seem, even the British Commander-in-Chief of India's Army, Sir Rob Lockhart, who, after all, was a servant of the Indian Government and thus could not give himself a supra-national role, supported Mountbatten's arguments on the grounds that such a step would be a grave military risk. But Nehru and Patel held firm and, finding them adamant, Mountbatten gave in, only stipulating that military help by India should be made conditional on the maharaja's formally acceding to India and on the clear understanding that the question of whether Kashmir belonged to India or to Pakistan should be ultimately decided by the will of the people of Kashmir, which would be ascertained as soon as law and order were restored.

While, in New Delhi, Nehru and his colleagues were resolutely fending off the arguments of their own Governor-General and Army Chief, the raiders were advancing rapidly over the main highway that led from Abbottabad, in Pakistan, into Kashmir. Within three days, they had captured Muzaffarabad and Domel and looted and burned the township of Uri. On 26 October they had reached Baramula, thirty-five miles from Srinagar.

Baramula was the sort of place where British colonels and their wives dreamed of settling down, because as likely as not that was where they had spent their honeymoons; a riverside town known for its mahseer fishing and houseboat living, for its strawberries and roses and dark shady walks, quiet, picturesque, unspoilt, it would have made the ideal setting for a period novel about the great days of the Raj.

On the morning of 26 October Baramula was all that. By the next evening, it was a smouldering ruin. Out of a population of 14,000, all but 3,000 had been massacred; the church, the convent, the mission hospital were burned down, the nuns publicly dishonoured, the patients in the hospital butchered where they lay. A British officer on leave was forced to witness his wife being raped before he too was hacked to pieces, and another man, a Muslim youth, was nailed to a cross in the town's main square.

On 26 October too, Sir Hari Singh announced that he had acceded to India, and there can be no doubt that, if only someone had explained to His Highness that India's response to his desperate call for help depended on this technicality, he would have done so much sooner.

The very next morning, Indian troops were airlifted into the Srinagar valley, and by the evening were in action against the raiders. It now turned out that the raiders were equipped with the latest in conventional infantry weapons, that they had been ferried right up to the borders of Kashmir in Pakistani military lorries, and that their mysterious leader, 'Jebel Tariq', was none other than one of the most highly rated Pakistani generals, Akbar

Khan.[1] If the Indian leaders had not allowed themselves to be held back by their own Governor-General and their Army Chief, their troops would have been in action two days earlier, and the invaders stopped somewhere beyond Uri. The rape of Baramula would certainly have been prevented.

Was it the fate of Baramula that shocked Mountbatten into the realization that what was at stake was not a fine point in political etiquette, but a bid for annexation by methods reminiscent of Ghengis Khan, 'a trick', as he angrily told Ian Stephens, the editor of *The Statesman,* to enable 'Jinnah to rid in triumph into Kashmir'? From being an aloof observer, he now became, if not a protagonist, at least someone who took a more sympathetic view of whatever Nehru and Patel had done. He told Ian Stephens that it was India's intervention that had saved Srinagar from the savagery of the raiders, including the massacre 'of a couple of hundred British residents'.

Lockhart's warnings against sending troops into Kashmir soon proved to have been so grossly exaggerated that they gave rise to rumours that he might have been deliberatedly misleading his political superiors to give Jinnah a free hand in Kashmir, and even that he must have had advance knowledge of Pakistan's plans to send raiders into Kashmir, which knowledge he had kept to himself. Be that as it may, the fact remains that, though Lockhart had barely completed four months of his four-year contract to serve India, the Indian Government found it expedient to terminate his services.

So the Kashmir war began; the Kashmir problem was born. It was a lusty child, and still survives.

If Sir Hari Singh had acted promptly on Mountbatten's advice, certainly there would have been no Kashmir problem. But, as far as India was concerned, there would have been no Kashmir either. And there can be no doubt whatsoever about what the Indian public would rather have, no matter what Nehru and others have found it necessary to say in their public pronouncements. Kashmir, for better or worse, was Hari Singh's gift to India.

The Kashmir war placed Mountbatten in an invidious position. Being an outsider who was making a sincere effort to maintain an even-handed stance between the two dominions, he could not take on the direction of the war on India's behalf, even though it is difficult to imagine anyone else being better fitted to do so. His principal contribution to resolving the 'imbroglio', as he called it, was to prevent it from developing into a full-scale war between India and Pakistan. In the prevailing atmosphere of racial hatred, this itself was an amazing feat; in the light of subsequent history, it can be seen only as a miracle.

But Mountbatten's immediate worry at the time was that the war had suddenly deprived him of the troops with which he had so confidently expected to put down the communal violence in the country. Accustomed to having at his beck and call a large number of crack combat units, he was now reduced to looking on helplessly at the charts and graphs of the refugee movements and the spread of riots in the 'map room' which he had set up in a wing of Government House. The picture they presented was grim and getting worse every day.

Not that, in the capital itself, one needed artificial aids to get an idea of the dimensions of the problem. In the six months that had elapsed since the announcement of the 'Mountbatten Plan', the city's population of a little under a million had more than doubled with the influx of refugees. But mere numbers don't tell the full story, because the refugees were not ordinary people. They were angry, deeply embittered, even desperate people; men and women caught up like insects in a tide and who had been exposed to the most barbaric atrocities committed by man against man. Here is what one of them, a young man called Madanlal Pahwa, who was later sentenced to imprisonment for life for his part in the murder of Mahatma Gandhi, stated on oath: 'We walked night and day. There were men and women of all ages and all conditions. Many could not stand the strain. They – mostly women and children – were left on the road.'

Madanlal reached a place called Fazilka, in Indian territory, and discovered that another refugee column in which his father and other relatives had set out had fared much worse. They had been attacked by Muslim mobs: 'Only 40 or 50 had survived out of 400 or 500 and even these were in hospitals. My aunt had been killed, more than a hundred girls abducted, and my father rescued from a heap of the dead.'

While in Fazilka, Madanlal saw other refugee columns coming in; one of them he says was 'forty miles long', and in another marched 'five hundred women who had been stripped naked... I saw women with their breasts, noses, ears and cheeks cut... one of them told me how her child was roasted and she was asked to partake of the same... another was ravished in the presence of her husband who was kept tied to a tree.'

These were the experiences of one man. There were, at a rough estimate, seven million refugees in India, and of these a million were concentrated in Delhi. Here they discovered that their miseries were far from over. They were herded like cattle in barbed-wire enclosures, and even these enclosures were so overcrowded that those who came after them had been ordered to move on to other parts of India. Above all, an incredible rumour was doing the rounds that there was some kind of a move afoot to compel them to go back to Pakistan to inhabit their old homes and to take up their vocations as though nothing had happened.

The rumour had a basis in fact. It was Gandhi, they learned, who was trying to pressurize the government to send the refugees back, so that the Muslims who had left India could return and live in peace among the Hindus. Gandhi, the Mahatma, saviour, freedom fighter, saint, the man who could do no wrong; to the refugees he now stood revealed as a Hindu-hater, a Muslim-lover, an enemy.

At first they merely cursed him and the other sheep-like leaders of India who listened to his crazy counsels. Then, as they began to wander the streets of Delhi in search of food and shelter, they were horrified to see that, in this ancient city that was their country's proud capital, a large number of Muslims lived as though by right; there were influential Muslims in the government, in the services, in the professions, in trade; there were even compact, all-Muslim localities right in the heart of the city. And Gandhi

Delhi received the highest number of refugees for a single city. Housed in various locations such as the Old Fort, Red Fort and military barracks in Kingsway, life in the city was difficult. Though the fire of discontent was spreading, the Muslim population in Delhi was quite safe, as Gandhi had also moved to Delhi during this period to champion the cause of the Muslims. Seen here is Gandhi in the refugee camp at the Old Fort pacifying the refugees.

himself had come to camp in the city for the avowed purpose of championing the cause of the Muslims. He was exhorting the Muslims to remain where they were, and he was prevailing upon Nehru and Patel to disarm the Hindus and Sikhs so that the Muslims might live without fear.

All this, to the refugees who had flocked into Delhi, represented a form of perversity, a manifestation of a total lack of guts on the part of their leaders. This was not how Pakistan had treated *them*!

They fell upon the Muslims with a rage that knew no bounds, and it did not make any difference to them that the Muslims of India had done them no harm. In their eyes, they were all enemies, though their only crime was that they had been born Muslims. The Hindu and Sikh residents of Delhi now joined their brethren from Pakistan in this war of retaliation. They formed themselves into bands, collected whatever weapons that came into their hands and began to attack the Muslims. They drove them out and took over their houses; they then went and occupied the mosques and the numerous Muslim shrines dotted all over Delhi. This was one way of making sure of having a roof over their heads for the hard winter months.

Delhi was thus, if anything, a nodal point of the communal violence rather than just a representative sample. There had been a massacre at Delhi's Willingdon airport, barely a mile away from town; and right within the compound of Government House, in Mountbatten's own backyard as it were, the Muslim servants had been attacked by an infuriated mob of Hindus and Sikhs.

Mountbatten was alarmed. 'If we go down in Delhi,' he told one of his colleagues, 'we are finished.'

Gandhi, too, had said something on the same lines to one of his callers. 'If Delhi goes, India goes, and with that goes the last hope of world peace.'

Both had convinced themselves that they would win or lose the battle against violence in Delhi itself.

With India's Army and Air Force totally committed to the Kashmir war, Mountbatten could see that his government had little hope of suppressing the riots by force. He must have voiced these fears to Nehru; but did he also mention them to Gandhi and, in particular, did he suggest to Gandhi that he should try to do something on his own to stop the riots?

According to Mr J.N. Sahni, a prominent New Delhi journalist who, in those days, kept himself fairly close to where the action was: 'Mountbatten was creating pressure on both Mahatma Gandhi and Pandit Nehru that they should do something spectacular... [to make it safe]... for Mohammedans to stay in India... a great gesture for Pakistan to act in the same way.'

If Mountbatten did 'create pressure' on Gandhi, he was only showing that he had, in the few months that he had spent in the country, acquired a better grasp of the 'mind' of India than any other British head of state before him. He had assessed the amazing power that Gandhi wielded over the masses. And, even if what he was asking Gandhi to do amounted to a miracle, he was being altogether practical, for Gandhi had done just that, in Calcutta as well as East Bengal – performed a miracle. He had halted a similar wave of communal violence by undertaking a moral crusade to bring about a change of heart in the embattled communities. There was no reason why he should not try out his methods in Delhi as well.

Whether at Mountbatten's urging or on his own,[2] that evening in January when Gandhi had gone to see Mountbatten he had made his decision. At his daily prayer meeting which he had concluded only minutes earlier, he had announced his intention to go on an indefinite fast.

In the course of a long and rambling address that was something between a fireside chat and a multi-religious sermon, interspersed with a public reading and answering some of his private mail, Gandhi had told his audience: There is a fast which a votary of non-violence sometimes feels impelled to undertake by way of protest against the wrongs done by society ... and this he does when he has no other remedy left... [My fast] will end when and if I am satisfied that there is a reunion of hearts of all communities.'

To Gandhi, a fast was the last weapon in his armoury. Whether it would bring about results, remained to be seen. But one thing was certain. If Gandhi's fast could not bring about 'a reunion of hearts of all communities', nothing else could.

Gandhi belonged to the *bania,* or trader caste, a people known for their shrewd business sense; and to try to make one weapon, even a last weapon, do the work of two was sound business sense.

One of the consequences of Partition was that the movable property left behind by the Raj had to be divided between the successor dominions in an agreed proportion. Everything from ships, aeroplanes, guns (and ammunition), railway engines and wagons, down to office furniture and even office files was to be shared out. And, of course, this included money too. The cash possessed by undivided India, which was held in the Reserve Bank of India, amounted to Rs 220 crores and it was agreed that a quarter of this amount or Rs 55 crores, should be paid to Pakistan.

As with the division of other spoils, there had been a good deal of hard wrangling over the sharing of these 'cash balances' as they were called, and it was not till the end of November 1947, and thus more than two months after Pakistan had already come into existence, that agreement was finally reached.

By this time the Kashmir war had been going for a full month, and it had become known to the Indian Government that the tribal raiders had been aided and abetted by Pakistan and were led by a Sandhurst-trained General of the Pakistani Army. And, even though Pakistan publicly disclaimed all responsibility for whatever the raiders were doing, in private conversation Jinnah had all but admitted to Mountbatten that the raiders were his own creatures. At one of their periodic meetings, Mountbatten had remarked to Jinnah that the Indian Army had so strengthened its position in the Kashmir valley that the raiders stood no chance of capturing Srinagar. Upon this Jinnah had coolly suggested that they should proceed to normalize the situation by both sides withdrawing simultaneously. And when Mountbatten had expressed doubts that the raiders could be pulled back by a mere order Jinnah had blandly assured him: 'If you do this, I will call the whole thing off.'

Knowing all this, Nehru felt that to hand over Rs 55 crores to Pakistan was to provide her with 'sinews of war', and his deputy premier, Patel, was in complete agreement with him. On 28 November, Patel had bluntly told the Pakistani representative that 'India would never agree to any payment until the Kashmir affair was settled'.

And no Indian would have quarrelled with this view. You did not hand out large sums of money to a country at war with you. But Mountbatten did not see it in that light. 'A step both unwise and unstatesmanlike,' he told Campbell-Johnson. He must have held forth about this to Gandhi who not only agreed with him but found the whole thing morally wrong. 'Like an elder brother hanging on to the rightful share of the patrimony of the younger,' was the way he saw it. How could the Indian Government, which had come into being amidst protestations of so many pious declaration stoop to such outright skullduggery?

Gandhi had heard what he wanted to hear. He told Mountbatten that he would 'take up the matter with Nehru and Patel', and also reassured him that he would make it clear to them that it was he who had sought Mountbatten's views. As Gandhi rose to go, Mountbatten told him that his decision to go on a fast was a 'brave move' and that he hoped it would create the new spirit that was so badly needed.

And with that Gandhi left, 'to give effect to his great decision'.

It had worked before; there was a good chance that it might produce results this time too.

In 1921, when the Prince of Wales (the future Duke of Windsor) had come on his official tour of India, Gandhi had called upon the public to observe *hartals* wherever he went. A *hartal* is a peaceful protest; it involves the closing of shops and the people remaining indoors so that the streets should present a deserted appearance, and indeed it is looked upon by everyone almost as a holiday. But in the very first place that the Prince had come to Bombay, the *hartal* had gone out of control. Mobs had gathered and waved black flags and shouted slogans, and the severity with which the police dispersed them had made them go berserk. In the ensuing firing, fifty people were killed and several hundreds injured, and there were signs that the disturbances would spread to other parts of India.

Gandhi was shocked. To restore peace, he had gone on an indefinite fast. Within five days, the riots had subsided.

One of the consequences of the Partition was the division of moveable property left behind by the Raj – from ships, aeroplanes, to office furniture and files, and even the cash from Reserve Bank – everything was to be shared. Seen here is a railway official meticulously checking the priority luggage carried on the special train to Pakistan.

Three years later, he had undertaken a fast again. But this time it was what he called a 'penitential' fast, with no conditions attached; and it was for a fixed period, twenty-one days. He was punishing himself for the sins of his people. There had been bloody Hindu-Muslim conflict in a distant town called Kohat in the North-Western Frontier Province which had incensed both communities all over India, and it was feared that the riots would spread to other places. Gandhi's fast had an instant sobering effect on both communities, and, at least for the time being, they were held in check.

Since then there had been other fasts, for other purposes – one in 1932 to protest against the principle of separate electorates that the British had come out with, under which what were then known as the Depressed Classes or the Untouchables would elect their own representatives to the legislative bodies in the country. This, Gandhi was convinced, would only succeed in driving the Untouchables even further away from caste Hindus and nullify his lifelong struggle to unite the community. This one, too, was to be a fast unto death unless the principle of separate electorates was abandoned. Within five days – again that magic number – the leader of the Depressed Classes, Dr Bhimrao Ambedkar, had agreed to a compromise solution which Gandhi found satisfactory. Separate electorates were given up.

And yet again in 1943, as a gesture of self-chastisement against the nationwide uprising that had followed the police and military excesses with which the Raj had put down his 'Quit India' movement. 'The disturbances were crushed with all the weight of the Government,' Mr Churchill had gloated. Gandhi's answer was to go on a fast; but this time too, it was for a definite period, twenty-one days. Gandhi was then in his seventy-fifth year. Miraculously he survived the ordeal.

The last occasion on which Gandhi had gone on a fast had been only three months earlier, on 1 September. He was in Calcutta then, where again the majority community – this time the Hindus – had gone berserk. Mr C. Rajagopalachari, the Governor of Bengal, had tried to talk him out of it, and when Gandhi had come out with one of his stock explanations about the promptings of his inner voice had snapped: 'If you put yourself in God's hands, why do you add lime juice to the water you allow yourself?'

'You're quite right,' Gandhi had answered. 'Lime juice is a weakness. I shall not even take lime juice.'

That time, the fast had achieved its purpose within seventy-three hours.

All in all, this ultimate weapon in his armoury had served Gandhi well. But would it work now, in the face of the seething anger of the refugees and their supporters? They had seen thousands of men and women die. What was Gandhi's life to them? They wanted revenge, 'Blood to wipe out blood with,' as they yelled in the streets of Delhi. They did not want peace, and Gandhi himself was acutely aware of this. 'We are bidding fair to say good-bye to non-violence,' he told his secretary Pyarelal at about this time.

The truth was that Gandhi's non-violence had lost out to violence; no one else believed in his 'ahimsa' any longer, inside or outside the Congress. Whatever its force in normal times, these were not normal times; and to censure the refugees for having fled from Pakistan and to exhort them to go back was to many a form of perversity if not madness; or the action of a saint bent on martyring his flock in a grand gesture of idealism.

'There was a time when India listened to me; today I am a back number,' Gandhi had complained a few weeks earlier. Now, by going on a fast, he was testing out the strength of his enfeebled arm. His fast was non-violence's last-ditch stand.

It was a heroic gesture. Gandhi was in his seventy-ninth year. How could he hope to survive? And would not his death introduce a new and explosive element into a situation that was already clearly out of hand?

Anyone else might have preferred to stay put in Delhi and see the crisis through; but not Mountbatten. True to his reputation for coolness under fire, he did not cancel a visit to the princely state of Bikaner which had been planned many weeks earlier. He went off on schedule, to shoot sandgrouse with the maharaja and to talk about the future of his state. The only concession to the crisis – or to the mood of fasting – was that the state banquet arranged by the Maharaja in the Governor-General's honour was cancelled.

DELHI EDITION

The Hindus[tan Times]

LARGEST CIRCULATION IN NORTHERN,

VOL. XXV NO. 1 — NEW DELHI: THURS[DAY]

NO PAYMENT TO PAKISTAN

Supply Of Military Stores Stopped

INDIA AGAINST IMPLEMENTATION OF FINANCIAL SETTLEMENT

DEMAND TO GIVE UP KASHMIR ADVENTURE

(By Our Special Representative)

NEW DELHI, Wednesday.—It is gathered [th]at Pakistan has been informed by the Govern[m]ent of India that implementation of the recent [f]inancial settlement being contingent on the con[t]inuance of cordial relations between the two [St]ates it is not possible for India to supply the [ca]sh and military stores which may only be used [in] the war in Kashmir against her. The supply [of] these will be resumed after Pakistan has given [up] its Kashmir adventure.

It is said that, following this decision of the [Go]vernment of India, Pakistan is trying to raise [fu]nds by pledging its securities with the Reserve [B]ank of India. This method of raising money [ha]s its limitations and no doubt the Reserve Bank [an]d the Government of India authorities will [w]atch developments.

[R]aiders Withdraw [I]n Jhangar Area

[In]dian Army patrols encounter-

"British Gurkhas"

At midnight on December 31, units of Gurkha troops were for the first time in history being transferred for service with the

REACTION IN KARACHI

Pakistan Wants All Issues To Go To U.N.O.

KARACHI, Dec. 31.—It is learnt that the Government of Pakistan welcomes the reported decision of the India Government to raise the Kashmir issue before the Security Council. But it is stated that Pakistan will insist that all outstanding points in dispute between the two Dominions should be referred to U.N.O. and not merely the question of Kashmir.

In political circles it was pointed out here today that the action of the Government of India towards Junagadh State, which had acceded to Pakistan, must have become the subject of an impartial international verdict, as also the accession of Kapurthala to the Indian Union, without reference to the wishes of the Muslim majority.

It is argued that the Government of India has failed to stop what is described as the wholesale slaughter and savagery perpetrated on the Muslims of Kashmir by the Sikhs and Dogras in spite of the fact that the India Government claims Kashmir as part of its territory.

These circles also ask why the Indian Government, if it had a strong case in Kashmir, could not first refer the issue to U.N.O. before its armed intervention. They point out that the allegations of Pakistan's active assistance to raiders have already been categorically denied by the Pakistan Government.

Pakistan Move To Open Second Front

EAST BENGAL GUERILLAS BEING ENCOURAGED

CALCUTTA, Dec. 31.—Guerilla activities by supporters of the Pakistani movement for entering the Assam border via Tripura and Sylhet portion of Assam and Garo Hills are being carried on for the last few days, according to reports received at Gauhati, writes the *Hindusthan Standard* correspondent from Gauhati.

It is stated that satellites of Mr Jinnah are putting pressure on the East Bengal Premier, Khwaja Nazimuddin, to give facility to the penetrators into Assam, but Mr Nazimuddin is reported to be resisting such pressure on the ground that it would

Philippine[s] ... By Seven

(MANILA, Dec ... earthquake com... "Christmas (Typ... Peninsula, near ... has laid waste ... devastated the ... the Philippines. ... layed reports re... day.

Hospitals, co... docks and hous... port in the Phili... molished.

The 5,000-t... steamship "Tigre... to the beach n... later reached he...

Terror reigne... Bicol provinces ... and people soug... churches.

An additional ... ter was a fire o... origin" which ra... Tacloban, capital... —Reuter.

Foreign ... Confe[rence]

U.S.A. RESPO[NSIBLE FOR] FAILURE, SA[YS MOLOTOV]

MOSCOW, Dec ... Soviet Foreign Mi[nister] ... Pressmen that the ... ence of Foreign M[inisters] ... cause the United S[tates] ... of dictation which ... evitable rebuff from ...

The United Sta[tes] ... toration of comple[te] ... and the re-establi[shment] ... unity conditional ... the American plan ... Europe," he said ... tions by *Pravda* ... pondents.

The time had n... attention of the ... Ministers should ... problem of the p... Germany in the W... in the East.

The United Stat[es] ... ed the most stu... this and "no longe[r] ... ate the solution of ... London conferenc[e] ... tain and France ar... road."

M Molotov said ... the London talk... were untrue. Pr... co-ordinating th... Governments in ... —but this wa... "since the Ameri[cans] ... riedly undertook t... work of the Conf...

Regd. No. E.P. 18

...an Times

...-WESTERN AND CENTRAL INDIA

...UARY 1, 1948. PRICE TWO ANN...

Sheikh Abdulla, Mr V. V. Giri, Indian High Commissioner in Ceylon and Mr Senanayake, Ceylonese Prime Minister, at a buffet dinner given by Pandit Nehru on Monday. On Sheikh Abdulla's left is Mr R. T. Chari, First Secretary to the Indian High Commissioner in Ceylon. (See also back page.)

FIERCE FIGHTING WEST OF MUKDEN

GOVT. BOMBERS POUNDING RED CONCENTRATIONS

NANKING, Dec. 31.—Heavy bombers of the Chinese Government have been thrown into incessant action against Communist troops attacking Mukden, the largest city in Manchuria, reports reaching here said today.

More than 100,000 Communist troops were today lining the banks of the Liao River, north-west of Mukden, ready for attack. Fresh reinforcements were sent up by both sides as furious fighting raged west of the city.

In North China, Government troops

The division of all property also included the sharing of cash possessed by undivided India. Though it was agreed that out of Rs 220 crores, a quarter of this amount, i.e. Rs 55 crores would be paid to Pakistan, Nehru in the face of the ensuing Kashmir problem felt that to hand over the money to Pakistan would be providing her with 'sinews of war'.

NO. 11. VOL. CX. BOMBAY: TUESDAY, JA

MAHATMA GANDHI STA

SURPRISING DELHI ANNOUNCEMENT

Move To Bring About Hindu-Muslim Unity

ORDEAL FOR "INDETERMINATE PERIOD"

NEW DELHI, Jan. 12.

MAHATMA Gandhi told his prayer meeting this evening that he was undertaking a fast from tomorrow for an indeterminate period to bring about Hindu-Muslim unity.

"One fasts for the sake of health under laws governing health or fasts as a penance for a wrong done and felt as such," said Mahatma Gandhi, announcing his decision.

"In these fasts," he added, "the fasting one need not believe in 'ahimsa'. There is, however, a fast which a votary of non-violence sometimes feels impelled to undertake by way of protest against some wrong done by society, and this he does when he, as a votary of 'ahimsa', has no other remedy left. Such an occasion has come my way."

Proceeding, he observed: "When on September 9, I returned to Delhi from Calcutta it was to proceed to West Punjab. But that was not to be. Gay Delhi looked a city of the dead. As I alighted from the train I observed gloom on every face I saw.

"Even the Sardar, whom humour and the joy that humour gives never desert, was no exception this time. The cause of it I did not know.

"He was on the platform to receive me. He lost no time in giving me the sad news of the disturbances that had taken place in the metropolis of the Union. At once I saw that I had to be in Delhi and do or die. There is apparent calm brought by prompt military and police action. But there is storm within the breast. It may burst forth any day.

"This I count as no fulfilment of the vow to 'do', which alone can

Mahatma Gandhi

Indian Army's Gallantry

KASHMIR ACTION

Defence Minister's Tribute

NEW DELHI, January 12.

"I wish to express the admiration of the Prime Minister, of myself and of our colleagues in the Government of India, for the work of the troops and Air Force operating under your command in Kashmir," says Sardar Baldev Singh, Defence Minister, Government of India, in the course of a special message to Major-General Kalwant Singh, General Officer Commanding, Jammu and Kashmir Force, and Air Commodore Mehr Singh, Air Officer Commanding No. One Operational Group, R.I.A.F., respectively.

The message reads: "Moved out at short notice, and fighting against considerable odds, all units have

Mahatma's Friends Express Anxiety

"NOT IN BEST OF HEALTH"

NEW DELHI, January 12.

Mahatma Gandhi's announcement to go on a fast for an indefinite period came as a complete surprise to his colleagues and the members of the Government

SHI

The 2,327-

REFUGE IN

Six-Ho P

LAHO

Nearly 1C killed and m ed as a res clash betwee cort of a n train coming

ING FAST FROM TODAY

ROUND ON GOODWIN SANDS

teamer, "S llvia Onorato," hard aground on the Goodwin Sands, off the South-east ngland. The vessel was bound for Rotterdam with a cargo of lead ore.

Construction Of Buildings

BOMBAY CONTROL

New Ordinance Issued

An Ordinance for the control of erection and re-erection of buildings in the Bombay province has been issued by the Government of Bombay with a view to conserving materials for small tenement housing, says the Director of Publicity, Bombay.

The obligation to obtain a permit is confined to structures involving the use of essential building materials. All permits for the continuation of works in progress must be obtained before January 31. Contravention of the Ordinance is punishable with imprisonment extending to three months or with fine which may extend to Rs. 1,000 or with both.

Criticism has often been made that while there is an acute shortage of building materials, they are being allowed to be frittered away on unessential buildings like cinemas and theatres. The Government of Bombay have not issued or permitted the issue of any building material for structures of this kind.

ORTS

t In

ry 12.
s were
wound-
six-hour
rasi es-
refugee
nu and

U. S. Aid To Foreign Countries To Check Totalitarian Rule

PRESIDENT'S PROPOSALS IN BUDGET ESTIMATES

WASHINGTON, January 12.

PRESIDENT Truman today uttered a warning that the United States would have to rearm "if Europe should succumb to totalitarian rule," when he presented Congress with a 139,700 million-dollar budget for the fiscal year 1948-49.

The non-payment of the cash balances to Pakistan was one of the reasons Gandhi decided to undertake a fast. Covered extensively by the national media, this fast was also for the unity of Hindus and Muslims.

LARGEST NET SALES of any Daily Newspaper Printed in Northern, Sou

The Times

NO. 14, VOL. CX. BOMBAY: FRIDAY, J

INDIA'S GESTURE TO PAKISTAN

Immediate Payment Of Cash Balances

BID TO REMOVE CAUSE OF SUSPICION

NEW DELHI, January 15.

THE Government of India have decided to implement immediately the financial agreement with Pakistan in regard to the cash balances with a view to removing "the one cause of suspicion and friction" between Pakistan and India.

"This decision," says a "communique" issued by the Prime Minister's Secretariat late tonight, "is the Government's contribution, to the best of their ability, to the non-violent and noble effort made by Gandhiji, in accordance with the glorious traditions of this great country, for peace and goodwill."

The Prime Minister of India, Pandit Jawaharlal Nehru, in a separate statement said: "We have come to this decision in the hope that this gesture, in accord with India's high ideals and Gandhiji's noble standards will convince the world of our earnest desire for peace and goodwill.

"We earnestly trust also that this will go a long way towards producing a situation which will induce Gandhiji to break his fast. That fast, of course, had nothing to do with this particular matter, and we have thought of it because of our desire to help in every way in easing the present tension.

The Government communique reads:

"The Government of India have fully clarified their position in regard to the financial settlement arrived at between them and the Government of Pakistan.

They have declared that they abide by that settlement, but that the implementation of it, in regard to the cash balances, must be considered as a part of an over-all settlement of outstanding questions in issue between India and Pakistan.

They regret that the Finance Minister of the Pakistan Government should have advanced arguments which are unsupported by

tion to end his fast and add still further to his unparalleled services to India.

The Government have decided to implement immediately the financial agreement with Pakistan in regard to the cash balances. The amount due to Pakistan on the basis of this agreement, i.e., Rs. 55 crores, minus the expenditure incurred by the Government of India since August 15 on Pakistan account, will therefore be paid to the Government of Pakistan.

This decision is the Government's contribution to the best of their ability, to the non-violent and noble effort made by Gandhiji, in accordance with the glorious traditions of this great country, for peace and goodwill.

PANDIT NEHRU EXPLAINS

The Prime Minister in his state-

Mahatma Weak

LOSS OF WEIGHT

Objects Of Fast Reiterated

NEW DELHI, January 15.

On the third day of his fast, Mahatma Gandhi is growing weak and was unable to be present at the prayer meeting. However, a large gathering was present and the prayers were held as usual.

In a message which was read out to the congregation, Mahatma Gandhi repudiated the suggestions of any difference of opinion between himself and Sardar Vallabhbhai Patel and emphasised that the Sardar was a friend of the Muslims. Mahatma Gandhi also said that the fast had nothing to do with the Kashmir dispute and the U. N. Security Council meeting. The fast was undertaken for the objects he had already set out and for self-purification.

People who had come to the prayer were allowed to see Mahatma Gandhi. They filed past in single and paid their obeisance to the Mahatma who was seated on a cot.

VISITORS TO MAHATMA

The Congress President Dr. Rajendra Prasad, the Burmese Ambassador U Win, Mr. B. G. Kher, Premier of Bombay, Mr. Shankerrao Deo, Acharya Jugal Kishore, Mr. Khurshed Ahmed Khan, Chief Commissioner of Delhi, Mr. V. T. Krishnamachari, Dewan of Jaipur and Dr. Syud Hossain saw Mahatma Gandhi this evening.

A bulletin issued at 4-30 p.m. today by Dr. B. C. Roy, Dr. M. D. D. Gilder, Dr. Jivraj Mehta and Dr. (Miss) Sushila Nayyar, says;

"Today is the third day of Gandhiji's fast. He is losing weight. The weakness has considerably increased. He had to be carried out of the bathroom in an arm-chair this morning. His voice is feeble. Acetone bodies have appeared in the urine. He is still able to drink plain hot water in sufficient quantity.

"We once again request friends and the public not to disturb him by seeking interviews and 'Darshan'

Secu

Dr. P. P. Pil... the Secu...

Soviet

SECRE... ORDE...

"Daily T...

AN amazin... "Protocol... ing strike ac... come into B...

The orde... precis and ... been passed ... in the Brit... channels of ...

cr Western India." REGD. No. B111

of India

FOR PURE DIAMONDS K. Wadia GRANT ROAD, BOMBAY—Ph. 42483

ED 1838

16, 1948. PRICE TWO ANNAS DO NOT PAY MORE

Council Hears India's Case On Kashmir Against Pakistan

MR. AYYANGAR URGES EARLY SOLUTION

Sir M. Zafrullah Khan Granted Short Adjournment

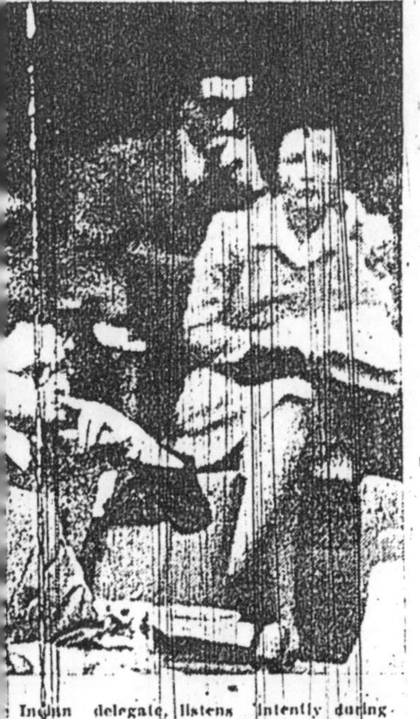

Indian delegate, listens intently during initial discussion on the Kashmir issue.

LAKE SUCCESS, January 15

AFTER hearing India's 6,000-word complaint that Pakistan was at no time willing to do anything to stop the raiders of Kashmir from using Pakistan territory, the U. N. Security Council adjourned further consideration of the dispute until tomorrow at the request of Sir M. Zafrullah Khan, Pakistan Foreign Minister.

In making his request for adjournment of the debate Sir M. Zafrullah said the picture did not appear to him "in the same colours" as the Indian spokesman had painted.

Mr. N. Gopalaswami Ayyangar, Indian Minister without portfolio, complained that Pakistan's unwillingness to dissociate itself "openly and categorically" from the tribesmen who invaded the State three months ago was the reason no agreement had been reached.

Mr. Ayyangar called on the Council to prevent Pakistan personnel from participating in the invasion of the State, and to ask Pakistan to deny the invaders the use of Pakistan territory for operations against Kashmir.

When the Cabinet met the President, M. Fernand van Langenhove, invited Mr. N. G. Ayyangar for India and Sir M. Zafrullah Khan for Pakistan to take their places and announced he would give the floor successively to India and

Mr. N. G. Ayyangar

"NO YIELDING TO PARTITION"

Kashmir Leader's Assertion

NEW DELHI, January 15

Strong resentment at reports regarding the possibility of partition of Kashmir was expressed

to Wreck Marshall Plan"

CUMENT REVEALS STRIKES IN RUHR

nd "Times of India" Correspondent.

BERLIN, January 15.

ominform order of 1,200 words, called gives detailed instructions for foment- Ruhr to "break the Marshall Plan," has at a centre in Western Germany.

into a ... have ... ist cells ... hrough ... t Unity

Bulgarian Premier Warns Opposition

The last weapon in the armoury of Gandhi, undertaking a fast, had served him well and on 16 January 1948 the government decided to 'implement immediately the financial agreement with Pakistan ... with a view to removing the one cause of friction and suspicion' between the two nations.

The news that Gandhi had decided to go on a fast to force India to transfer Rs 55 crores to Pakistan, was being broadcast over the news media in all languages. Pandit Nathuram Vinayak Godse and Narayan Dattatray Apte – the editor and manager of the Marathi daily, the *Hindu Rashtra*, were sitting in their office and reading it on their teleprinter, when they suddenly made their 'great decision' – Gandhi had to be killed.

TWO

There was no legal machinery by which
[Gandhi] could be brought to book...
I felt that [he] should not be allowed
to meet a natural death.

— NATHURAM GODSE

Even as Gandhi was talking to Mountbatten, the news that he had decided to go on a fast was being broadcast over the news media in all of India's fourteen languages. In Poona, two men sitting in a shoddy newspaper office read it over their teleprinter. Read it and suddenly made *their great* decision: Gandhi had to be killed.

Their names were Nathuram Godse and Narayan Apte; they were the editor and manager respectively of a Marathi-language daily newspaper, the *Hindu Rashtra*. No one knows which one first thought of murdering Gandhi because to the end they maintained that only one of them, Nathuram, was responsible for the killing, it is more than likely that they both thought of it at the same moment for, in matters such as this, their thoughts were strangely in accord. More than a year later, and only days before he was hanged, Apte was to tell Nathuram Godse's brother Gopal:

> In the four and a half years that Nathuram and I worked together, we found that we often thought of the same things at the same time. Nathuram would send a leading article from wherever he had gone to, and it would turn out that I had already written on the same subject and on the same lines. And as to our devotion to the cause, we were like one mind in two bodies.

'The cause' was Hindu Sanghatan, which envisaged the unification and revitalization of the Hindus so that they should stand up and fight for their political rights instead of giving in to the Muslims as they had done in the past. And the supreme, almost sacred, goal of the Sanghatan movement was to prevent the dismemberment of India.

It was thus a cause already lost, for India had been divided and there was nothing they could do to put it together again. They were bitter, angry, frustrated. The British had perpetrated a fraud, and the Congress had betrayed the nation. The Independence of India to them was a mockery, an insult, because had not a limb from Mother India's body been torn away in the process? August 15, the day of Independence, they had observed as a day of mourning.

For weeks, months, they and their few companions had sat and brooded and racked their brains to think of doing something spectacular that would rock the nation. They had talked of destroying an ammunition train on its way to Pakistan, of killing Jinnah and his Assembly in one fell swoop, of blowing up bridges, of carrying out commando-type raids into the Hyderabad state (which, until then, had not been absorbed into India), and they had even begun, at considerable expense and risk, to stock up the explosives and weapons that would enable them to undertake these tasks.

Now, suddenly, their target was revealed to them as in a flash.

'I thought it to be my duty to put an end to the life of the so-called father of the Nation,' Nathuram Godse was to testify with visible pride.

By carrying out this duty, Nathuram has qualified himself for a sort of odious immortality.

Nathuram Godse was born into an orthodox Brahmin family which came from a small village called Uksan, which is ten miles from the wayside railway station of Kamshet, on the Bombay-Poona line. Nathuram's father, Vinayak Godse, was a minor official in the Postal Department. In 1892, when he was seventeen, he was married to a girl who was barely ten years old. Vinayak's first child was a boy, and the second a girl. This first son died before he was two years old. After that there were two more sons, both of whom died in their infancy.

At the turn of the century, to families such as Vinayak Godse's, the fact that three sons had died one after the other while a daughter had survived held a clear warning: their male children bore a curse. One remedy, which had often proved effective, lay in offering to bring up the next boy as though he were a girl. That might appease the Fates.

So Vinayak and his wife offered prayers. The next child, if it were a boy, would be brought up as though he were a girl. His left nostril would be pierced to take a *nath* or nose-ring.

The next child was a boy, born on 19 May 1910. Even though he was named Ramchandra, which name is customarily shortened to Ram; because his nose was pierced to take a *nath,* the pretence that he was a girl was taken a step further by his parents, who began to call him Nathuram, or 'Ram who wears a nose-ring.' The name stuck.

As far as placating the evil spirits was concerned, the artifice was wholly successful. Nathuram lived through infancy and grew up to be a strong child, and so did three other brothers who followed him, among whom only Gopal, who was born in 1920, figured in the assassination of Gandhi. Psychologists may find some explanation for his warped mental processes in the fact that Nathuram was brought up as a girl.

The family was large – four sons and two daughters – and poor. The father was constantly transferred to be Postmaster in small, out-of-the-way townships all over the Bombay Presidency. After Nathuram had finished primary schooling in his mother-tongue, Marathi, he was sent to Poona to study for the matriculation examination. As a child, his parents and brothers believed that he possessed oracular powers. He would sit before the family goddess, staring fixedly at a spot of soot smeared in the exact centre of a copper tray, and soon fall into a trance. While in the trance, he would see some figures or writing in the black spot before him, much as a crystal-gazer is supposed to see in his glass ball. Then one or other member of the family would ask him questions. His answers were believed to be those of the goddess, who spoke through his mouth.

His brother Gopal, who saw several of these performances, writes: 'He would recite parts of scriptures or Sanskrit hymns which he never remembered to have memorized... and nor, when the trance was over, could he repeat them, or indeed remember what he had recited.'

It was not till he was nearly sixteen that Nathuram gave up the practice of serving as a medium between the family deity and the family. He had become more worldly and less devout, his brother Gopal laments, and his powers of concentration must have been diminished.

There were other interests. Despite his early upbringing as a girl, he had grown into a strapping youth who was fond of physical exercise and who took special pride in his prowess as a swimmer. His instincts were almost abnormally wholesome. He revelled in being the neighbourhood do-gooder, devoting himself to such chores as might have been taken on by an eager boy scout. He was always being called upon to fish out lost vessels from village wells, rescue cats, run errands for the sick, serve at temple functions and in the marriage festivities of the poorer neighbours. While the family lived in Lonavla, he rescued an Untouchable child that had fallen into a well. When later in the day he told his parents about it, he was scolded for having come into the house without first taking a purifying bath – he had been polluted by the touch of the child!

At the time, such sentiments in a Brahmin family were quite normal, but Nathuram himself was not bothered by them. Later, much to the distress of his parents, he was to come out as a fierce protagonist for the removal of Untouchability.

He read voraciously, but only in subjects which interested him, such as mythology, scriptures and history, and only in the Marathi language. He neglected his normal schoolwork and found the English language difficult to learn. The consequence was that he failed to pass the matric.

The matriculation examination was, in those days, an essential qualification for the lowest grades of clerical jobs in government offices, and Nathuram's father, who was now close to retirement himself, was anxious to get his son employed in his own department. He implored Nathuram to sit for the examination again, but Nathuram, who by this time had already come under the influence of Gandhi's movement for non-cooperation with the British Raj, shrank at the thought of taking a government job. He was fed up with schoolwork anyway and wanted to start earning his own living. He left Poona and came to live with his father, who was then in Karjat. There, for a year or two, he tried his hand at learning to be a carpenter, but just as he was getting to be proficient his father was transferred, and the family had to move again.

The year was 1929, and Nathuram was nineteen years old. This time they were going to Ratnagiri, a sleepy town on the west coast, so obscure that it was not even listed in Murray's exhaustive *Guide to India*. Ratnagiri's principal claim to a place in history was that the British had exiled the last ruler of Burma, King, Thibaw, there. Thibaw had died thirteen years earlier, and Ratnagiri had lapsed into what it had always been – a backward place where minor government officials were sent to mark time for their pensions.

Nathuram had rejoiced. He had heard that Ratnagiri now housed another political prisoner, an Indian brought back from the penal station in Andamans to serve out the remaining years of his sentence of fifty years' imprisonment. Here the British had given him a bungalow and the freedom to move about within the confines of the district; he was required to abstain from all political activities, but was permitted visitors.

He was Vinayak Damodar Savarkar, the man who had burst suddenly on to the Indian political scene and had been despatched by the British to the penal colony in the Andamans; scholar, historian, poet, religious reformer, a trained barrister, but, above all, a firebrand patriot who had galvanized the youth of his generation by his open advocacy of an armed uprising against the British.

Within three days of his arrival in Ratnagiri, Nathuram went to see Savarkar.

Once he had come under Savarkar's influence, Nathuram was never the same man again. The high school dropout who would have been willing to live out his days as a village carpenter was transformed into a fiery champion of all the causes that Savarkar stood for, political, social, religious; freedom from British rule, the inviolability of the motherland, the purification of the Marathi language, the abolition of the caste system, the emancipation of the depressed classes and, a hitherto unheard of thing, the reconversion of Hindus who had been enticed into Islam or Christianity. Nathuram venerated Savarkar as a guru, as someone who bore a touch of divinity. And it was his blind devotion to the potent preachings of the master, and his shattering disillusionment at the way everything in Savarkar's scenario had gone wrong, that ultimately led Nathuram to the insane expedient of murder and self-immolation.

But conversely it is also true that, while his meeting with Nathuram Godse could not have made much difference to Savarkar's life at the time, nineteen years later Nathuram's continuing attachment to him was to provide the excuse to the police (and possibly to his political enemies) for dragging him into the Gandhi murder case. The strain of the trial, and the year spent in prison while it lasted, wrecked Savarkar's health and finished him as a force in India's politics.

Vinayak Damodar Savarkar was born in 1883 in a small village near the town of Nasik; in 1910, he was shut up for life in the penal colony in the Andamans. It is difficult to think of anyone else who has crammed so much activity into the twenty-seven years that he had lived as a free man, or of anyone who had lived them more dangerously.

He was only twelve when he organized a gang of his schoolmates to fight off the village bullies. At sixteen, while he was kept in Nasik for his higher schooling, he formed a revolutionary society to overthrow the British Raj. He barely made the grades at school but knew far more than his teachers about Indian history and the Sanskrit classics, and gave regular talks on these subjects at local functions. In 1903, when after passing his matriculation examination he left Nasik to join a college in Poona, the leading men of the town joined together to give him a hearty send-off.

As a college student in Poona, he became 'a notable figure in political gatherings', and thus inevitably came under police surveillance. In his final year, he flung himself with gusto into the Swadeshi movement which, among other things, required the burning of British-made articles of clothing in public bonfires. For these activities he was rusticated from his college and thus became the first Indian student to be sent down from a college for political reasons.

When, however, the time for the BA examination came, the authorities relented and let him sit for it. He managed to pass and immediately set out to try to bring his various organizations together and to win converts to his movement for an armed revolt against the Raj. He went from village to village, giving rousing talks, composed and sang patriotic ballads, and published a stack of pamphlets propounding his views on the problems facing the Indian people. These publications were summarily proscribed and their possession made an offence.

Thus, at the age of twenty-two, Savarkar had made himself one of the most intrepid opponents of British rule in India. At this stage, realizing that he did not possess a broad enough base of knowledge for the role he had taken on, and anxious to equip himself more adequately for it by a few more years of study and travel, he decided to leave India and go to England to qualify as a barrister.

The Indian Government, which was on the point of arresting him on a charge of sedition, must have breathed a sigh of relief at this turn of events. Savarkar could now be written off as a troublemaker. It was almost certain that England would transform him into a 'wog', a Westernized Oriental Gentleman.

That was the general pattern of the times. Indian boys went to study at the great colleges of England, goggled at the wonders of the western world

Vinayak Damodar Savarkar, popularly known as Veer Savarkar, was a great influence on people who believed in the ideology of the Hindu Sangathan. Nathuram Godse came in contact with Savarkar while his father was posted in Ratnagiri and was completely transformed by him whom he venerated as his guru. Savarkar, during this period was working to bring about social and religious reforms among the Hindus, and under his leadership the sangathan movement blossomed as a political party, the Hindu Mahasabha. Sitting in the centre is Veer Savarkar with Nathuram Godse (sitting second from left) and other Hindu Mahasabha members.

Nathuram Godse

Narayan Apte

Veer Savarkar

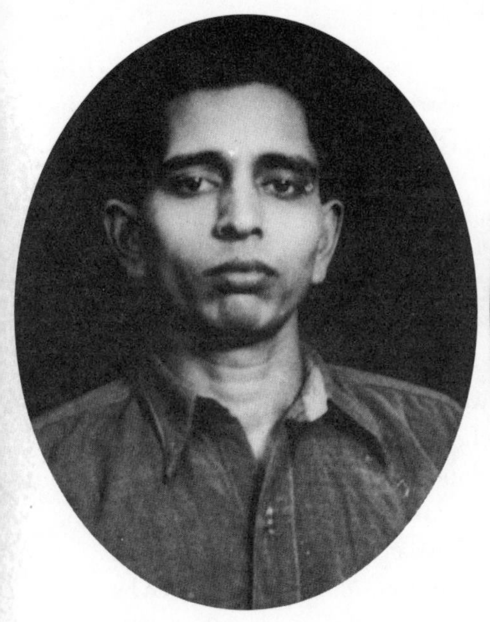

Gopal Godse

Vishnu Karkare

'India should be essentially a secular state in which (all citizens) should have equal rights and duties irrespective of religion, caste or creed. (But we) refuse to tolerate that Hindus should be robbed to enable the Muslims to get more than their due simply because they were Muslims and would not otherwise behave as loyal citizens.'
—Veer Savarkar

The credo of Hindu Mahasabha was to keep India as one undivided nation and a Hindu land, had a number of faithful followers especially in cities like Poona and Nagpur. Veer Savarkar was their undisputed leader who wanted them to learn to be proficient in the use of arms. It was this Hindu cause that brought these people from different walks of life together.

Nathuram Godse, who started as a tailor in a small town called Sangli, shifted to Poona and started a Marathi daily, *Agrani*; Narayan Apte left the Royal Indian Air Force and joined Godse as the manager of *Agrani*; Gopal Godse, younger brother of Nathuram, though not directly involved in the Party work, was effected by his brother's fervent zeal; and Vishnu Karkare an orphan who had always toiled to survive in this world, worked tirelessly to provide food and shelter for the refugees in Ahmednagar.

and were tamed by the civilizing influences of their environment. They invariably returned as brown sahibs. Many fell in love with English girls, and some brought back white wives.

Savarkar conformed to the pattern only by falling in love with an English girl, whose name was Margaret Lawrence. Otherwise he remained defiantly Indian. He joined Gray's Inn and four years later qualified to practise at the Bar. Throughout his time in England, he pressed on with his political activities at the same relentless tempo. He started what was called the Free India Society, whose weekly meetings were conducted quite openly. But, from among the members of the society he formed an inner circle of young men who, like himself, believed in revolutionary methods. Between them they raised a fund to learn the secret of making bombs, and despatched three volunteers to Paris to find 'some Russian revolutionist who might initiate them into the mysteries'. In Paris, they were 'duped and deceived by a bogus professor', and their search seemed destined to end in failure. But, 'At last a man was found, a Russian exile. He taught them the art of making explosives and the best way of utilizing them in revolutionary work, handed over an authoritative booklet describing and illustrating all sorts of bombs and their uses – and did not take a pie.'

This manual for making bombs was, according to the police in India, printed and distributed by Savarkar from London. Copies soon reached India and were to turn up in police searches in several widely distant parts of the country: Calcutta, Allahabad, Lahore, Nasik and Poona. A year later, one was discovered in the house of Savarkar's eldest brother, Babarao, and clinched the government's case that he was preparing to 'wage war against His Majesty the King Emperor'. Babarao was sentenced to transportation for life.

In 1908, the home-made bomb made its first appearance in India's struggle against the Raj. Its intended victim was a Mr Kingsford, the District Judge in a place called Muzaffarpur, in Bengal; Kingsford was singled out for this punishment because he had ordered the whipping of a boy named Sushil Chandra Sen for getting into a fight with the police. A young man called Khudiram Bose stationed himself at the entrance of the British Club in Muzaffarpur and threw the bomb into a carriage which he believed to be Mr Kingsford's. It was the wrong carriage and contained two women, a Mrs Kennedy and her daughter. Both were killed.

While the bomb was being tried out in India, Savarkar had gone on working tirelessly. Spaced between the 'daily discussions', the weekly meetings, the ceaseless work of writing, printing, packing and posting thousands of revolutionary pamphlets and booklets to hundreds of addresses in India', he contributed regularly to a newspaper called *Talwar* or 'The Sword' which was published in Paris, and brought out a Marathi translation of the life of Guiseppe Mazzini, the Italian revolutionary. The book became an instant success in India, and the government found it necessary to proscribe it and 'to hunt out its copies' wherever they could be found.

His next project was the writing of what he called the true history of 'the war of Independence of 1857', which the British had always referred to as 'the Mutiny of 1857'. This book, too, Savarkar wrote in Marathi and as he completed the chapters would read them out at the weekly meetings of the Free India Society, translating the sentences into English as he went along. British secret agents who had infiltrated the Society managed to steal two chapters of the book, which they sent to India. The Indian Government considered the material so inflammatory that it took the quite unprecedented step of banning the book before it was published, or even fully written.

Savarkar rewrote the two missing chapters and completed the book in time for publication in 1907, the fiftieth anniversary of the revolt. A copy of the manuscript was smuggled into India, where an obscure publisher in Sholapur undertook to print it secretly. But the police were already on the lookout for the book. Tipped off in advance by a friendly policeman that his premises were about to be raided, the publisher hastily distributed his type and sent the manuscript to Savarkar's friends in Poona for safekeeping. After that it was impossible to find another publisher in India.

Meanwhile, in England, Savarkar was busy translating the book into English. The English edition was eventually published in Holland. Patrons of the Free India Society enthusiastically bought hundreds of copies for free distribution in India. They were sent out in covers which bore the titles of the more popular works of Charles Dickens and Sir Walter Scott. Supporters of the cause in America soon brought out an edition of their own and began to compete with their counterparts in Europe in sending free copies to addresses in India.

Many of these copies were discovered by the Indian police; and the Indian Government, now convinced that Savarkar, despite his infatuation for an English girl, was not going to be turned into a docile sahib, served an order on him forbidding him to return to India.

In London, in 1909, Madanlal Dhingra, an active member of the Free India Society and a close friend of Savarkar, shot and killed Sir Curzon Wylie, who had been the government's prosecutor in the cases against Khudiram Bose and the other terrorists in Bengal. Dhingra gave himself up and was found to carry in his pocket a statement that he had killed Wylie 'to avenge the inhuman sentences passed by the British officials on Indian youths...' whose only crime was that they had taken up arms to free their motherland. Savarkar, who in any case had been too close to Dhingra to escape the suspicion that he was somehow connected with the murder, made himself even more conspicuous to the police. He sought an interview with Dhingra while he was held in custody, raised a fund for his defence, and openly opposed a resolution sponsored by other Indians in England to condemn the murder.

Scotland Yard began to keep a close watch on him, and in India the police stepped up their efforts to root out his movement. At this stage, someone threw a bomb at Lord Minto while he was on a visit to Ahmedabad, and even before the police had discovered the culprit, in Nasik, Savarkar's home town, a man called Kanhere shot and killed Mr A.M.T. Jackson, the British Collector, 'to avenge the sentence of transportation passed on Savarkar's elder brother, Babarao'.

The police suspected that the pistol with which Jackson was killed was supplied by Savarkar from London, and the Anglo-Indian press angrily demanded why 'the man who was at the bottom of all this nefarious revolutionary activity [was not] made to pay the penalty for all these crimes?' Sensing that his arrest was imminent, Savarkar's friends hustled him off to Paris, where for a few weeks Savarkar, according to an anonymous biographer, busied himself with 'infusing a new life into the small but influential colony of Indians living there'. But soon Paris began to pall. He longed to go back to India and take up the fight on the actual battleground. But India had been forbidden to him and he knew that he would be arrested even before he stepped on its shore. So he decided to go back to London, which seemed nearer the scene of action. Many people believed that he had gone back because he was pining for Margaret Lawrence. In the event he never saw Margaret again.

He was arrested as his train pulled into Victoria Station. He was remanded in Brixton Prison where he was served a warrant for extradition to India: it seemed that the Indian Government had reversed its decision to extern him and now wanted to try him in India for the offence of waging war against the King. He was to be taken back as a maximum-security prisoner and with a police escort headed by a Deputy Superintendent of the Bombay police, C.L. Power, who had been sent all the way from India to bring him back. In London, Scotland Yard deputed their own man, Detective Inspector Edward Josh Parker, to assist Power and his men in guarding their prisoner on his homeward journey. As a precaution against the possibility of Savarkar's influential friends in Paris moving a French court to secure his release on a petition of habeas corpus while he happened to be on French soil, it was decided not to take him by the normal overland route through France. Instead special accommodation was engaged on a ship going all the way to India, *SS Maurea,* and in her Savarkar was kept under watch night and day. Even when he went to the toilet two guards were required to sit outside the door and watch him in a mirror that had been specially fitted to the ceiling in front of a small opening cut into the door.

For some unexplained reason the *Maurea* put in to Marseille. All night Savarkar lay awake, thinking of some way to escape and, just before dawn, asked to be allowed to use the toilet. The two guards took him to it and stood outside the door. Savarkar bolted the door and hung his dressing-gown over the opening. Then he made a grab for the porthole, wriggled through the narrow opening and hurled himself into the sea even as the guards were trying to break open the door.

He had always been a strong swimmer and reached the shore before his pursuers, who had to wait for a boat to be lowered. He was now on French soil, and all he had to do was to find a policeman and demand political asylum.

The dockside streets of Marseille were already astir and the trams had begun to ply. Savarkar, clad only in a pair of wringing wet striped pyjamas and barefoot, ran over the cobbled streets, pursued by a posse of frantic English and Indian policeman yelling 'Stop thief! Stop thief!'. Some people in the street joined the chase, but Savarkar managed to reach a gendarme all the same. He grabbed hold of him and told him in broken French to take him to a magistrate. The policeman, convinced by his appearance that he was some lascar trying to run away from his ship, handed him back to the ship's officers instead.

The bid to escape at Marseille was the last bit of drama in Savarkar's life. After that he was caught up in the toils of the law of the Raj. He had believed that, for his revolutionary activities in London, the maximum sentence that any court could give him was seven years' imprisonment. He was given fifty years and sent to serve them in the cellular jail in the Andaman Islands to which his brother Babarao had already preceded him.

He nearly died in the Andamans. Ten years later, his health shattered and close to a mental breakdown, he was brought back from the penal colony and put into an Indian jail. After another four years, he was released on parole and confined to the district of Ratnagiri. He had already served fourteen years in various prisons, a period of time which, in India, constitutes a normal 'life' sentence.

Savarkar never made any apologies for adopting the methods of the anarchists in Europe to fight India's battle against the Raj. In an article he contributed to *Talwar* he asserted:

> We hold that whenever the open preaching and practising of truth is banned by enthroned violence, then alone are secret societies and warfare justified... whenever the natural process of national and political evolution is violently suppressed by the forces of wrong, revolution must step in.

Such was the man Nathuram Godse met in Ratnagiri in the summer of 1929. Savarkar was forty-six years old, a soft, bald man with the face of a family priest. In the five years he had been out of jail, he had regained his full bodily and mental vigour. He was working to bring about social and religious reforms among the Hindus; he read voraciously and wrote innocuous articles and plays and novels which were required to bear a publisher's declaration that they were wholly divorced from politics. But the torrent of energy was far from fully engaged, nor had it found its natural outlet, politics.

Nathuram came under Savarkar's spell. Savarkar had been forbidden political activities but he could not be prevented from talking about politics in private conversation to anyone who was willing to listen.

Nathuram sat and listened and was thrilled when, a few months later, Savarkar asked him to serve as his secretary. In this capacity he learned to write English well, to assemble his thoughts and to deliver speeches. By the spring of 1931, when Nathuram's father retired from service and the family had to leave Ratnagiri, Nathuram had become a disciple of Savarkar.

Nathuram's father settled down in Sangli because he believed that 'living would be cheap in a small town'. To supplement the family's income, Nathuram took lessons in cutting and sewing and set himself up as a tailor. Later he added a fruit stall to his tailoring business.

At this time, some leading Hindus in Nagpur started a movement called Hindu Sanghatan. Its object was to unite the Hindus to guard their political interests which, they felt, were being eroded by Muslim intransigence on the one hand and, on the other; by the excessive meekness of the Congress leaders like Gandhi and Nehru who were anxious to placate the Muslims at all cost. It called upon the Hindus to give up non-violence as a creed because it was emasculating them, and to learn to stand up and fight for their rights.

Hindu Sanghatan, of course, was a stepchild of Savarkar's own revolutionary movement against the Raj and, in his talks with Savarkar in Ratnagiri, Nathuram had discovered that it had the Master's full support. So when, a year later, a branch of Hindu Sanghatan was opened in Sangli Nathuram eagerly volunteered to work for it. He was appointed its secretary.

Nathuram was now in his early twenties and earning a modest living, and his parents thought he should get married and settle down. He told them that he had no intention of marrying, ever. It was a resolve he stuck to, and it, too, was all of a piece with his Spartan lifestyle. He neither smoked nor drank, wore the simplest clothes, read a lot of books on politics, history and Hindu religion and worked hard.

In 1937, when the British were trying out a new constitution for India, the first elected government was formed in what was then known as the Bombay Presidency. One of the first acts of this government was to release Savarkar unconditionally; to them he was no seditionist but a freedom fighter, even if of a different brand from themselves. Savarkar's trip from Ratnagiri to Bombay was a triumphal lecture tour in all the major towns along the route, of which Sangli was one. Here Nathuram rejoined Savarkar's staff and then went along with him on his tour. What he saw convinced him that Sangli was too small a place for his field of activities. He shifted to Poona and set up his tailoring shop there; but here, too, his time was taken up in the work of Hindu Sanghatan, which now, with Savarkar's return to the political arena, was fast gathering momentum, strength and, even more, direction. The British officials were no longer the villains; the real enemies were the Muslims, who seemed bent on carving out a piece of India for themselves and by extension the weak-kneed leaders of the Indian National Congress who looked as though they were going to give in to this demand. Under Savarkar's leadership, the Sanghatan movement blossomed as a political party, the Hindu Mahasabha, whose declared aim was to keep India whole and a Hindu land; but, it is only fair to explain, not a *purely*

Hindu land. As Savarkar, who was now acclaimed by his adherents as 'Veer' or 'The Warrior', explained, the Mahasabha wanted that

> India should be essentially a secular state in which (all citizens) should have equal rights and duties irrespective of religion, caste or creed. [But we] refuse to tolerate that Hindus should be robbed to enable the Muslims to get more than their due simply because they were Muslims and would not otherwise behave as loyal citizens.

In 1938 the Mahasabha decided to carry out a protest march into the princely state of Hyderabad where the Hindu citizens were being discriminated against, and Nathuram Godse was given the leadership of the first batch of protest marchers. He was arrested and sentenced to a year's imprisonment. By the time he came out, the Second World War had begun, and the political scene in India had suffered a startling transformation.

During the First World War, Gandhi had vigorously championed Britain's cause and had recruited troops in India to fight for it, and the British had rewarded these services by granting him the Kaiser-i-Hind medal. Since then, Gandhi had become the foremost leader of India's struggle for freedom from Britain, and when Hitler's war had begun he had called upon his followers to boycott the war effort. A little later, he had followed this up with a nationwide campaign of non-cooperation and had demanded that the British should quit India forthwith. And Nehru, who at the outset of the war had declared that India 'should offer unconditional cooperation to the British', shifted his stance and aligned himself with Gandhi's campaign, which sought to strangulate the Indian Government's war effort. For this, Gandhi and Nehru and other Congress leaders had been rounded up and given stiff jail terms.

Savarkar, who during the First World War had been a prisoner in the Andaman jail and had longed for a German victory, had now given a call to his followers to offer their fullest cooperation to the British war effort and to join the armed forces in large numbers. His motive was openly stated. He wanted the Hindus to learn to be proficient in the use of arms so that they would be able to hold their own in the battles that they were sure to be called upon to fight in the near future. Here was Britain, which had inflicted inhuman punishment upon Indians for possessing arms and trying to learn how to use them, offering to train them in the use of the latest weapons of war. It would be foolish not to take the fullest advantage of such an opportunity. Savarkar was looking into the future, beyond the Second World War, to a time when the British would have gone and left the country to the Hindus and Muslims and when the Hindus would be called upon to fend for themselves.

The Raj did not care why Savarkar was being helpful so long as he was being helpful; if he was no friend of the British, for the moment he was not an enemy, either. They allowed him to remain free but, as will presently appear, kept him under surveillance. It was the Congress leaders who now tended to look upon him as a renegade, if not an enemy; the man who was helping the British at a time when the Congress had called upon them to quit India. Outspoken as always, Savarkar made many powerful enemies among the leading Congressmen, and was to pay dearly for these indiscretions.

Savarkar concentrated on building up his party, the Hindu Mahasabha, into a national organization to compete with the Congress and the Muslim League. It made some limited progress all over India, but developed rapidly in the parts of India where the Marathi language was spoken, and the cities of Poona and Nagpur became its principal centres.

After. his release from the jail in Hyderabad, Nathuram Godse had returned to Poona and resumed work in the Party's office. Here in 1941 he was visited by a dynamic young man who had been active in the Party's work in Ahmednagar, a cantonment town only seventy miles from Poona. His name was Narayan Dattatray Apte. Over the next two years, Nathuram and Apte became close friends.

At thirty-one, Nathuram Godse was a quiet man of simple, almost austere tastes and a serious turn of mind. Pledged to celibacy he shied away from the company of women and deliberately shunned the temptations of life. He was bothered by even small lapses of middle-class morality and strove to keep his thoughts on a high plane. His favourite reading was books on religion and philosophy, his secret pride his ability to sway crowds with his speeches, and his admitted weakness a liking for coffee.

Narayan Apte was altogether different. He was quick-witted, lively and intelligent, well educated, and with a family background of pure scholarship. He smoked and drank, wore expensive clothes, and was fond of the good things of life. Though he came from the same sort of middle-class Brahmin background as Nathuram, he scoffed at the scruples and prohibitions of both his class and caste. He was good-looking in a somewhat effeminate way, and was vain about his prowess with women.

One can imagine Narayan Apte as the sort of man who might some day commit adultery (which he did) but not as a murderer; and Nathuram is difficult to imagine as one who would even think of reusing a postage stamp that had remained unfranked. That two men who were so different should become the closest of friends seems almost unnatural, but people who knew them well assert that neither was a homosexual and that the friendship was due entirely to a total identity of views on the Sanghatan movement.

Narayan Apte was born in 1911 and was thus a year younger than Nathuram. His family lived in Poona, and his father was a well-known historian and Sanskrit scholar. Narayan, the eldest male child among three sisters and four brothers, was educated in Poona. In 1932 he graduated from Bombay University as a Bachelor of Science. In those days of depression jobs were not easy to come by and he had to mark time for three years before finding an opening as a teacher in the American Mission High School in Ahmednagar, run by a Miss Bruce.

But before the job came marriage, to a girl named Champa from the Fedtare family of Poona. The marriage, arranged by Narayan's parents, is described as being one of convenience, for the Fedtares were an old and influential family and relatively affluent. It was considered a good match for a jobless youth even if the youth himself may never have given his approval to it or even been consulted beforehand.

Narayan worked hard at his job, and soon became popular with his colleagues and students alike. In 1938, he thought of opening a rifle club in Ahmednagar 'with the object of training young men in the use of firearms', and the Congress Government which had come into office in Bombay gave him leave to do so. The 'firearms' were in fact airguns with slugs, but even those in Indian hands were looked upon with suspicion in the days of the Raj, and clubs formed to train young men to use them regarded as positively dangerous. Apte's club became popular and the idea caught on. Within a year, Poona and half a dozen other towns had their own rifle clubs.

In 1939, Apte joined the local branch of the Hindu Mahasabha and met for the first time another man who was to be drawn into the conspiracy to murder Gandhi, Vishnu Karkare, a spry little Brahmin with wavy black hair and sharp piercing eyes who, with very little outside help, had established the branch of the Mahasabha in Ahmednagar, and had by now become its leading light. But initially Apte and Karkare were cool towards one another. To Karkare Apte's job in a Christian school was reason enough to suspect his credentials as a good Hindu, and Apte for his part must have tended to look down on Karkare who, for all his importance in the Party's office, was a man with no family background and almost illiterate. It was Nathuram who later brought the two together.

At this time Apte was not really keen on Party work. He was actually thinking of settling down and making a career of teaching, and had gone to special trouble to improve his qualifications for it by passing the BT (Bachelor of Teaching) examination. His wife Champa had borne him a son whom he adored. He had given the son a conventional Hindu name but called him Pappan, which is merely a term of endearment.

It took him almost two years to discover that his son was mentally retarded. People who knew him then say that he was shattered by the discovery. He wanted to leave Ahmednagar and all its memories and give up the teaching profession.

In the spring of 1942, most of the Congress leaders were behind bars and Savarkar's party, the Hindu Mahasabha, was making excellent progress.

Savarkar now thought of setting up a secret organization for doing work 'that could not be openly undertaken by a political party'. This organization, which was given the name of Hindu Rashtra Dal and which later gained notoriety as merely the 'Dal' was set up in May 1942, and both Nathuram Godse and Narayan Apte were selected to be its office-bearers. Both subsequently held training camps in their respective areas. According to the report of the CID (Criminal Investigation Department) informers who had wormed their way into the Dal, the camps 'trained volunteers in Indian games, physical exercise, shooting practice with airguns, and also classes in Savarkar ideology.' But, even according to these informers, the total membership of the Dal 'never exceeded 150'.

Meanwhile, Apte, who was still keen to get away from Ahmednagar, had applied for a job as a recruiting officer. He was taken on in early 1943, and appointed an assistant technical recruiting officer for the Royal (as it then was) Indian Air Force. He was gazetted a flight-lieutenant and posted to Poona. The job was temporary and meant to last only for the duration of the war, but he was now entitled to wear the insignia and uniform of an officer holding the King's commission, and to all the rights and privileges that went with it.

At last Apte could turn his back on Ahmednagar and the teaching profession.

It was, from all accounts, a touching farewell, for he had been an extraordinarily popular teacher. The High School was a coeducational institution, and many of the senior girls who came to see him in a batch actually had tears in their eyes. Apte made a suitably humorous speech and told them to stop being silly. It was not as though he was being posted to some distant theatre of war but only to Poona. For a few of them he scribbled the address of his Poona office in case they felt like writing to him some day to let him know how they were faring.

One of these girls was Manorama Salvi, then aged seventeen. She belonged to an Indian Christian family, and was brought up in the rigidly orthodox manner typical of such families, to the daily singing of hymns and in an atmosphere crackling with missionary piety. She was studious and moody and painfully shy. She was dark and plain. She carefully made a note of Apte's address and, more than a year later, while she was a student in a Bombay college, wrote to him. They met several times after that and eventually became lovers.

In Poona, the Air Force was sufficiently impressed by Apte's performance as a recruiting officer to offer him a permanent commission, which he eagerly accepted. To be an officer of the Royal Indian Air Force was to be launched on a sound, respectable and fairly lucrative career with a guaranteed pension at the end of it. But within a few months Apte resigned his permanent commission, preferring to go on working as a wartime officer. The reason he gave for doing so was good enough to satisfy the Air Force authorities. It was that his father had died a few months earlier and that, as his eldest son, all the responsibilities of the head of the family, or *Karta,* of looking after his widowed mother and several brothers and sisters had become solely his. This was, of course, quite true. But there was a far more compelling reason which made it out of question for Apte to remain in a service in which he was liable to be transferred away from Poona. His wife Champa, who had become somewhat abstracted in her behaviour, seemed to live only for their son Pappan, who was showing increasing signs of a virulent form of insanity. Apte had been resisting pressure from friends and neighbours and the advice of doctors to have the boy committed to a mental asylum. Apart from the fact that he himself could not bear the thought of consigning his small son, so innocent and trusting except during his fits, to the mercies of an institution, he knew that it would break his wife's heart.

It was the sort of problem that has no solution except through death. But at least, by remaining on the spot, he could keep things from getting worse, and the thought of what might happen to his family if he was posted away to some remote place was too horrifying to think about.

That was why Apte had to reject his permanent commission in the Air Force, but there was no reason why he should not go on working as a recruiting officer so long as they kept him in Poona.

Once the major decision was made and the prospect of an Air Force career thrown away, Apte had to think of something else to do after the war. Even as it was, recruiting had all but stopped and he had plenty of spare time on his hands. So, when his friend Nathuram asked him if he would like to join a venture that he was about to start to propagate the Party's ideals, he jumped at the offer.

Nathuram was starting a newspaper, and Veer Savarkar had made him a loan of Rs 15,000 to do it.

The Marathi daily *Agrani* (which means The Forerunner) began publication on the day of the Hindu New Year, which that year (1944) fell on 28 March. On its front page it bore a picture of Savarkar and a Sanskrit motto: 'Public good, not mere popularity'. Nathuram Godse was its Editor. Narayan Apte, who still held his job as a recruiting officer and still wore uniform, was its Manager. Right from the start, the paper ran into difficulties: wartime shortages, control on newsprint, censorship, CID surveillance and, above all, a desperate lack of money. But the Editor and the Manager worked hard in a spirit of dedication. The difficulties only brought them closer; they cheerfully shared one another's work, and borrowed from friends and moneylenders to keep the paper going.

Initially, there was not much difference between the sentiments of the Indian National Congress and the Hindu Mahasabha; both wanted Swaraj, or self-rule, and both wanted India to remain undivided. The only difference was that the Congress was prepared to make considerable concessions to the Muslims to keep India undivided, and the Mahasabha was opposed to any such concessions. Gandhi for his part had repeated his cry, 'Vivisect me before you vivisect India', and Nehru and others, if less dramatic in the way they expressed it, were equally firm against partition. Later, when it turned out that the Muslim League was altogether unappeasable, the Congress began to show signs of giving in to their demand for Pakistan, but Savarkar and his followers remained staunchly opposed to it till the very end, and so, to be fair, did a large number of people within the Congress itself.

Even as late as March 1947, Gandhi had insisted: 'If Congress wishes to accept Partition, it will be over my dead body. So long as I live, I will never agree to the Partition of India.'

But these were like the words of a charm repeated again and again in the hope that they might work a miracle. For Gandhi had already accepted the inevitability of partition a whole three years earlier, soon after he had been released from jail in 1944. In those days it was his habit to spend a few weeks every year in the hill resort of Panchgani, a bare fifty miles away from Poona. And here Narayan Apte had led a batch of his followers to confront him and denounce him for reneging on his promises.

The *Times of India* of 23 July 1944, under the headline 'MR GANDHI HECKLED', carried a report that a Poona journalist named N.D. Apte had led a demonstration of Hindu youths to express their resentment at Gandhi having given his 'blessings' to the formula of partition. The *Times* went on to say that there were at least four armed police officials in mufti close to Gandhi. As Apte and his party shouted slogans and waved black flags, and the small crowd of about four hundred people began to grow restive, the policemen swooped and hustled Apte to the local station for questioning. Deputy Superintendent N.Y. Deulkar, a tall, athletic man with a fruity unctuous voice and a persuasive manner, who was on duty in Panchgani at the time and who later played a crucial part in the investigation following Gandhi's murder, questioned Apte closely. These details assume an importance only because they prove that, at least from July 1944, Apte was well known to the police as a man who detested Gandhi. Subsequently too, both Godse and Apte were repeatedly pulled in by the authorities for some infringement of the Indian Press (Emergency) Act. Despite this, and even though the police had at least a week's advance warning that the editor of a Marathi journal called the *Hindu Rashtra,* as the *Agrani* was later renamed, was among those who had planned to kill Gandhi, they were unable to prevent the murder. The information got caught up in a tangle of procedure and in departmental rivalries and never filtered through to Deulkar who, at the time of Gandhi's murder, happened to be the Deputy

Superintendent of the CID in Poona itself, and lived within walking distance of the paper's office.

The *Agrani's* own reporting of the Panchgani incident was far more dramatic. It carried on its front page a photograph of Apte posed against one of Gandhi, and bearing the caption: 'I denounce you a hundred times because you have conceded Pakistan!'

What with this deep involvement in the politics of the Mahasabha, in addition to holding down his two jobs, Apte might be thought to have had his hands too full for anything else. But he was a man of extraordinary energy and had time for other pursuits as well. So when, on this return from Panchgani after heckling Gandhi, he received a letter from one of his erstwhile pupils, Manorama Salvi, to come and see her, he responded with alacrity.

'I wrote to Apte at Poona,' Manorama was to testify before a Bombay magistrate, 'and a few days later he called at the hostel to see me and two other former students.'

The hostel was the Ramabai hostel for girls in Bombay, attached to the Wilson College. Apte, a dashing figure in his Air Force uniform, came in the middle of the afternoon, charmed the warden of the hostel, a Mrs Hewat, who was known for her strictness towards her wards, with a snappy salute and a dazzling smile, and took all three girls out. They saw an afternoon movie and later walked on the sands in front of Wilson College. By 7.30 all three girls were back in their hostel.

When, a few days later, Apte called at the hostel again, he only asked for Manorama. This was the first of many such meetings, as a result of which she later admitted becoming 'very friendly with him'. They began to correspond, Apte writing his letters in a feminine handwriting and signing himself Nirmala, as though he were a girl, to ensure that they were not intercepted by the eagle-eyed Mrs Hewat. By the end of the year, she had taken to spending nights with him in various seedy hotels. In the hotel registers, he boldly entered their names as Mr and Mrs Apte.

दैनिक अग्रणी

Agrani, literally meaning the 'Forerunner' began publication on the day of the Hindu New Year in 1944, with Savarkar's photograph on the masthead with a motto in Sanskrit, 'Public good not mere popularity'. Veer Savarkar was the guiding force who was often requested by Godse and Apte to write articles for *Agrani* to increase its circulation. Seen here is Savarkar (sitting in the centre) with Nathuram Godse (sitting second from right), Narayan Apte (sitting second from left) and other staff members of *Agrani*.

म्रांतराष्ट्रवाद्यांना हिंदुराष्ट्र द

पांचगणीच्या पर्जन्यवृष्टींतून पाकिस्तानवर अ

चरकली खलांची हृदयें । संतुष्ट जाहले सुजन ॥

लेखक—ना. द. आपटे, संचालक 'अग्रणी'

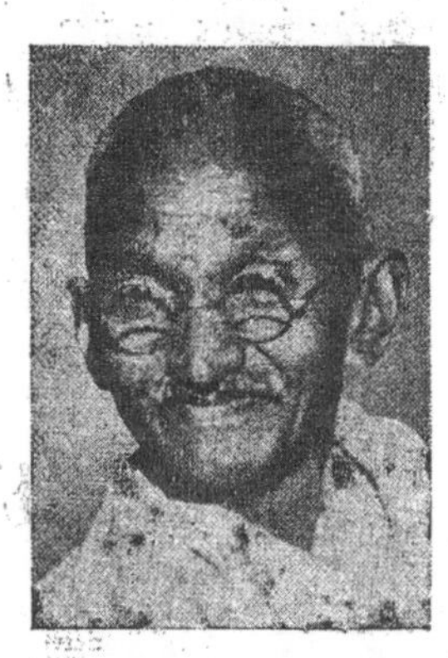

गांधींजी—होय, मी पाकिस्तानाला संमति दिली आहे.

[पांचगणीचे प्रशांत पठारावर पाकिस्तानी प्रचारकाची प्रत्यहीची प्रार्थना झाल्यावर झालेल्या विरोधी निदर्शनाचे नाद अराष्ट्रीयांचे अंतःकरणांत बराच काळ घुमत राहातील अितक्या दणकेदार रीतीनें तो कार्यक्रम झाला. गांधींजींच्या दिव्य अध्यात्म शक्तीच्या अफवा अनेकांनीं अैकलेल्या आहेत. पण त्यांचें तोंडावर त्यांच्या देशघातकी योजनेचा धिक्कार भर सभेंत यत्किंचितहीं न डगमगतां करणें ही कांहीं सामान्य कथा नाहीं. श्री. आपटे नि त्यांच्या श्री. गांगुर्डे प्रभृति हिंदुराष्ट्रवादी सहकारी युवकांना हें निदर्शन करण्यापूर्वी काय काय विचार करावें लागले आणि प्रत्यक्ष तेथें काय काय घडलें यांचे 'सत्यं शिवं सुंदरम्' शब्दचित्र श्री. आपटे यांनीं खालील लेखांत रंगविलें आहे.]

आपटे-

शतवार धिक्का

प्रयाणाची पार्श्वभूमी

भारताचें अखंडत्व प्राणपणानें राखिलें पाहिजे या अंगीकृत तत्त्वाचा प्रचार 'अग्रणी' करीत असल्यामुळें भारतभंगी योजनांविरुद्ध अतिशय तीव्र टीकेचे लेख 'अग्रणींत' वारंवार येत असतात. त्यांचा अंशतः परिणाम म्हणूनच कीं काय अनेक हिंदुत्वनिष्ठ तरुण येऊन आम्हाला विचारूं लागले "हिंदूपतपादशाहीचीं स्वप्नें सत्यसृष्टींत उतरविलेल्या महाराष्ट्रावर ब्रिटिश सत्तेची अवकळा आलेलीच आहे आणि आता तर आपल्या

वरील संभाषणाची आठवण मला यावेळीं झाली. आणि आतां दिव्य अध्यात्मशक्तीची प्रचीती आपणास पहावयास मिळते कीं काय असा विचार मनांत चटकन येऊन गेला. पण माझें अंगीकृत कार्य हें [illegible]त्र राष्ट्रीय कर्तव्य असल्यानें माझा आत्मविश्वास नि अंतःप्रेरणा यत्किंचितही ढळली नाहीं.

आहिंसा भक्तांची पूर्वपीठिका

आम्हाला ही पण कल्पना होती कीं, सहा सातशे श्रद्धेनें जमलेल्या बहुसंख्य कॉंग्रेसवाल्या श्रोतृसमुदा-

प्रकार तेथें दिसून आला. अहिंसा—चार्यांभोंवतीं चार सशस्त्र गुप्त पोलीसच त्यांचें रक्षणार्थ असल्याचें आढळून आलें. धन्य महात्मा नि महाधन्य अहिंसा !

खाजगी नको प्रकट बोला !

माझे प्रश्न नि गाधींची उत्तरें सुमारें ५ मिनिटांनी संपलीं. आणि अखंड भारताच्या धनगर्ज घोषणा सुरू झाल्या. एका प्रश्नावर गाधीजी म्हणाले कीं, 'आपण नंतर खाजगी बोलूं' पण मी लागलीच उत्तरलो I dont want your private

दिसले माझे
बरोबर म्हणू
दर्शवीत आ
तर योग्य ते
आपला उघ
वरील
लोकांनीं अ
सांगितलें कं
मधून शिष्टमं
खतीसाठीं ये
स्तान-संमती
अतिशय धो
पटवत दे

आपल्या प्रांताचा परामर्ष

जुगाऱ्यांची गुंडगिरी
सरकारनें कडक उपाय योजावें

(आमच्या वार्ताहराकडून)

बार्शी, दि. २३—येथील वृत्तपत्र व्यवसायी भाई पिंपरकर यांचेवर येथें चालू असलेल्या सुमारें चार महिन्यापासूनच्या जुगारावरच्या लोकांनीं 'तूं आमच्या जुगाराच्या बातम्या कां देतोस आम्हीं तुला भोसकूं असा दम भाई पिंपरकर सिनेमाहून रात्रौ येत असतां दिला. अशा प्रकारच्या दमदाट्या वाटेल त्या माणसास येथील जुगारी देतात. जुगार उघड उघड चालतो जुगार बंद होण्याबाबत येथील कॉ. पिंपरकर वगैरे लोकांनीं बराच प्रयत्न चालविला. जुगार बंद होण्याबाबत अखेर येथील प्रतिष्ठित नागरिकांच्या स्वाक्षऱ्यानिशीं मा. कलेक्टर यांचेकडे पुन्हां आवेदनें जाणार आहेत; थोड्याच दिवसांत येथें चालू असलेल्या जुगाराचें पर्यवसान असंतोष वाढण्यापर्यंत जाईल असें कळतें.

डॉ. चिटणीस यांचें शोचनीय निधन

कोपरगांव येथील लोकप्रिय डॉ. चिटणीस L. C. P. S. यांस पुणें मुक्कामी रक्तक्षयाच्या विकारानें दि. २४ जुलैला सकाळीं १०॥। वाजतां देवाज्ञा झाली. डॉक्टरांचा स्वभाव

सांगलीचें वृत्त
शिरगांवकर बंधूना काढणार

दि उगार शुगर वर्क्सचे मॅनेजिंग डायरेक्टर श्री. शिरगांवकर बंधू यांचे कडून कांहीं अंतस्थ. भानगडीनें डायरेक्टरशिप काढून घेण्यांत येणार असल्याचें समजतें. त्यामुळें श्री. केळकर यांची धावपळ चालू आहे.

आबाराव जोशी जाणार

येथील नवें हायकोर्ट जज्ज रा. सा. आबाराव जोशी हे येथून दुसऱ्या मोठ्या पगाराच्या जागेवर जाणार असल्याची वार्ता आहे.

'विश्वास' पत्राचें प्रकाशन

येथील 'विश्वास' पत्र सरकारनें खटला भरून, जामिन मागितल्यानें बंद पडलें आहे. तें दि. २ पासून पुन्हा सुरूं होणार असल्याची वार्ता प्रसिद्ध झाली आहे, पण राजसभेनें अद्यापि जामिनकीची प्रसूचना परत न घेतल्यानें वरील पत्र ती प्रसुचना परत घेईपर्यंत सुरूं होऊं शकत नाहीं.

दुधाचें भाव कडाडूं लागले

सांगली नगरांतील दुधाचें भाव अतिशय कडाडूं लागले असून; आतां रुपायास शेर याप्रमाणें भाव पडला आहे. इतकें होऊनही दूध भेसळ विकलें जातें. त्यामुळें नागरिकांचे अत्यंत हाल चालू आहेत. सरकार

आजची नभोवाणी

बुधवार दि. २६

मुंबअी १ सकाळीं ८-० बरसातीं गीत, -८-३० रहमतखां सतार ९-१५ रोशनारा बेगम ललत ९-५० वाद्यमु १०-० बंद. १२-३० भावगीत मु. १-० हिंदी कार्यक्रम ४-२० शालेय कार्यक्रम, ५-० पुरुषोत्तम सोलंकर पूरिया, गीत, ५-३० व्हायोलीन; ५-४० भजन मु. ६-० मुलांचा मराठी कार्यक्रम ६-४५ चंदावरकर मधुतर गणिला कशी राधिका ७-० नये नये फिल्म ७-१५ रहमतखान, सतार, ७-३५ पुरुषोत्तम सोलंकर नंद, ठुमरी, ८-५ गोतुवाद्यम् ९-४५ दिल्ली रिले, १०-० वाद्यवृंद १०-१५ रोशनआरा बेगम बिहाग, दादरा ११-० बंद.

'The Meaning of Hindu Nation for Misguided Nationalists', was how *Agrani* reported Narayan Apte's interview of Gandhi when he met him at Panchgani in July 1944. Below the headline posed against the photograph of Gandhi with the caption, 'Yes I have consented to Pakistan', was dramatically placed the photograph of Apte saying, 'And therefore I condemn you a hundred times.'

Quick-witted, lively and intelligent, Narayan Apte was good looking and was vain about his prowess with women. Married to Champa Fedtare at a young age, he was very popular with his students in American Mission High School in Ahmednagar where he taught for a few years. Manorama Salvi, his student, later became very close to him. It was during her stay in the Ramabai Hostel in Bombay that Apte used to come to meet her and take her for nights out in Bombay hotels, always checking in as Mr and Mrs Apte.

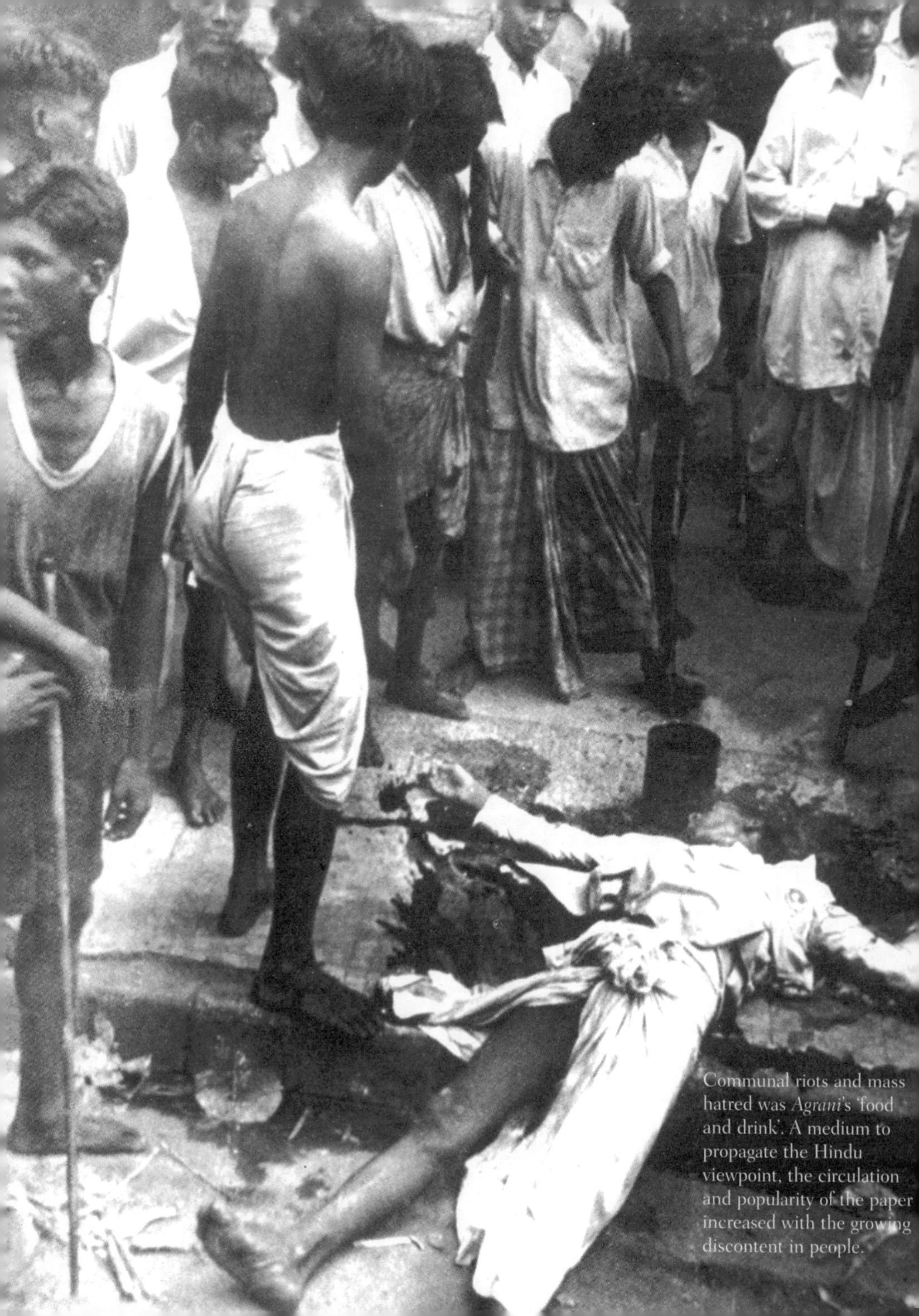

Communal riots and mass hatred was *Agrani*'s 'food and drink'. A medium to propagate the Hindu viewpoint, the circulation and popularity of the paper increased with the growing discontent in people.

THREE

Is it [non-violence] not a futile experiment I am conducting? What if, when the fury bursts, not a man, woman or child is safe, and every man's hand is raised against his neighbour?

— M.K. GANDHI

For two years the *Agrani* was like a patient on his deathbed, barely twitching with life and hardly breathing; it was the will-power of its Editor and Manager that kept it alive. At least once every month Nathuram wrote to Savarkar about the *Agrani*'s affairs, and in between he as well as Apte kept pressing him to write an article or two for it which, they firmly believed, would enhance its prestige and improve its circulation. But, after he had provided a part of its initial capital, Savarkar had had little to do with the *Agrani* and certainly did not, as he was later to protest, contribute 'even a small note' to it.

Meanwhile the war had ended, and with it had ended Apte's job as a recruiting officer. The British were eager to quite India, but Jinnah and the Muslim League wanted them to partition the country first.

Tension among the Hindus and Muslims grew into mass hatred. The *Agrani*, which fervently propounded the Hindu viewpoint, gradually began to make converts; its circulation improved and advertisements trickled in. Its monthly losses were reduced and it even began to think in terms of expanding. It acquired a printing press of its own and installed a teleprinter. Apte and Nathuram began to look for a site where they could put up their own building. Ultimately they found a vacant plot in a good area, 495 Shanwar Peth, and drew up plans to build a shed there to house their press and office.

Thus, on a high note, they entered the year 1946, the year before Independence and Partition; and the year in which the massacres began.

In the spring there were elections, both for the provincial legislatures and for the Constituent Assembly in New Delhi. The business of the Constituent Assembly was to hammer out independent India's constitution so that Britain could hand over power to a government in authority and not merely a political party. Till such time as the new constitution came into force, the Viceroy would rule the country with a caretaker all-Indian Cabinet.

As a result of the provincial elections, Bombay once again got a Congress government; and this government at once turned its attention to the *Agrani's* misdemeanours. On 26 June, Nathuram reported to Savarkar that it had stopped the *Agrani's* 'advertisements by a single order and transferred them to the *Lokashakti*' a rival Poona daily. Nathuram and Apte were discovering that the Indian ministers were far more intolerant of their views and methods of reporting than the guardians of the Raj had shown themselves to be.

Both were convinced that the reason behind the *Agrani's* chastisement was party jealousy, for the Congress was now also the Government. But, even if there was an element of truth in this, it cannot be denied that the *Agrani* for its part had consistently flouted the requirements of the Press Act, which sought to black out all news of communal rioting and also to prevent the publication of such sentiments as would arouse communal passions.

In fact, communal ferment was the *Agrani's* food and drink. As the champion of Hinduism, it considered it its duty to keep its readers informed about the atrocities that the Muslims were committing upon the Hindus all over the subcontinent, to censure the government for its inability to protect the Hindus and, above all, to exhort the Hindus to stand up for themselves. To keep the *Agrani* in check the government ordered it to pay Rs 6000 as a security for good behaviour. The sum, modest as it was, was altogether beyond the resources of the *Agrani,* but Nathuram and Apte managed to raise it all the same by desperate borrowing from friends and moneylenders. After paying it, however, they went on just as before and the government retaliated by 'forfeiting their deposit, to His Majesty', and ordered the paper to be closed. Apte and Nathuram, who must have been prepared for this, obeyed the order but the very next morning started another paper, the *Hindu Rashtra.* What they had done was, of course, to bring out the *Agrani* under a new name. This paper, too, was called upon to pay Rs 5000 as an earnest of good behaviour and, much to the government's surprise, the editor and manager were able to put up the money in time. With the spread of communal riots in the country, many affluent Hindus had begun to fall in line with the Mahasabha's stand; and were coming out to support its paper with funds. The fear of government disapproval made some of these donors give their contribution secretly, but the fact remains that, from the middle of 1946, neither the paper nor its editor and manager were short of ready cash. As will be seen, they began to spend money much more freely on themselves and even branched out into the clandestine buying of arms and explosives for furthering their political objectives. Despite government threats of further reprisals they went on publishing their paper right up till 31 January 1948. The last issue carried the news of Gandhi's murder.

The blacking out of news about the riots in the press and the radio did little to ease the communal tension. In any case, the Congress Government in Bombay was quite powerless to control the Muslim League which, in the summer of 1946, decided to resort to what it called 'direct action'.

Direct action, according to its initiator, Mr Jinnah, was bidding 'good-bye to constitutional methods'. Frank Moraes, in his biography of Nehru,

सोमवार विनाप्रतिदिनी प्रसिद्ध होतो

वर्ष १ लें अंक १२३] डाक पेटी क्र. ५०६ ÷ पुणें मंग

पराभूत गांधीवाद समूळ उखडून ट

आखिल हिंदूंना

भगव्या ध्वजाखालीं अेक होण्याचा आदेश

वेळ आलीच तर भोपटकरांबरोबर नरकांत जाअीन; पण नेहरू-पटेलांबरोबर स्वर्गांत जा

कश्मीरवर आफ्रीडी टोळ्या धाडण्यांत केवळ काश्मीरवर अधिराज्य प्रस्थापित करणें हाच एक हेतु पाकिस्तान सरकारनें ठेवलेला नाहीं; तर कामवासनेनें बेफाम बनलेल्या टोळीवाल्यांकडून काश्मीरी स्त्रियांच्या अब्रूचे धिंडवडे काढण्यासाठींच ह्या टोळीवाल्यांच्या सेना अमूप शस्त्र सामुग्रीनिशीं काश्मीरच्या दऱ्या खोऱ्यांत धुडगूस घालीत आहेत. आणि याची दखल जर वेळीच हिंदु समाजानें घेतली नाहीं तर हिंदु समाजावर भीषण प्रसंग ओढवणार हे निश्चित. ह्याकरितां स्पष्टपणें हिंदु समाजानें शिवाजींचें नांव घेऊन भगव्या ध्वजाखालीं अेक झालें पाहिजे अशी आशयाचें तळमळीचे मौलिक विचार आज सायंकाळीं सहा वाजतां शिवाजी मंदिरामध्यें भरलेल्या विराट सभेत महाराष्ट्राचे प्रमूख विचारवंत पुढारी प्रा. बापूसाहेब माटे यांनीं काढले. या सभेचे अध्यक्षस्थान हिंदुराष्ट्रपति धर्मवीर अण्णाराव भोपटकर ह्यांनीं मंडित केलें होतें. त्याचप्रमाणें या सभेंत आचार्य बबुराव अत्रे ह्यांचाहि परिस्थितीची योग्य कल्पना देणारे आणि कॉंग्रेस नेत्यांच्या पराभूत मनोवृत्तीवर विदारक प्रकाश टाकणारे भाषण झाले

पुणे, दि १:- हिंदुराष्ट्रपति अण्णा साहेब भोपटकर, प्रा. बापूसाहेब माटे आणि आचार्य अत्रे ह्या तीन विचारवंतांची भाषणे आज अेकाच व्यासपीठावरु [illegible]

आतां हिंदुसभावादी झालोंत. तो हिंदुसभावादी झालो ! हिंदुसभावादी म्हणजे महारोगी की काय? (हंशा व प्रचंड टाळ्या) मंझ्यांत कांहीं बदल आलेला नाहीं पूर्वी मी जसा होतो

काळ्यांच्या विरुद्ध आहे, अहिंद वर्षे मी [illegible] याविरुद्ध प्रचार करतो आहे. देशाची फाळणी करून कॉंग्रेसने मोठी चूक केली आहे [illegible]

[illegible] आहे ते [illegible] पाकिस्तान [illegible] ठाढले ते [illegible] पणाचे [illegible] राज्यात [illegible] आहे असें त्यांनीं [illegible] तीनावर [illegible] बोलताना थोडे [illegible] आतां ते [illegible] कशी मुक्त [illegible] घेऊन निघू [illegible] आणि हिंदूंनी [illegible] केली.

R. No. B, 50

वरं जनहितं ध्येयं / केवला न जनस्तुतिः वीर सावरकर.

दैनिक

[हिं]दुराष्ट्र

[ग]ोडसे संचालक ना. द. आपटे

'दैनिक हिंदुराष्ट्र

—ःवर्गणीचे दरः—

पुण्यांतः—	वार्षिक	रुपये
,,	सहामाही	रुपये
,,	तिमाही	रुपये
बाहेरगांवीं	(पोस्टेजसह)	
,,	वार्षिक	रुपये
,,	सहामाही	रुपये
,,	तिमाही	रुपये

मागील अंकाची किंमत दो

[दिन]ांक ४ नोव्हेंबर १९४७ [मूल्य १

[.]तरच देश जिवंत राहील—आचार्य

—अत्रे

अ. भा. संस्थानी हिंदुमहा

काश्मीर, जुनागड, हैद्राबाद ...

घेणार

Godse and Apte's publication was consistently flouting all requirements of the Press Act, and was thus ordered by the government to close down. The editor Godse and manager Apte, as though prepared for this, obeyed the order, and the very next morning started another paper, the *Hindu Rashtra* — it was the same old newspaper under a new name.

suggests that it had 'a sinister purpose'. It was, he goes on, 'to set in train massacres, violence and bloody riots which were to extend beyond August 15,1947, culminating in the mass migration of 11,500,000 souls ... in a two-way trail of blood between India and Pakistan.'

Jinnah may not himself have realized that his call for direct action would let loose the terror it did; and certainly he would not have wished for it. His followers ran amuck. Calcutta saw what The *Statesman* described as 'The Great Killing.' Within days the fire had spread to the other towns and villages of Bengal wherever the Muslims had the upper hand. A district called Noakhali became a synonym for genocide; here Muslim mobs went from village to village, setting fire to houses and killing the men and taking away the women as though they were herds of cattle.

The Indian news media continued to black out all mention of who was killing whom. Even Gandhi deplored what he called 'this hush-hush policy'.

He was living in Delhi then so as to be close to the scene of action where momentous decisions concerning India's future were being made. He decided to leave it all and go to Bengal to try to stop the massacres. 'The heart of every man who believes in God bleeds for Bengal,' he announced.

Even as Gandhi's train was speeding through the famine-parched land of Bihar, he could see the smoke and flames of villages burning. In Bihar, the Hindus were in a majority, and they had decided to answer Bengal's direct action by a call of 'blood for blood' against the Muslims. As soon as he reached Calcutta, Gandhi issued a statement denouncing the Biharis for their 'barbarities', and threatened to go on a fast unto death if, within twenty-four hours 'the erring Biharis have not turned over a new leaf'.

'A fast unto death.' Coming from Gandhi the words held the threat of an unbearable calamity. In the event Gandhi did not even have to resort to a fast; the mere threat was enough to send the Biharis stampeding to make amends – at least till Gandhi's attention was engaged elsewhere. Gandhi stayed in Calcutta for a few days and then went on to Noakhali.

There were other men whose hearts bled for Bengal and who wanted to do all they could to help the victims of the holocaust. One of these was Vishnu Karkare, the little man from Ahmednagar who, it will be recalled, had organized the Hindu Mahasabha office there.

Karkare was born of Brahmin parents, which is about all he knew of his early days. He did not even know the date of his birth, because both his parents had died when he was a small child, and he had been brought up in the Northcote Orphanage in Bombay, which put down his approximate date of birth as 1910. As a boy he had received little or no schooling even though later he taught himself to read and write Marathi and to speak Hindi. At ten he began to work as a tea shop drudge in Bombay, and later ran away to Poona. After fifteen years of hard work, he moved to Ahmednagar, carrying all he possessed in a gunny bag slung over his shoulder. Here, in a disused cowshed near the motor stand, he started his own tea shop. The only food he served beside tea was puris (fresh unleavened bread) and, to go with it, a chilli concoction which he called 'blood-purifying sauce'.

How any man who had been treated so shabbily by life should have come to feel passionately about abstract things such as religion or the motherland is difficult to imagine. The fact remains that both were the driving forces – even obsessions – of his life.

The tea shop was a success, and Karkare was able to expand it into a cheap hotel or what, in this part of the world, is invariably described as a 'lodging and boarding house'. The hotel, too, did well, and Karkare erected his own building to house it. He married, and employed servants to work in his hotel. Now he had time to do what he was later to describe – perhaps with excessive licence – as 'social service'.

Himself uneducated, he thought he would help the cause of education by giving concessional rates or at times even free rooms in his hotel to students. He got together an amateur dramatic company and also began to take a keen interest in the work of the Hindu Mahasabha.

In 1938, Savarkar came to Ahmednagar for his party work, and Karkare decided to treat him to a special performance of his theatre group. Savarkar happened to be extremely busy, but in the end agreed to come for fifteen minutes. He sat through the full show, three hours. Karkare was thrilled.

In 1939, when Apte first came into contact with him, Karkare had already become the District Secretary of the Hindu Mahasabha. Three years later, he stood as a candidate for the municipal elections and was elected unopposed. Thus at the age of thirty-two, Vishnu Karkare was the owner of the Deccan Guest House, Kapad Bazaar, Ahmednagar, as well as a municipal councillor.

The child from the Northcote Orphanage had come a long way when the massacre of Noakhali began.

'I wanted to do something,' Karkare later told a friend. To bring back into Hinduism those who had been forcibly converted, to set free some of the women who had been abducted – anything. I had no idea exactly what I could do. I thought I'd get there first and see what needed to be done.'

He was conscious that by himself he could do nothing; he needed others to go with him. And for this he did not have enough money. So on the day of the *Bhaubij* or the Hindu festival of 'Brothers' day' on which it is customary for brothers to give presents to their sisters, he called upon the public of Ahmednagar to come to his shop and donate whatever they could for their 'sisters' in Noakhali. By the end of the day he had collected more than Rs 3000.

He confessed that, when he saw how the people had responded to his call, tears came to his eyes. He and six Mahasabha workers went off to Noakhali. They wore typically Hindu turbans and dhotis and conspicuous caste-marks daubed on their forehead. Knowing that they were likely to be singled out for attacks, under their shirts they wore chain-mail jackets which they had bought from a man in Poona whom Karkare knew, Digambar Badge. Once in Noakhali, they travelled from village to village, and at places opened up relief centres in the name of 'Veer Savarkar'. They were horrified by what they saw and heard. At first the policemen would come into a village and force the villagers to surrender whatever arms they possessed by telling them that the government had made even the possession of swords and knives an offence. Then the mobs would swoop down on the defenceless villages. Accomplices would point out the houses of the richer Hindus. They would be looted and burned and the men killed, the women raped. Hindu women were regarded almost as a kind of perquisite of the Muslim elite. Karkare was given photographs of processions of naked women made to march through village streets followed by their swaggering abductors.

They were able to restore a few women to their families, save a handful of lives, feed a few children, reconvert perhaps a score of men in all. The problem was vast. Nothing that they were able to do looked as though it had made the slightest dent in it. Karkare once flew back to collect more funds. But when that money ran out they returned, humbled and despairing, and talking of revenge. This was a problem that had no solution; it was something that had to be prevented from happening ever again. The trouble in Bengal would not have been so bad if the Hindus had not been rendered incapable of standing up for themselves by repeated doses of Gandhi's *ahimsa,* non-violence. The answer was to fight back. That was the teaching of the Mahasabha; blood for blood.

So the little men brooded as their train rumbled through the heart of India. Meanwhile, the man whom they held responsible for the suffering of Bengal was himself walking from village to village in the Noakhali district; and his coming had stopped the carnage as though a switch had been turned off.

Gandhi toured Noakhali for seven weeks, taking in a village a day, and, when he felt sure that the trouble had really subsided, turned to Bihar. Unlike the Mahasabha, who only stood for the Hindus, Gandhi regarded himself as the champion of all sufferers. In Bihar, even though his threat to go on a fast had held the Hindus in check, it was feared that they were only waiting for Gandhi to go back to political work before attacking the Muslims again. To forestall this Gandhi toured all over Bihar, admonishing the Hindus and reassuring the Muslims, and he collected a fund for the Muslims who had suffered in the Bihar riots. He was still in Bihar when Lord Mountbatten came to India as the new Viceroy. At Mountbatten's pressing invitation, Gandhi went to Delhi on 30 March 1947. By then the riots had already broken out in the Punjab, and the refugee exodus had begun.

Ahmednagar is situated on a branch line, and to get to it from almost anywhere it is necessary to pass through Poona. Karkare, who was bursting with anger and eager to tell the world about the terrible things he had seen in Noakhali, took time off in Poona to see his two friends who ran the Party's newspaper. He knew that at least he could rely on them to publish his reports without watering them down for fear of the Press Act. He was greatly moved when he discovered that Apte and Nathuram, even though they themselves had not seen the atrocities, were just as worked up about them as himself. More, that they had already thought out several plans for retaliation. Karkare was so dazzled by the sheer audacity of these plans that he prevailed upon his friends to accept his services in their execution.

From the summer of 1947, Karkare became the team's messenger and contact man for nosing out suppliers of explosives, firearms and, as often as not, cash. In the pursuit of these clandestine activities, he had to shuttle constantly between Ahmednagar and Poona and make frequent trips to Bombay and other places at short notice.

Early in 1947, with their paper doing well, Apte and Nathuram decided to take on an extra hand as assistant editor, B.D. Kher, a close friend of Karkare. In fact Karkare actually seems to have shoehorned Kher into the job. Anyhow, what is significant here is that whenever Karkare came to Poona to see Apte, he stayed with this man, Kher.

The house in which Kher lived, No 2 Narayan Peth, had begun life as one of the city's *wadas,* or mansions of the grandees: a double-storeyed building with an inner *chowk*, or courtyard, which was the size of a badminton court. Over the years, the *wada*'s fifty-odd rooms had been divided up into a dozen or so flats of different sizes, and perhaps the largest of these flats was occupied by a senior police officer, Deputy Superintendent N.Y. Deulkar, the same Deulkar who had been on duty at Panchgani when Apte had heckled Gandhi at a public meeting, in the summer of 1944, and who knew by sight both Nathuram and Apte, as hot-headed Hindu Sanghatanites who looked upon Gandhi as an enemy of India.

The flat Deulkar lived in adjoined that of Kher, and in fact, a partition wall that divided their two flats had a grilled window to allow the free flow of air. As neighbours, Deulkar and Kher knew each other well... and exchanged pleasantries. What is more, Deulkar had also come to know, if only by sight, the man from Ahmednagar who frequently stayed with Kher, Karkare.

On one occasion, when Karkare had brought his drama group with him to Poona to give a few performances, some local friends had given a dinner party for the players in the courtyard of the house, and Deulkar had actually attended this dinner.

So here we come across a plot-twist which would seem too contrived in a work of fiction: a senior and highly competent officer of the Secret Police had personally known three principal conspirators in the Gandhi murder plot: Apte and Nathuram, whom he had to deal with when they heckled Gandhi in Panchgani and Karkare, a frequent guest of his neighbour, Kher. Which means that if only Deulkar had been given some inkling that such a plot was suspected and that Apte, Nathuram and Karkare were implicated, he could have nabbed them at short notice. To have defeated such a plot would surely have been the crowning achievement of Deulkar's career as a policeman.

As will be seen, even though the vital facts about the plot and the names of the people involved in it were known to the police in Bombay at least a week before the murder, that information never percolated to Deulkar in Poona.

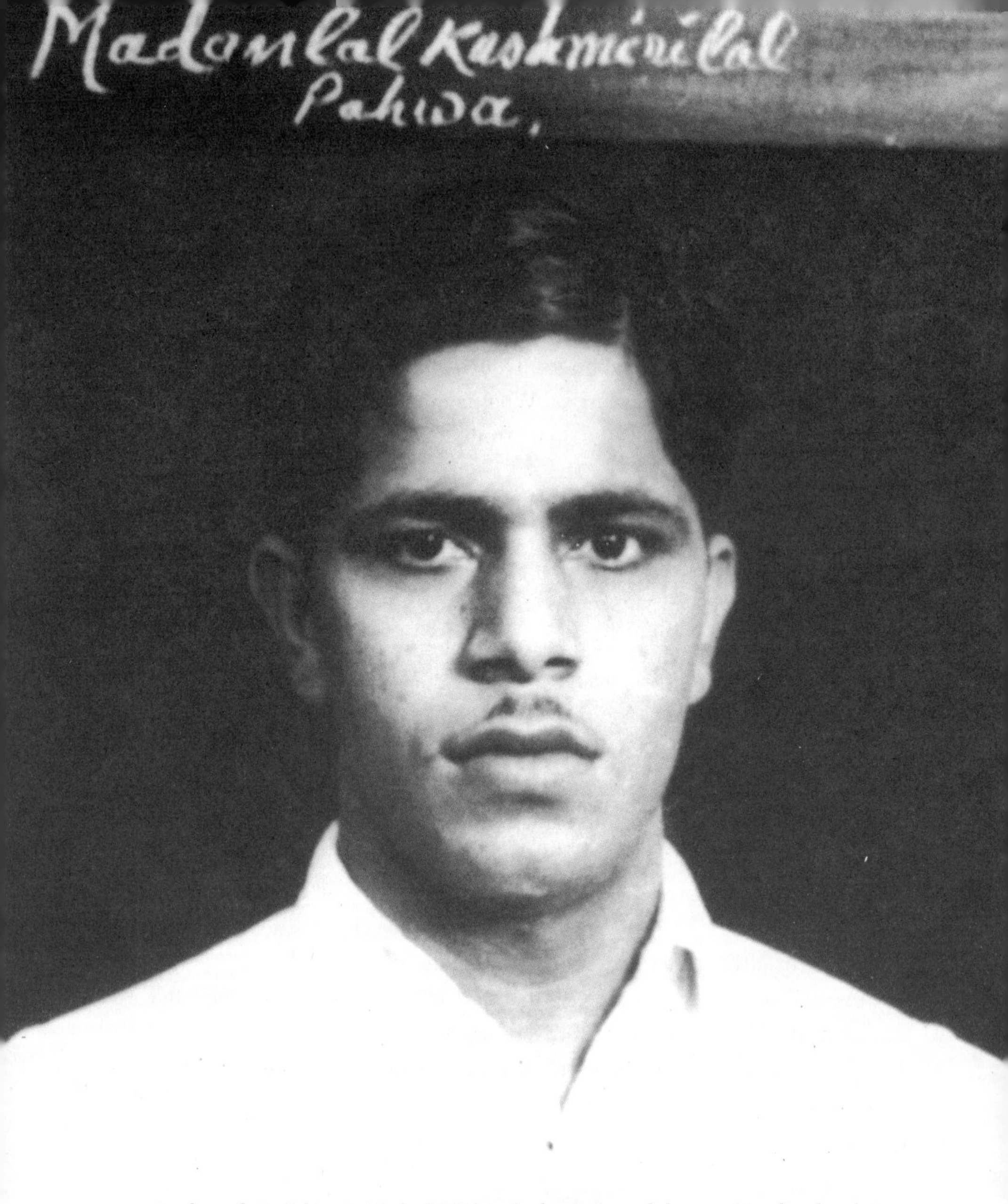

A refugee from Pakistan, Madanlal Pahwa had experienced the atrocities first hand. An accused in the Gandhi's murder case, for throwing a bomb at his prayer meeting on 20 January, he came in contact with Godse and Apte through Vishnu Karkare, who took him from a refugee camp in Bombay to Ahmednagar and helped him earn his living.

FOUR

I have joined the fire-cracker business.

— MADANLAL PAHWA

Karkare coming to tell them of the horrors he had seen was to Apte and Nathuram an experience similar to that of staff officers at some safe rear headquarters being told about front-line fighting by a private soldier. Both were acutely aware that they had done nothing practical in the service of the cause that was so dear to their hearts. They had written a series of fiery editorials condemning the Congress leaders for trying to placate Jinnah and, in defiance of the Press Act, had gone on publishing lurid accounts of the atrocities committed by the Muslims against the Hindus. And, if they had not actually commended similar atrocities on the part of the Hindus and Sikhs against the Muslims, they certainly had not denounced them.

In Poona, Apte lived in the family house, Anandashram, a two-storeyed building in Budhwar Peth. He had a large family to look after, consisting of his own wife and child as well as all of his six brothers and sisters, and it is said that he took his duties as the head of the family fairly seriously. But away from his family he instantly became obsessed by his role as a worker for the Hindu cause. His stint as a wartime officer in the Air Force, even in

Anandashram, the family house of Narayan Apte in Budhwar Peth, Poona, where he stayed with his six brothers and sisters, and wife Champa.

MS-CIT
Vision Infotech Tel.: 24454835
द्वारका शारदापीठम्

बेडेकर
नूपुर
मसाले, लोणची, चटण्या

नुपूर स्टोअर्स

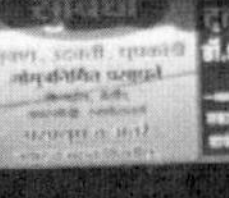

DR. S.G.PALSULE'S
HOMOEOPATHIC DISPENSARY
Dr. S.S.BHADBHADE
होमिओपॅथिक दवाखाना

a purely administrative capacity, had brought him into daily contact with other officers who had flown missions over enemy territory and who talked casually about bomb runs and blowing bridges and busting dams. That was the sort of punishment that he now dreamed of inflicting upon the enemies of Hinduism. The role he fancied himself in was that of a stern and dauntless leader of a band of dedicated men who were blindly devoted to him and whom he would dispassionately order to carry out the most dangerous of missions.

While Nathuram concentrated on the day-to-day work of their paper, Apte bustled about all over the place trying to raise funds to keep it going. He was a glib talker with a salesman's irrepressible manner and a ready smile, and his sincerity was undeniable. In Bombay he was able to make several useful contacts among the richer Hindu merchants who, themselves soft and ease-loving, were ready to pay conscience-money to a man who was so obviously doing something for their common religion.

During his frequent trips to Bombay, Apte combined business with pleasure by taking Manorama Salvi out. They would take in a film, eat dinner at a moderately priced western-style restaurant, and spend the night together in a hotel room. Apte bought himself a motorcycle and thought nothing of the 120-mile journey to Bombay just to be with Manorama for a few hours, and once he brought her with him on his motorcycle all the way to Poona.

If Apte's donors in Bombay had known about these escapades, they might not have been quite so generous to him; the fact that he was the lover of a Christian girl would, in their eyes, have tarnished his credentials as a worker for a Hindu cause.

For someone who thought of himself as a hard-boiled commando leader Apte was shockingly unsecretive. In Poona as well as in Bombay, he would hold forth over a drink about his favourite schemes to a circle of admiring friends, and often create the impression that he was about to give the go-ahead signal to some dramatically daring assault upon the enemy. The result was that several people who had not even met him had come to hear of his plans.

Among these was Dada Maharaj, the head of a sect of affluent Hindus known as the Pushtimarg Vaishnavas. He was forty-two years old, and lived in Bombay in a house in the precincts of the famous Bhuleshwar temple, which is one of the city's landmarks. A man called Mukund Malaviya told Dada Maharaj that he knew someone who was going to 'destroy the whole of the Pakistani Constituent Assembly', and that his name was Narayan Apte.

For someone who belonged to a holy order, Dada Maharaj was extremely worldly. He had gone to a university and taken a degree in Sanskrit, but he also held a pilot's licence. He took his position as the religious head of his sect very seriously, regarding himself as a spokesman and guardian of Hinduism itself. He was well read, businesslike and shrewd. Above all, he was an extremely rich man, with an annual income exceeding Rs 300,000 which was derived mainly from cash offerings left at his feet by his devotees 'out of their love and respect' for him.

Dada Maharaj, too, had like Karkare, travelled through the Noakhali district to see things for himself and had come back full of thoughts of retaliation. He went from place to place preaching what was more or less Savarkar's doctrine – that the Hindus must fight for their religious and political rights. But there was a hard, practical side to his resolution too, and to assist the Hindus to become militant he had secretly started to collect arms and explosives. The arms were to be distributed freely among the Hindus who lived in the areas bordering the Nizam's territory, and the explosives were for carrying out operations right inside the Nizam's territory.

But this side of his work Dada Maharaj entrusted to his younger brother, Dixitji Maharaj, who also lived nearby in an apartment on the temple property. The two brothers were close to one another and worked as a team, Dada Maharaj being the organizer and the financier and the man who made the decisions, Dixitji the one who looked after the details. Even though he chose to remain in the background, Dada Maharaj always had a good idea of what his brother was doing and who his callers were, particularly since Dixitji, for his part, always accepted Dada's superior status and kept him fully informed.

Dada Maharaj thus knew that, among Dixitji's suppliers of what were regarded as 'permissible' weapons, in that a licence was not required to buy or sell them, was a man called Digambar Badge, who lived in Poona and ran a small business somewhat grandiosely called Shastra Bhandar or the 'Storehouse of Weapons'. This Badge was the man who had supplied the six chainmail jackets to Karkare's group for their trip to Noakhali. Dada Maharaj had never spoken to Badge, but had seen him a few times.

Digambar Badge was also known to Narayan Apte and Nathuram Godse, and was later to join them in the conspiracy to murder Gandhi. But in July 1947, when Dada Maharaj first heard about Apte's plan to destroy Pakistan's leadership in one stroke, both Apte and Nathuram were a little standoffish towards Badge. At any rate, they had not bought anything other than 'Permissible' weapons from him, and certainly had not told him anything about their secret plans.

Dada Maharaj was so thrilled to hear about what Apte planned to do that he rushed to Poona to make his acquaintance and see if there was something he could do to help. In July 1947 he held at least two separate discussions with Apte, and in one of these they were joined by that enthusiastic new member of the team, Vishnu Karkare, who had been specially sent for by Apte to meet Dada Maharaj. Apte, now very much the Air Force Officer, spoke professionally about the plans in hand and asked Dada Maharaj for Rs 5000 for the purchase of two mortars with which to blow up the Pakistani Assembly. Dada Maharaj, who at the time had no idea what a mortar was, blessed the venture and drove back to Bombay deeply impressed. Later, he was to deny having paid Apte any money for the mortars, but this, under the circumstances, seems unlikely.

Whether Apte did indeed have the two mortars on offer never became clear. He had told Dada Maharaj something about their being available in Goa, which was then in Portuguese hands. On the face of it, it was an unlikely story. The fact remains that he never got the mortars.

What is perhaps more to the point is that, even if he had been able to get them, he would not have known how to make use of them, for he had received no training whatsoever in the use even of what the Army calls 'small arms' and certainly did not know much about its more destructive weapons such as mortars or (something which he thought of using later) a flame-thrower. No doubt some friend in the Army or a discharged soldier could have explained to him how a mortar was fired, but it is hardly likely that he would have been given a demonstration in its use; of how to get it firmly in position and find the right range without wasting too much ammunition. Even in expert hands, a mortar is a far from accurate weapon, and for the purpose Apte had in mind, which was the slaughter of all the members of the Pakistani Constituent Assembly while they were in session, it was a most impracticable one. There were two kinds of mortar then in general use in the Indian Army, the two-inch and the three-inch, and assuming even that the one he had in mind was the smaller type how was he going to sneak it into the Assembly Hall, set it up, sight it without a trial round and fire it without being detected? Or, was he thinking of shelling from outside, in the hope of destroying the building itself, which was an even more impracticable proposition?

Obviously the mortars were no more than a Walter Mitty dream, a device which his mind had endowed with capabilities it never possessed. And, unable to get hold of them, Apte turned to something only a little less Grand Guignol, a Sten gun. A Sten is a modified and mass-produced Thompson sub-machine gun and it had come into general use as an infantry soldier's weapon in both the Indian and British armies towards the end of the war. Apte and Karkare must have seen soldiers in Poona and Ahmednagar carrying Stens slung over their shoulders, and heard stories about the damage they were capable of doing. At least Stens were not too difficult to acquire. With the confusion attendant upon general demobilization, the repatriation of British troops from India (who were glad to unburden themselves of all surplus gear) and the division of the Indian Army as well as its stock of weapons, a large quantity of Stens and other easily concealable weapons had found their way into private hands. In the summer of 1947, therefore, it was fairly easy to buy a rifle or a Sten if you knew where to go.

Karkare, who had come to Poona to assist Apte in his talks with Dada Maharaj, had stayed on, and he now suggested to Apte that they should go and see if Digambar Badge could provide them with a Sten gun.

Up till now Apte and Nathuram had been chary of Badge. He was not the sort of person who inspired confidence at first sight. A face with its features askew as though seen in a mirror, Badge is small, almost diminutive, but thick-set and well built, so that he looks like a stunted wrestler. As the result of some childhood injury, one of his eyes is much smaller than the other, giving the impression of a cast. He has the swagger of a warrior in a shadow-play, and he is an inveterate name-dropper and a big talker who is all but unsnubbable, so that people must often have bought his knives and daggers merely to get away from him. Because of his short stature and the mismatched eyes, he is easy to locate even in a crowd.

Nonetheless, he fancies himself as someone who could escape detection by resorting to the oddest disguises, and as proof of this ability keeps an album full of theatrically posed photographs of himself in the garbs that he had supposedly worn while carrying out some especially hazardous mission. The photographs, usually taken in studios, show him dressed up variously as a Muslim butcher, a Brahmin priest doing pooja, a Sikh farmer and even as a prisoner in a barred cell guarded by a sentry. Once he turned up in Dixitji Maharaj's place dressed up as a professional musician, with his servant carrying the twin drums, *tabla* and *dugga* which invariably accompany true professionals. In the presence of Dixitji 'Badge opened the drums and took out daggers'.[3]

No description of Badge as he was at this time can be complete without bringing in his servant, Shankar Kistayya, and no generality can show up the workings of Badge's mind better than his relationship with this servant. Both might have stepped straight out of the pages of *Kim*.

Shankar, who was born in Sholapur and spoke only Telugu, was illiterate. In 1945, he lived with his mother and was working as an apprentice carpenter when Badge came upon him during one of his selling trips. Badge, who was looking for someone who could put handles on the dagger blades that he bought at cut rate from a supplier, offered Shankar the job. The salary was to be Rs 20 per month, plus food and clothes. Shankar joined Badge and went to Poona.

In Poona he did not even know the local language, Marathi, and was almost completely dependent on his master, who communicated with him in a mixture of broken Telugu and Hindi for all his needs. According to Badge, Shankar's duties were to prepare the handles for the daggers, to pedal the bicycle rickshaw in which Badge rode and carried his wares, and to act as his delivery boy and domestic servant.

The domestic chores, it turned out, included everything that a diligent housewife could conceivably be called upon to perform such as the washing of Badge's clothes and massaging his limbs, drawing water from the tap in the street, sweeping the floors, helping with the cooking and marketing, and anything else that Badge or his sister, who lived a few doors away, ordered him to do.

The salary that Shankar had been promised, Rs 20 per month was low even for those days. But, in actual practice, Shankar seldom if ever received his full salary. Badge would give him a couple of rupees once every week or so, and if Shankar protested Badge would berate him as a slacker and a bungler and his sister would call him even worse names. Once Shankar's mother came from Sholapur to plead for the payment of his arrears of salary, but fared no better than her son. In the middle of 1946, Shankar found that he was owed six months' wages and that there was no prospect of ever being paid them. In desperation, he fled.

But Badge had the answer to block that particular escape hole. He promptly filed a complaint with the police that his servant had stolen Rs 200 and run away. Shankar, who had gone straight back to his mother's house in Sholapur, was arrested and brought back in chains. A few nights in the police lock-up and his experience of police methods of interrogation convinced Shankar that Badge was too powerful a man even to run away

Shankar Kistaya, servant of Digambar Badge, became a part of the conspiracy without even being aware of it. He was the only member of the group who didn't even know who Gandhi was.

Digambar Badge, not the kind of person who inspired confidence, was the owner of Shastra Bhandar, the 'Storehouse of Weapons'. An 'inveterate name-dropper and a big talker', he came in contact with Godse and Apte through Dixitji Maharaj.

बाल गजा

Shastra Bhandar, or 'Storehouse of Weapons', at 300 Narayan Peth, Poona, was from where Digambar Badge ran his business of supplying 'Permissible' weapons. This photograph shows the present day site of the Shastra Bhandar. Badge became a part of the conspiracy to kill Gandhi when he supplied Godse and Apte with a revolver.

from: that, no matter how he was treated, he had to stick with his master for the rest of his life. He appealed to Badge for mercy; and his master, after arranging for him to be released on bail, took him back and magnanimously raised his salary to Rs 30 per month. Shankar resumed his job as Badge's man of all work with the total resignation of a lamb entering a slaughterhouse. He was then eighteen years old.

When the case against Shankar finally came up for a hearing Badge never showed up to press the charges. After adjourning the case several times for want of the complainant, the magistrate finally dropped it. But by this time nearly a year had gone, and Shankar, despite the fact that he never saw much of the money he had been promised, had become firmly established in the Badge household as a permanent servant.

On a rainy afternoon towards the end of July 1947, Apte and Karkare drove in a borrowed car to the Shastra Bhandar, or the 'Storehouse of Weapons', at 300 Narayan Peth. As Badge was to testify later, Apte, after telling him that he was doing business on behalf of 'influential persons' asked to buy a Sten gun.

Badge called out to Shankar to mind the store, and got into the car. They picked up a Sikh called Gurdayal Singh and drove on to the road that skirted the rear wall of the great Yeravda Central Prison. Here Gurdayal told them to stop, and got out of the car. He returned after only a few minutes. Cradled in his arms was a Sten gun.

It was as simple as that. Badge, the little man whom they had never taken seriously before, had established his credentials; he could produce the goods. They dropped Gurdayal Singh and, back in the Shastra Bhandar, Apte gladly paid Badge the price he asked, Rs 1200. He and Karkare then returned to the *Hindu Rashtra* office, delighted with the day's work. The end was in sight.

A Sten is not the kind of weapon a man can fire without a good deal of preliminary instruction in the manner of loading it and handling it and, of course, firing it. It is used mainly to spray a large quantity of ammunition in a single burst, and since it is normally fired from the hip, aimed in a general direction, it is a far from accurate weapon. Above all, it uses up enormous quantities of ammunition. Even granting that Apte might have managed to get a dozen or so loaded magazines for his Sten, he still had to get someone who was trained in its use and would be prepared to risk his life in an attempt to spray the Pakistani Constituent Assembly during one of its sessions in Delhi. In the event, the Sten was never used.

Meanwhile, time was running out. The date set for the granting of Independence was fast approaching. All through July, the Pakistani leaders had been leaving India in planeloads and, by 10 August, Delhi was virtually empty of them. On 14 August, Jinnah and his assembly were safely installed in their new capital Karachi.

And on 15 August freedom came to India. A 'tryst with destiny', Nehru called it; a 'historic hour', said Mountbatten. Nathuram Godse and Narayan Apte and their friends boycotted the festivities because they were 'painful and disgraceful' to them, 'while the whole of the Punjab was set by the Muslims in flames and Hindu blood ran in rivers'.

And the Mahatma too, for reasons of his own, observed Independence Day as a day of fasting and prayer.

In Bombay, Dada Maharaj, who was nothing if not practical, had been making his own inquiries about the capabilities and limitations of mortars. But, before his confidence in his new-found daredevil, Apte, was irrevocably shaken, Apte himself, accompanied by the devoted Karkare, turned up at his house with some elaborate explanation as to why the plan had to be abandoned. But, at the same time, they reassured Dada Maharaj that they had two other equally daring plans ready which they had come to discuss.

One, was to carry out a midnight raid on a busy octroi post on the Hyderabad side of the border, kill the officials with a couple of bursts from their Sten and make off with the day's collection of cash, which was believed to be considerable. This fund they would set aside to pay for further adventures. All the help they needed to carry out this plan was the use of a large car for the raiding party to travel in, something like Dada Maharaj's own Chevrolet station-wagon. The other plan, far more daring, was to lie in wait and destroy a train that was carrying a part of Pakistan's share of the stocks of ammunition left by the British. But, to put this one through, they would need Rs 10,000 to buy a couple of flame-throwers.

Dada Maharaj, now certainly less enthusiastic than at his first exposure to Apte, offered him his car for the raid on the octroi post but declined to put up the money for the flame-throwers 'unless I saw them'. Further, as though to show him that he too was not entirely a novice in such matters, he hinted that he knew where to lay his hands on 'some hand grenades and dynamite', if Apte needed them.

But Apte, who could not have seen a flame-thrower in action other than in a wartime newsreel, had pinned his hopes on that outlandish weapon. He declined the offer of grenades and dynamite, but accepted the loan of the car, and drove off in it to see Manorama Salvi.

For the next two months, Dada Maharaj heard nothing more from Apte, and at the beginning of October he went to Poona to find out what was happening, and to reclaim his car. Here Apte but on another show for him by inviting couple of dozen earnest young men from his Dal to meet him. He told him that they were all only waiting for the flame throwers to arrive before setting out to destroy the next ammunition train on its way to Pakistan. Apte also placated Dada Maharaj by inviting him to perform the opening ceremony of the new building that he and his partner had put up to house their press and staff. The *Hindu Rashtra* was going into its own premises.

Nothing was said about the raid on the octroi post, but Dada Maharaj must have considered himself lucky to see his car again. Also he must have been considerably flattered by the invitation to perform the opening ceremony. By rights it should have been Savarkar's privilege, but for the past few months Savarkar had not been in good health, and had stopped accepting engagements outside Bombay. Anyway, Dada Maharaj once again showed his readiness to help Apte, but declined to put up the money for the flame-throwers unless they were produced for his inspection. As Dada Maharaj later testified, there followed 'a talk about explosives for the purpose. Apte then suggested that he would send for Badge, through whom explosives could be obtained.

Dada Maharaj had, of course, known who Badge was and had even seen him once or twice when he came to do business with his brother, but had 'had no dealings with him'. He arrived loaded with 'gun-cotton slabs, fuse wire, detonators, and "808" packets containing explosive substances'. (This last was Nobel's nitroglycerine.) Dada Maharaj bought nearly everything that Badge had brought with him but most of it to one side to take back to Bombay for distribution to the Hindus in Hyderabad through his brother, Dixitji. Apte then produced a crudely made pistol which he said he had bought for Rs 400, and asked Dada Maharaj if he could have it exchanged for a more reliable pistol or revolver of a fairly large calibre. Dada Maharaj accepted Apte's pistol and promised that he would either get him a serviceable revolver in exchange or, failing that, reimburse the price of his pistol. After that he drove off in his car with the parting command: 'The ammunition train to Pakistan must be destroyed.'

But there was more on Apte's mind than the destruction of the ammunition train. In fact, he was quite frantic with domestic worries.

For one thing, his son's madness had become steadily worse and, a couple of months earlier, he had hardened his heart and had him committed to the mental asylum in Poona. His wife's grief when she discovered that he had come back without the boy was inconsolable. There were hysterical outbursts every day, and their weekly visits to the asylum were periods of torment. The son and the mother would cling together and sob bitterly and had to be torn apart by sheer force when the visiting-hours ended. The boy would mumble horrifying stories of the humiliation to which he had been subjected by the other inmates. Convinced that a few more weeks of life in the asylum would kill his son, Apte had persuaded the authorities to let him take him back on the promise of never letting him out on his own. The homecoming took place in an atmosphere of neighbourhood hostility and made little difference to his son's health, but at least the mother and son were together again, and she had ceased to look upon Apte as some kind of monster.

Then something else had happened to shatter whatever peace of mind Apte still had left. A couple of weeks earlier his mistress, Manorama Salvi, had told him that she was pregnant.

She was still at Wilson College, but no longer in the women's hostel. Now she lived with her parents in a Police Department flat in Byculla, almost next door to the Northcote Police Hospital in which her father, Daulatrao Salvi, worked as the medical assistant. She was in the senior BA class, and thus in her final year before graduation. Her romance with Apte had been going on for the best part of three years.

The Salvis were Christians. More, the family had lived in what, in India, is called a 'mission compound' and thus were full of missionary taboos. They were typical of the low-income, lower-middle-class Christians in India who were still too close to their conversion to allow for any liberal thinking on matters of sex and religion. The daughter had violated both. Not only was she going to have an illegitimate child, but the father was a Hindu who, if not an orthodox practitioner of Hinduism, yet took his obligations to it with terrifying earnestness. In the closed-circuit community of local Indian Christians, the shock of such a transgression would be altogether shattering.

Manorama Salvi had not told her parents that she was pregnant and, amazing as it might seem, in October 1947 the family still did not know of her long-standing romance with Apte.

Apte's less extroverted partner, Nathuram, had no such embarrassing problems, even though he, too, had numerous relatives in Poona. In fact, his father had left Sangli and brought his entire family to Poona, and his brothers and sisters had married and started *their families.* One of the brothers had set up his own house in Poona, and another, Gopal, in Kirkee, which is a suburb of Poona barely four miles from the centre of the town. Though Nathuram saw all these relatives fairly frequently and was particularly close to Gopal, he lived alone, in a single room which he had rented from a friend at 334 Shanwar Peth. This room was within walking distance of his new office, which was at 495 Shanwar Peth. His austerity, too, had, if anything become more pronounced. He ate the simplest of meals, and slept on a single blanket which, as often as not, was flung directly on to the floor. His one indulgence, as always, was coffee, of which he drank at least six cups every day. He spent much of his day in his office, which was in a tent pitched behind the main *Hindu Rashtra* building.

If, in the partnership of unlikes, Nathuram was very much the backroom boy, the man who did all the hard work and struggled with the day-to-day problems, it was a relationship that he accepted. He and Apte had if anything come closer. Both were totally convinced of each other's dedication to the cause and, after all, that was what mattered.

In everything except running the paper, Nathuram accepted Apte as the leader, or at least the senior partner. He knew all about the plans that Apte was hatching and, indeed, they held long and earnest discussions about their possibilities in Nathuram's tent. Since Nathuram knew even less about firearms and explosives than Apte did, he left such matters entirely to Apte and carried out his orders without question.

Apte and Nathuram and, at a different level, Badge and his servant, Shankar, were both integrated two-man teams. It was difficult to think of any one of them without the other. Karkare was the odd man out, unattached. Now he, too, was to acquire a partner and form a team.

Karkare was endowed by nature with quite phenomenal energy, which was perhaps the one quality that had enabled him to raise himself from the gutter to at least the lowest rung of the middle-class ladder and the fringe of respectability. Doubtless he could have gone on making money and expanding his business, but, as far as he was concerned, he had arrived. His Deccan Guest House was being run by a manager and making a handsome profit. Now he wanted to devote all his energies to the service, by his lights, of his country and religion.

After his return from Noakhali, he had taken to visiting Poona at least once every week at Apte's bidding, and he had several times accompanied Apte to Bombay; but he still lived in Ahmednagar and ran his Deccan Guest House as well as the Hindu Mahasabha office. But routine work no longer interested him or kept him occupied. Then, towards the middle of the year,

With an increase in the popularity of the *Hindu Rashtra* and its endorsement by many rich Hindu families, money was flowing in. Godse and Apte were able to buy a plot of land to start their own press and also bought a teleprinter. 495 Shanwar Peth was the address from where the press operated, this was at a walking distance from 334 Shanwar Peth, where Godse stayed alone in a room he rented from a friend. The main street of Shanwar Peth as it is today.

During these years of political turmoil there was something more happening in the life of Narayan Apte that stripped him of his peace of mind. While on the one hand was his son and his deteriorating mental condition, on the other was his mistress Manorama Salvi, who had now shifted to stay with her parents to a Police Department flat in Byculla in Bombay, was pregnant. Seen here is the flat where Manorama stayed with her parents.

advance elements of a refugee column reached Ahmednagar and suddenly Karkare found the sort of work that he craved for: refugee relief. He plunged into it with gusto.

One of Karkare's associates in this work, Ghanashyam Gilda, has described how, when the refugees first started to arrive in Ahmednagar, the government had made no arrangements for them whatsoever. They were dumped beside the railway track to fend for themselves and forgotten. Gilda borrowed a few lorries from haulage contractors to bring the refugees into town and even managed to find some tin shelters for them. But the problem of feeding them seemed quite insoluble until

> Karkare took on the responsibility. I would bring the refugees into town, and he would give them a meal in his hotel. After a few days, Karkare even managed to borrow some tents from the army and had them set up. For nearly a month, till the Visapur refugee camp was established by the government, Karkare must have given between 25,000 and 30,000 free meals.

The Visapur camp was an abandoned jail, situated twenty-six miles from Ahmednagar, and in it at least 10,000 refugees had been crammed. The refugees, according to an official report, 'were in an angry mood', for here, too, as in Delhi they could see the Muslims 'enjoying their properties and pursuing their avocations and politics in peace and even under official protection'.

If anything, here in Ahmednagar, the refugees had even more cause for anger than the refugees in Delhi. The district of Ahmednagar bordered on the princely state of Hyderabad which, even though 85 per cent of its people were Hindus, happened to be ruled by a Muslim prince, His Exalted Highness the Nizam. The Nizam had always favoured his co-religionists so outrageously that 80 per cent of all government jobs in his state were held by Muslims. Further, the Nizam had no intention of letting his dominion become a part of an independent India, and as the independence talks progressed his agents in Europe had been buying arms secretly to start what he sought to pass off as a people's rebellion. This irregular army of fanatics whom he had armed called themselves the Razakars – Volunteers. They had now come into their own and terrorized the Hindu population of Hyderabad and even carried out raids into the neighbouring districts. The leader of the Razakars, a firebrand maniac called Kassim Rizvi, who claimed that 'Hyderabad was a Muslim state by right of conquest,' had openly boasted that he would lead his Razakars and conquer Delhi itself.

The refugee camp buzzed with talk of retaliation. Their handiest targets were the unfortunate Muslims of Ahmednagar. They had the jobs, the houses, the shops, everything which, the refugees felt, should have been distributed among themselves. They began to wander about the streets, shouting slogans and uttering threats, and they formed processions to voice their demands. Their mood so alarmed the authorities that they immediately passed an order forbidding anyone in the whole of Ahmednagar district from carrying arms.

Karkare considered that the order was perverse; its only consequence would be that the Hindus of his district would find themselves defenceless against the raids of Kassim Rizvi's thugs. He, Karkare, had no intention of abiding by it. On the contrary, he was at the time busy making preparations for the raid on the octroi post that Apte had planned. That raid was to be launched from Ahmednagar, and everyone hoped that it would provide enough money to finance even more spectacular future operations. Karkare was looking out for someone who would sell him a few hand grenades cheaply. Badge's price for them had gone up, and he demanded anything up to Rs 200 apiece.

He had heard that in Bombay it was easier to buy grenades cheaply, because several people there manufactured them. He went to Bombay to find out, and there in the refugee camp at Chembur discover his man – someone who actually made hand grenades.

His name was Madanlal Pahwa, some of whose experiences as a refugee have been related in an earlier chapter. He came from a small town called Pakpattan, now deep in Pakistan. He had passed his matriculation examination and had served in the Royal Indian Navy as a wireless operator. He was honourably discharged from the Navy in 1946, and had gone back to his home. A few months later, when the Hindus were routed out of his part of the Punjab, he became part of a refugee column.

While in the Navy, he had been for a time posted in Bombay. So when, after his horrifying experiences in the refugee column, he finally reached India in the summer of 1947, he at once made for Bombay in the hope of finding a job.

Madanlal was now twenty years old. He was a thick-set, muscular man with dark brown hair and a wine-red smudge of a moustache who was not averse to using his hands to make a living and his fists to get what he considered his due. He wore the belligerent scowl of a man who bears a grudge against the world. He was, in short, the sort of young tough whom any commando captain would be glad to enlist in his unit.

In Bombay, Madanlal found himself shoved into the Chembur refugee camp, which was like a vast scrapheap of unwanted humanity that, for the sake of decency, had to be kept out of sight. He did not make a good, docile refugee. Every morning he would set off for the city and tramp its steamy streets in search of a job. A fellow-refugee took him to see a professor who taught Hindi in the Ruia College at Dadar, a Dr J.C. Jain. Dr Jain, who was the author of several Hindi books on esoteric subjects and who must have been looking for a strong young man who would peddle his books from house to house, is said to have taken pity on him and 'in order to help him monetarily' engaged him as a salesman. Madanlal was to receive no salary, but retain a 25 per cent commission on the sales he made.

The books were not easy to sell – nor, to be sure, did Madanlal try very hard to sell them. In the two months that he worked as Dr Jain's salesman, his commission did not exceed Rs 50.

While Madanlal was hawking Dr Jain's books, a social worker of Bombay, a lady called Mrs Modak, who was thinking of starting a drama group of amateur artists for providing free entertainment to the refugees, offered to engage him as her private secretary. But Madanlal declined because, as he told Mrs Modak, he had joined 'the fire-cracker business'.

Indians love noise; it is an index of high spirits, even a status symbol, for in olden days the right to beat the loudest drums was a privilege enjoyed only by the highest in the land. Our festivals during which fire-crackers are let off in their millions can be a trying time for foreign visitors, and even many Indians run away from the cities and into the country. The manufacture of fire-crackers is therefore a thriving business, and it was true enough that Madanlal Pahwa had found employment in a factory which was licensed to make them, Messrs Vassen Puspasen.

But this part of the firm's business was no more than a front for its more profitable and less legitimate activity, the turning out of hand grenades. In those days of communal conflicts, there was a ready demand for such handy missiles and, judging from the number of crudely made bombs that were for ever turning up in police raids, there must have been dozens of factories making them.

It was this part of the fire-cracker business that Madanlal had wormed his way into. He not only worked on the factory's grenade-making machine, but also served as a salesman for the grenades it made – an activity for which Professor Jain's unsaleable books provided an excellent cover.

One of the men to whom Madanlal was able to sell a book was Dixitji Maharaj, the younger brother of Dada Maharaj who had been so carried away by Apte's schemes. The price paid for the book was Rs 5. Whether Dixitji also bought a few of the grenades which Madanlal usually carried in his bag of books was never revealed by either. That no such transaction took place seems unlikely. After all, it was Dixitji's job to buy explosives and weapons on his brother's behalf, and it was at just about this time (end of August 1947) that his brother had hinted to Apte that he could provide him with a few 'hand grenades and dynamite'. Be that as it may, the sale of just one book seems to have established a fairly cordial relationship between the two men. Madanlal was encouraged to call again and, on these later occasions, was given some clothes and cooking pots for distribution among the refugees in the Chembur camp.

As might be expected, the moment Madanlal's back was turned after that first visit, the elder brother, Dada Maharaj, was given a full report of whatever had transpired. And it is also likely that, during one of the subsequent visits, Dada Maharaj was given an opportunity to see Madanlal without himself being seen.

Karkare, who had come from Ahmednagar to look for a reliable source of hand grenades, met Madanlal in late September or early October. At this time, Madanlal could not have been actually working in the factory, because a few days earlier he had had an accident in which he had lost the top portion of the index finger of his left hand. The finger had got caught in the gears of a turntable when his hand had slipped. His assistant had immediately stopped the machinery, but the finger was wedged between the teeth of two rotary wheels, and was bleeding profusely.

'There were half-made bombs lying all over the place,' Madanlal told the author many years later. 'To send for a doctor would have been suicidal. So I picked up a knife and chopped the finger off.'

Karkare, who had the easy small talk of a small-town hotelier and a ready wit, was also free with his money, and he was able to persuade Madanlal to go with him to Ahmednagar. Ahmednagar, too, had its own refugees, he explained, more than 10,000 of them, and many of them were from Madanlal's own part of the Punjab. They would make ideal recruits for the work he and his partners had in mind – that of sending raiding parties into the state of Hyderabad. He also promised to set up Madanlal in business. He made Ahmednagar seem a land of opportunity; in Bombay, Madanlal was wasting his time.

Madanlal needed a new job anyway, while his finger healed. He went with Karkare, and with them they carried a steel trunk filled with the bombs that Madanlal had made, together with a few slabs of explosive and some fuse wire.

For Madanlal it was a fateful decision. Within days after he had left, the firm of Vassen Puspasen was raided by the police and the owners and workers were arrested. If Madanlal, too, had been caught in the factory, he was sure to have earned at least a year in jail. But, if he escaped imprisonment this time, ironically it was only to be drawn into a far bigger crime – the conspiracy to murder Gandhi and a term of life imprisonment.

Madanlal had left without settling accounts with Dr Jain, but wrote two letters to him from Ahmednagar, and when, in the middle of December, he happened to visit Bombay he went and saw Jain at his house, Mangal Nivas, in Shivaji Park, Dadar. Despite a slight unpleasantness over the accounts for the books, it seems that his relations with Jain continued to be amicable. According to Jain, Madanlal once told him that he 'considered me as his father'.

In Ahmednagar, Madanlal opened a fruit stall or, as he told Dr Jain later, occupied a fruit stall from which he and his friends had driven away its Muslim owner. His business was financed by his friend Karkare whom he invariably referred to as Karkara Seth; 'Seth' means a banker or rich trader. He admired Karkare for what he had done for the refugees in Ahmednager, and himself became active in all of Karkare's schemes. Within two weeks of arrival, he had made up his mind to stay on in Ahmednagar because, as he testified later, 'my business was in a flourishing condition'. What was more, in those two weeks he had also managed to become friendly with a local girl.

In the middle of December, on one of his periodic visits to Poona, Karkare took Madanlal along with him and introduced him to Apte and Nathuram. Apte was particularly pleased that they had at last found someone who was familiar with explosives. All four sat together in the editor's tent at the *Hindu Rashtra* office and went over their plans to raid the octroi post. Now all they needed to put it through was a large car. As soon as Apte managed to get hold of one he and Nathuram would drive down in it to Ahmednagar. They left it at that.

The order forbidding the people to carry arms was made applicable to most parts of the Ahmednagar district on 6 November 1947. And with that, the police hoped, they had prevented all possibility of communal disorders.

But it soon turned out that someone in Ahmednagar possessed a stock of hand grenades, and at least four of these were thrown between 24 November and 26 December. One of them exploded in a packed cinema, the Vasant Talkies, and another in the midst of a Muslim procession on the occasion of the Mohurrum festival.

Amazingly enough, none of these bombs caused any serious damage and no one was killed by them. The one at the Mohurrum procession was thrown when the procession was passing through Kapad Bazaar, which is Ahmednagar's most crowded thoroughfare. It is also the street where Karkare's Deccan Guest House was situated.

At first, no one connected these bombs with either Karkare or Madanlal. Even though, because of the lead taken by both in the several demonstrations organized by the refugees, their names were well known to the police, they tended to regard the pair as agitators and slogan-shouters rather than men of violence. There is also the factor that most of the police officials were Hindus. They felt sorry for the refugees and at the same time they had good reason to feel resentful against a section of the local Muslims whom they believed to be secretly in sympathy with Kassim Rizvi and his Razakars, and who seemed to delight in provoking the refugees by putting up the Pakistani flag on their houses and mosques. At least a few of the policemen were kindly disposed towards people like Madanlal and Karkare who, they believed, were only fighting for the refugees.

It was pure chance that enabled the police to connect Karkare's name with the bombs. In the course of investigating a murder which had been committed in Poona several months earlier, the police found it necessary to carry out a search of the house where Karkare's manager, a Mr S.V. Ketkar, lived. In the event they found nothing to connect Ketkar with this murder but, during the course of the search, came upon a steel trunk which contained 'country made hand grenades, a revolver, daggers, explosives, fuses and about a hundred rounds of ammunition for both pistols and rifles'. What was more, the grenades were identified by experts as being of the same type as the ones thrown into the cinema and at the Mohurrum procession. Ketkar told the police that the trunk had been kept in his house by his employer, Karkare. This discovery was made on 1 January and, needless to say, it led the police to search Karkare's house and his hotel, but nothing incriminating was discovered at either place. After this incident, Karkare was 'ordered to be kept under constant surveillance'.

Nevertheless, the police seem to have shown towards Karkare an unusual degree of indulgence. In normal circumstances he would have been arrested and kept in detention while further investigation proceeded. The crime of possessing explosives, arms and ammunition without a licence was a serious one.

In police reports Madanlal's name had already been coupled with Karkare's as a man who 'was always creating trouble'. The last time he had created trouble in Ahmednagar was on 5 January, when a prominent Congress leader, Raosaheb Patwardhan, had come to town to preach communal harmony. Madanlal heckled him repeatedly and, by his own admission, rushed upto the platform and 'snatched away the microphone from Patwardhan'. He was arrested on the spot and marched off to the police station where he was kept in the lock-up till the next morning.

On 9 January, Inspector Razak of the Ahmednagar police recommended to his superiors that both Madanlal and Karkare should be kept in detention. It took three days for the recommendation to be processed and the final order issued. By then both Karkare and Madanlal had fled – in fact, they had run away on the very day Razak had recommended their arrest.

There can be no doubt that some friend in the Police Department who had access to the secret files had tipped them off. Inspector J.N. Joshi, who at the time acted as the Secretary to the District Police Superintendent (DSP) of Ahmednagar, later stated that he had run into Madanlal at the Ahmednagar railway station 'on or about 10 January' (it must have been on the ninth) and had actually spoken to him, and that Madanlal had told him that he was going to Delhi to get married. Joshi, who over the next couple of days, could not have been unaware that a warrant was about to be made out for arresting Madanlal, never thought of telling his chief that Madanlal had already gone away. In fact, he did not say anything about it till 21 January. By that time Madanlal had already exploded a charge of gun-cotton at Gandhi's prayer meeting in Delhi, and was caught by the police red-handed, while he still nursed a live grenade in his pocket.

For his part, Madanlal had not gone to any special trouble to keep his movements a secret. In fact, what he had told Inspector Joshi was quite true. He was on his way to Delhi to see about his marriage. And, if he had not told the Inspector that on the way he would be stopping in Bombay for a while, within two days of his reaching Bombay he had written a letter to his girl friend and in it he had given her an address in Bombay at which she should write to him. This address was care of his author friend, Professor J.C. Jain: Mangal Nivas, Shivaji Park, Dadar.

The girl's name was Shevanta. All the police had to do, if they really wanted to arrest Madanlal before he could do any mischief, was to keep an eye on Shevanta's mail, and it would have led them to him. Intercepting the letters of everyone connected with a suspected criminal is quite a common practice in India. That the police were not aware of Shevanta's infatuation for Madanlal is difficult to believe; after all, they were supposed to have been keeping a close watch on his movements.

Poor Shevanta. Her identity was never revealed, and must remain for ever confined to the two letters she wrote to Madanlal in reply to his. All that is certain is that she was desperately in love with him, and, further, that she had no idea that he had decided to jilt her. She was barely literate, and yet wanted to tell him of her passion for him; for this she resorts to a time-worn device, the quoting of Hindi couplets which have a double meaning, capable of an interpretation which can be either dreamily romantic or daringly erotic.

The first letter written on 15 January is fairly innocuous. It acknowledges the one sent by Madanlal and assures him that 'she understand everything'. She accuses him of leaving after 'showing your love for only two days', and tells him that her heart yearns for him. She implores him to treat her letter as though it were a telegram and return at once, and to read in her words much more than they say.

The second letter written the very next day, sets out to describe the extent of her infatuation. After telling him that his memory haunts her, she asks him to return at once and to bring for her a sari and a pair of sandals. 'Come soon because my heart remains sad,' she concludes and then quotes:

> My flower garden looks desolate without you.
> Oh, come, my simple-minded hunter.
> Nights are passing, days are going,
> And my heart is sinking,
> Spring has come and the flower-bed waits to be looted.
> Oh, come, my simple-minded hunter.
> My life's companion, your love troubles me
> And says something else which I dare not tell.
> How can I live without you,
> Oh, come my simple-minded hunter.

This time Shevanta signs herself as Madanlal's darling, and scribbles yet another couplet which the translator appointed by the court found to be 'illegible'.

The hunter had left Bombay even before the first letter got there. He was to see both letters for the first time only when they were included by the prosecution among the documents on which they would rely to prove their case against Madanlal and others.

As for Shevanta, only four days after she wrote that love-sick letter she must have heard what Madanlal had been up to. On 20 January he was arrested by the police in Delhi for throwing a bomb in the compound of Birla House while Gandhi was holding his prayer meeting.

The cast of characters: Seven in number – the three pairs – Apte-Nathuram, Karkare-Madanlal, and Badge-Shankar; and the odd man Gopal Godse, who just wanted to be of some help to his brother. Veer Savarkar (sitting second from left), believed to be their leader and the brain behind the killing. An affidavit submitted by Savarkar in the Bombay High Court sites this picture as taken without his consent on 11 May 1948, at the CID office Bombay. He later testified in the affidavit that the police might use this photograph to 'prejudice his defence' in the trial.

FIVE

As regards non-violence, it was absurd to expect forty crores of people to regulate their lives on such a lofty plane.

— NATHURAM GODSE

January 9 was a Friday. Karkare and Madanlal left Ahmednagar by the afternoon train and were in Poona late in the evening. Now that their carefully hoarded stock of explosives had been confiscated, their first concern was to find more supplies. From the station they took a tonga to Badge's store and reached it at 8.30 p.m. As Badge testified later, he 'was introduced to Madanlal for the first time by Karkare. Karkare then asked me to show what *mal* I had with me.'

Badge and Karkare, of course, spoke in Marathi, and *mal,* which merely means 'goods' was a term they had started using in conversation to describe the contraband part of Badge's wares, such as explosives, arms, detonators and ammunition. Badge ordered his servant, Shankar, to bring out the goods from where they were hidden under a stone slab at the back of the house. When Shankar returned with an assortment of 'gun-cotton slabs, hand grenades, cartridges, a pistol, and fuse wire', Madanlal, after a professional look at it, pronounced that 'he knew how to operate the articles'. Madanlal and Karkare then went away, without buying anything.

The last train to Bombay left Poona just before midnight. That gave Karkare and Madanlal plenty of time to go and see Apte and Nathuram and hold a prolonged consultation with them. Madanlal had seen whatever Badge had to sell, and was satisfied that he could use it, but everyone was agreed that Badge's prices were far too high. Apte, who had to worry about the finances, was particularly anxious that they should find a cheaper source of supplies. Madanlal's old firm was no longer in business, but he had contacts among the refugees in the Chembur camp who, he felt sure, would lead him to someone who manufactured bombs and sold them cheaply.

He himself had no plans for returning immediately, for he was on his way to Delhi to take a look at one or two prospective brides about whom his uncle and father had written to him. But, in the few days that he would be in Bombay, he would try to locate a reliable supplier and introduce him to 'Karkara Seth', who was accompanying Madanlal as far as Bombay.

According to Karkare, once again the talk went round and round: a commando sortie into Hyderabad, the attack against the ammunition train, the raid on the octroi post. Now that they had an expert sitting in on their discussion they were much more down to earth. For the first two schemes they did not have the right kind of armaments, for the third they did not have the right kind of car.

They all felt indignant: about Kassim Rizvi and his fanatical challenges, and they reviled Gandhi and Nehru and the other leaders for not dealing firmly enough with Rizvi and his Razakars and the Muslims in general. But both Madanlal and Karkare told the author, after their release from prison and long after it could be of any conceivable advantage to either to be secretive about such details, that on the evening of 9 January there was no talk of murdering Gandhi.

In fact, nothing definite was decided upon. Madanlal and Karkare were to proceed to Bombay and look around for another supplier of *mal*. Apte and

Nathuram would stay on in Poona and think out the next move. The one thing they were all agreed about was that it was high time they struck somewhere. Apte and Nathuram knew where to contact Karkare in Bombay, for he either stayed with his wife's sister, a Mrs Lalit, in the Girgaum area or with a friend, a Mr G.M. Joshi, who lived in the suburb of Thana, but ran a printing press, the Shivaji Printing Press, in Dadar. They would contact Karkare immediately in case something urgent turned up. Not that anything was likely to turn up.

Madanlal and Karkare reached Bombay early on the morning of 10 January. After stopping at Mrs Lalit's house for a cup of tea, they went to the Chembur refugee camp and got down to work. The weekend was a good time to find everyone at home.

On Sunday afternoon, Madanlal ran into his professor friend Dr Jain in front of the Plaza Cinema in Dardar and told him that he would come and see him later in the evening. He turned up at eight, when another friend of Dr Jain's, a textile broker named Angad Singh, who had met Madanlal before, also happened to be there. According to Angad Singh, Madanlal was full of 'tall talk' about his exploits in Ahmednagar. He told them how they had formed a party in Ahmednagar with the object of hounding out the Muslims and that the party was financed by his good friend Karkara Seth; that they had already taken over the fruit and vegetable stalls that had belonged to the Muslims; and that, when the Congress leader, Raosaheb Patwardhan, had come to preach tolerance and told them that the Hindus should think of the Muslims as their brothers, he, Madanlal, had 'rushed up to him, whipped out a knife, caught hold of his collar and challenged him, if he dared, to repeat what he had said.'

Madanlal then 'took out from his pocket some Marathi newspapers and gave them to Dr Jain saying that they were full of praise for him.'

As it happened, neither Jain nor Angad Singh could read Marathi well, and in any case Jain was far more interested in what Madanlal had to say about the money he owed him than in what the papers had to say about Madanlal.

At about 8.30 Angad Singh left. Madanlal told Jain that he would call again in the next few days and pay him his dues. Then he went back to Chembur.

That night he wrote to Shevanta, his girl in Ahmednagar, and asked her to address her reply care of Dr Jain. But he did not post the letter till late on Monday, with the result that Shevanta did not receive it till the morning of Wednesday, 14 January.

And so the weekend passed; a quiet weekend. The news in the papers was chiefly about the discussions that Mountbatten was holding with the Indian princes.

It was not till Monday evening that things suddenly began to move. Gandhi announced his decision to fast, and as the news came clacking out over their office teleprinter Apte and Nathuram made up their minds to kill him.

So a target had presented itself. 'D-Day' was immediately fixed 20 January.

It was typical of the pair that nothing else was decided – how the killing was to be accomplished, with what weapons, and who else they would need to go to Delhi to assist them in the killing. The details were to be worked out as they went along, the weapons collected, the men assembled and allotted their roles.

Over the next week, in Poona, in Bombay and in New Delhi, in taxicabs and trains, and in the streets of Bombay, their imagination added the bits and pieces till they had created a many-limbed monster. The plan to kill one man became a plan of indiscriminate slaughter. To accomplish the death of Gandhi, they zestfully set out to kill or maim scores of men and women who, they knew for certain, would be crowding around Gandhi at the time. It was something that only sick minds could have conjured up, something that even the most brutal of commandos operating within enemy territory might have thought too callous. As it finally crystallized in the Marina Hotel in Delhi's Connaught Circus on the afternoon of 20 January, the scenario was a horrifying mixture that was part farce and part *Marat-Sade*. If it did not show up Apte and Nathuram as cowards, equally so it did not show them up as men of courage, either, for they had managed to farm out all the dangerous roles to their subordinates and themselves intended to remain in the background. They had even put a pistol into the hands of that most inoffensive of men, Badge's servant, Shankar Kistayya. Poor Shankar didn't even know who Gandhi was, or what he had done, or why he has to fire the pistol at him.

Nathuram's first act connected with the plot was an altogether practical one. Two years earlier, he had taken out two insurance policies on his life, one for Rs 3000 and the other of Rs 2000. On the morning of 13 January he wrote off to the insurance company that he had nominated his beneficiaries for both. The first was Sindhu, his brother Gopal's wife; the second Champa, Narayan Apte's wife. That Apte himself was not nominated is understandable; but it seems clear that Nathuram also knew that Gopal was going to share whatever dangers Apte and himself were going to be exposed to.

Gopal Godse was twenty-seven years old. A gentler, more soft-spoken and self-effacing man, someone who would more neatly fit into the definition of a quiet householder, would be difficult to imagine. Admittedly he had been influenced by his brother's fervent zeal for the Hindu cause, but so far he had never felt involved in it. He was far more concerned with the problems of day-to-day living, of bringing up his family, holding down his job, the good opinion of friends and neighbours.

After passing the matriculation examination, he had joined the Military Ordnance Service as a civilian clerk. When the war began he volunteered for service overseas and in 1941 found himself sent off with the British column that went to Iran and Iraq, PAIFORCE. He had remained with PAIFORCE for the next three years, and had returned to India in April 1944. Since then he had been posted as an assistant storekeeper in the vast complex that is the Ordnance Depot at Kirkee, four miles out of Poona. His service record was wholly unblemished, and he was hoping to be promoted soon. He was married and had two daughters, one aged two years and the other four months. He had rented a couple of rooms tucked away behind the bazaar of

Kirkee, where he and his wife lived, but his wife had gone away for a few days to her parents' house in Poona and taken the children with her.

Gopal had always been particularly close to Nathuram and so had a fair idea of the plans that Nathuram and his partner were constantly hatching, but he had never envisaged his own participation in them. Badge, who was a fairly frequent visitor to the *Hindu Rashtra* office and had had dealings with Apte and Nathuram, had never met Gopal.

The one reason why Gopal had been taken into their confidence was that he possessed a revolver. It was a service revolver that he had picked up while he was with PAIFORCE, and which he had managed to bring back to India. A service revolver is of a 'prohibited' bore and cannot be bought or sold by civilians. Nor were Gopal's social position and income such that he would have been granted a licence for a pistol or revolver even of a non-prohibited bore. On his return home he had buried it in the yard of his village house.

This bringing back of a revolver may have been some indication of a split personality, for as soon as Gopal heard what his brother and Apte were planning to do he seemed to be transformed into a blood-thirsty terrorist. It was almost as though his meekness had been a mask, that all his life had been a period of waiting for just such an opportunity to show his fangs. He declared that he would not part with his revolver unless he was himself allowed to use it, and that nothing Nathuram could do would shake his resolve. He became a member of the conspiracy, and promised that he would bring his revolver to Delhi in good time for the assassination, Nathuram advanced him Rs 250 for his expenses.

It was a fitting commentary of Gopal's Jekyll-and-Hyde personality that, even to commit a murder, he could not bring himself to go off without obtaining leave from his office. On the morning of the fourteenth, he put in an application for seven days' leave beginning from the fifteenth to attend to some 'immediate farm affairs in my village'. And when his commanding officer turned down the application Gopal put in another application asking for leave from the seventeenth instead. Only after his was sanctioned did he proceed with his mission.

So Gopal could be relied upon to contribute a revolver. The two leaders had also decided that they should take with them the grenades and explosives that Madanlal had been shown in Badge's shop and said he could use. Apte sent for Badge.

This was on the evening of 13 January. Badge who had returned from one of his excursions only a few hours earlier, went to see Apte, who told him he wanted to buy all the grenades and explosives he had shown to Madanlal, but that he would take delivery and pay for them in Bombay. It is possible that, at least as far as Bombay, Apte wanted to avoid all possible risk of being caught with a bag full of munitions. A more charitable explanation might be that he had no money to pay for the goods and was sure that he could raise it in Bombay. Badge had no objection to this provided, of course, that Apte would pay his and his servant's travelling expenses. They agreed to meet in the Hindu Mahasabha office in Bombay on the following evening.

The Deccan Express leaves Poona railway station at 3.30 in the afternoon and gets into Bombay's Victoria Terminus four hours later. On 14 January, Badge, accompanied by Shankar, got into a third-class compartment. Shankar carried a shoulder bag made of khaki cloth which contained the five hand grenades, two gun-cotton slabs, six detonators and a coil of black fuse that Badge had promised to deliver to Apte and Godse in Bombay. Badge, who had an idea that the police were showing an excessive interest in his activities, was being extra careful. He had ensured that, in case of a search, it would be Shankar who would be caught with the goods. He was also in one of his moods for affecting disguise. He had, for the past few weeks, let his beard grow, and today was dressed up in a saffron dhoti and a knee-length saffron robe. Around his neck he wore garlands of dried-up berries and he had daubed his forehead with wood ash. He was a *sadhu,* a holy man. No *sadhu* ever dresses up so fully, and even in the crowded third-class compartment Badge must have stood out like a flame-coloured danger signal. But, if his disguise only made him more conspicuous, such doubts could never have assailed Badge himself.

A few carriages behind him, in an otherwise empty second-class compartment, sat Apte and Nathuram. They had managed to find window seats facing one another. If Badge's efforts to hide his identity verged on the comic, neither Apte nor Godse seemed to be bothered about hiding theirs. Or, if they were, any such resolve must have melted when Apte looked up and saw that a very pretty woman was going up and down the corridor obviously looking for a window seat. Apte got up and offered her his seat and himself sat on the opposite bench, next on Nathuram. As soon as the train started, he asked the woman if she was not Bimba, the famous screen actress, and she admitted that that indeed was her screen name.

As the train neared Dadar, a suburb of Bombay, they struck up an amicable conversation, and Apte, who was getting out at Dadar, discovered that Bimba, too, lived there. He asked if he could take her to her destination, but it turned out that she was being met by her brother. She offered to drop Apte and Nathuram instead, if they were going somewhere close to where she lived, which was in Shivaji Park. Her house, she told them, was almost next door to Savarkar's house, which was called Savarkar Sadan.

Apte and Godse were actually headed for the office of the Hindu Mahasabha, which was about half a mile from where Savarkar lived, but Apte accepted Bimba's offer with alacrity. She dropped them in front of Savarkar's house, but never saw whether they went in.

By giving in to his vanity as a lady-killer, Apte was not only creating evidence against himself but was also tightening the noose around Savarkar, who had no idea of what they were planning to do. For Bimba remembered the dashing young man and his taciturn friend and where she had dropped them, and the evidence she gave in court strengthened the police case against Savarkar as the brain behind the conspiracy.

Their excursion in Bimba's car had actually taken them away from the Hindu Mahasabha office where they had told Badge to meet them, and it was well past 8.30 when they got there. It would have been unlike Apte if he had not gone on talking about his chance meeting with a well-known film actress even after they were joined by Badge and Shankar, with the result that Badge, too, came to know about the encounter.

Shankar Kistayya, who was greatly excited about his trip to the great city, was sorely disappointed when Badge told him that they were getting off at Dadar. 'Why?' he demanded.

'Because this is where we have to deliver the *mal*.'

It seems they had no idea that Apte and Nathuram had travelled on the same train as theirs, nor did they run into them on the platform at Dadar. As befitted a holy man, Badge decided to walk to the Hindu Mahasabha office.

The office consisted of a three-storeyed building. The main hall where the members came and sat and read papers and chatted (and, as will be seen, at times even stretched out on the floor and spent the night) was on the first floor, reached by a staircase which was common to all the floors of the building. When Badge discovered that Apte and Nathuram were not there, he decided to wait. After half an hour, just as he and Shankar were thinking of going down for a cup of tea, Apte and Godse walked into the hall.

Apte had not had time to raise the money to pay off Badge. They sat and talked for a while and it was decided that Badge should keep the bag somewhere safe for the night and bring it back the next morning; whereupon, according to Badge, they took a taxi and went to Dixitji Maharaja's house in the yard of the Bhuleshwar temple, getting there when it was well past ten o'clock and Dixitji had already retired. But Badge, who had visited the house several times earlier and knew Dixitji's personal servant, Narayan, left the bag with him, telling him that he would call for it the next morning.

It was nearing midnight by the time Badge and Shankar were taken back to Dadar and dropped at the Hindu Mahasabha office where Apte told them to spend the night, and where he promised to come and see them in the morning. As they walked into the main hall, in which most of the lights had now been turned off, they saw that three or four other men were sleeping on the floor. One of these men sat up and called out 'Badge, *kabh aye*?' ('Badge, when did you come?') So much for Badge's elaborate disguise.

Savarkar Sadan: According to Badge, who became the police approver, Apte and Godse had visited the Savarkar Sadan, to take his blessings before leaving for Delhi on 17 January. The house was attacked by an angry mob after it became public that Nathuram Godse, the man who killed Gandhi, was a Hindu fanatic. A present day photograph is of the Savarkar Sadan.

On their way to Delhi to accomplish the mission, the members of the team all collected in Bombay, where the office of Hindu Mahasabha became their common meeting point.

He glared at his questioner and haughtily told him that he must be making a mistake, but after a few seconds recognized him to be Madanlal Pahwa, whom Karkare had brought to his shop a few days earlier.

Credentials thus established, they chatted amicably, and Madanlal, who had plenty of bedding to spare, gave the other two a blanket and a sheet to sleep on.

At 8.30 the next morning, when Madanlal was barely awake, Apte and Nathuram turned up. They had stayed the night at the Sea Green Hotel (South) on Marine Drive and had been up for hours. They had already visited the Tata Airlines office in the Fort area where they had bought tickets for Delhi for the afternoon flight on 17 January, two days later. They had booked the tickets under false names, Apte calling himself 'D.N. Karmarkar' and Nathuram 'S. Marathe'.

In the Mahasabha hall, they told Madanlal that they would call for him later and dashed off with Badge and Shankar. In the street they took a taxi to the Shivaji Printing Press, run by Karkare's friend Mr G.M. Joshi and which was also in Dadar, barely a mile away. Near the entrance to the Press, they ran into Karkare. Apte and Nathuram took Karkare to one side and told him what they had decided to do, and then all of them got into the taxi and went back to the Hindu Mahasabha office. Here Madanlal was waiting for them, his bedding done up in a neat roll. Badge ordered Shankar to get out and wait for him upstairs, and Madanlal, after depositing his bed-roll on the luggage-carrier fixed on top of the taxi, got in. They told the driver to take them to the Bhuleshwar temple where Dixitji Maharaj lived.

Dixitji was in bed, suffering from a virulent form of scabies, and asked for his visitors to be shown into his bedroom. He had, at one time or another, met Apte, Nathuram, Badge and Madanlal, but did not know who Karkare was. Only after the others had vouched for Karkare did Dixitji call his servant and order him to bring out the bag that Badge had left the previous night.

Dixitji was greatly annoyed with Badge for having, without his knowledge, used his house for depositing incriminating material, and at the way Badge was now displaying the contents of his bag to his friends, without any attempt at camouflage or secrecy. He was about to say something sharp to Badge when he noticed that Badge was 'trying to explain to the others as to how to work a hand grenade', and was shocked that he did not even know that the striker handle had to be held down till the moment of throwing. It was not as though Dixitji himself had ever thrown a hand grenade, but he had seen it being done in films, and at least knew that to go on holding the grenade after the striker handle had been released was to invite a horrible death. He explained to them that it was 'important that the spring was to be kept tightly held down'. Then he told them – as he must have seen a film hero doing it – that 'the pin was to be pulled out with one's teeth'.

Incredibly enough, even Madanlal who, it will be recalled, had made and thrown bombs, had no knowledge of the proper way to handle a military-type hand grenade.

By all accounts, this was the only lesson that the conspirators ever received in the use of the 36 grenade; they went on believing that it was essential to pull out the pin with one's teeth. Having by his display of superior knowledge put his visitors in their place, the holy man shuffled off painfully for his medicinal bath; but his resentment was still unappeased and, as will be seen, when he joined them again he remained firmly un-cooperative.

In the bedroom, the five visitors were left to themselves. Here Karkare took Madanlal to one side and told him that they had decided to murder Gandhi. Madanlal, ever the man of quick decisions and instant action, pronounced it to be 'an excellent idea', and took charge of Badge's bag. Later he tucked the bag away in his bed-roll, which he had left in the entrance hall.

Madanlal, who was headed for Delhi anyway to be introduced to the several girls his relatives there had arranged for him to look over so that he should select one of them as his bride, was impatient to start. It does not seem to have occurred to him that he could not take an active part in the plot to murder Gandhi and still hope to go through with the plans for his marriage. Karkare, Madanlal's benefactor and guide, immediately agreed

Sea Green Hotel: An affordable hotel on Marine Drive, Bombay. It was in the Room No. 6 of this hotel that Godse and Apte stayed from January 14 to 17, 1948, before they left for Delhi. Apte even met up with his girlfriend Manorama Salvi here.

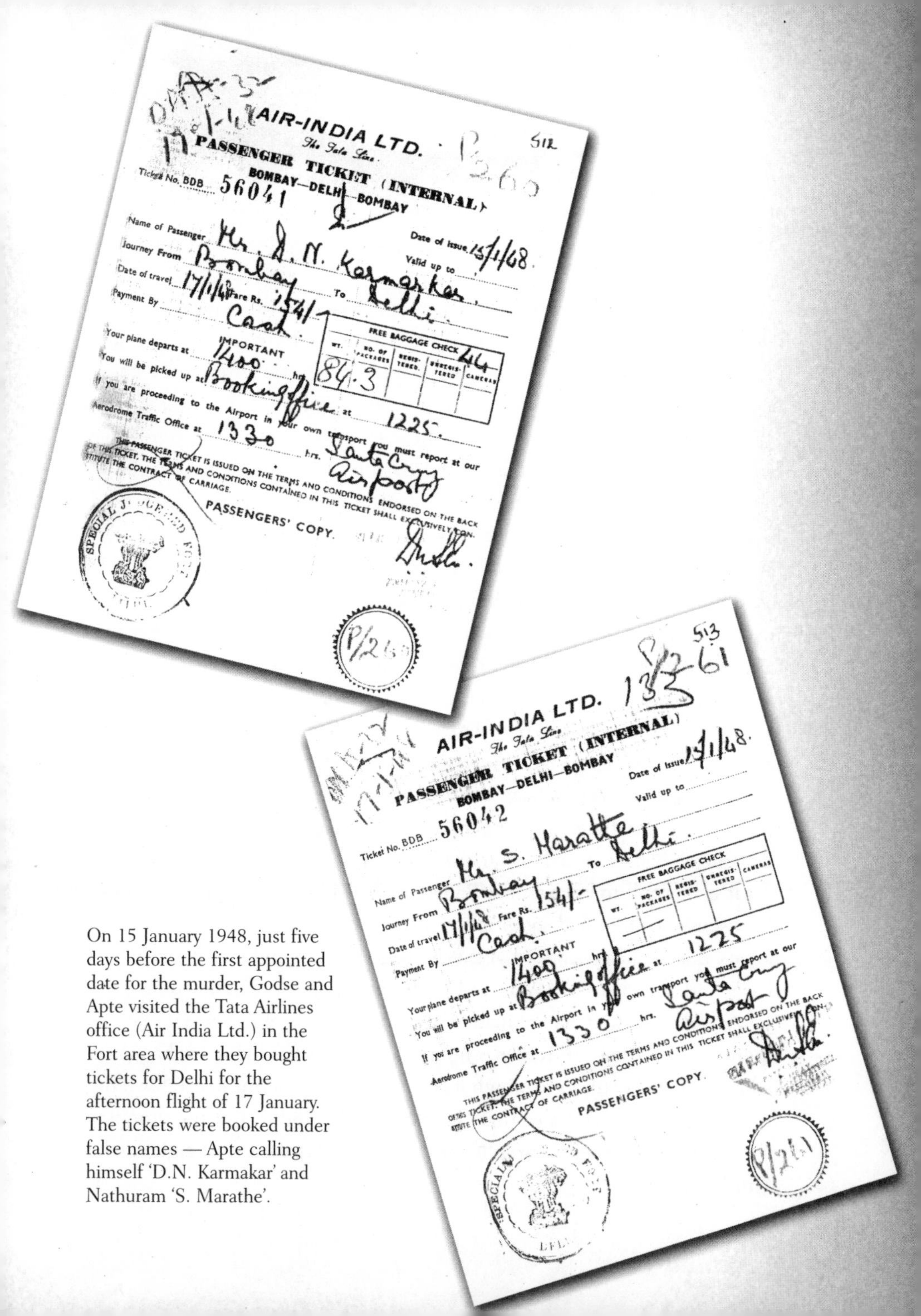

AIR-INDIA LTD.
The Tata Line.
PASSENGER TICKET (INTERNAL)
BOMBAY—DELHI—BOMBAY

Ticket No. BDB 56041

Name of Passenger Mr. D. N. Karmarkar, Date of issue 15/1/48
Valid up to
Journey From Bombay To Delhi.
Date of travel 17/1/48 Fare Rs. 154/-
Payment By Cash.

FREE BAGGAGE CHECK				
WT.	NO. OF PACKAGES	REGISTERED	UNREGISTERED	CAMERAS
84.3				

IMPORTANT
Your plane departs at 1400 hrs
You will be picked up at Booking office at 1225
If you are proceeding to the Airport in your own transport you must report at our Aerodrome Traffic Office at 1330 hrs. Santa Cruz Airport

THIS PASSENGER TICKET IS ISSUED ON THE TERMS AND CONDITIONS ENDORSED ON THE BACK OF THIS TICKET. THE TERMS AND CONDITIONS CONTAINED IN THIS TICKET SHALL EXCLUSIVELY CONSTITUTE THE CONTRACT OF CARRIAGE.

PASSENGERS' COPY.

AIR-INDIA LTD.
The Tata Line.
PASSENGER TICKET (INTERNAL)
BOMBAY—DELHI—BOMBAY

Ticket No. BDB 56042

Date of issue 15/1/48.
Valid up to
Name of Passenger Mr. S. Maratha
Journey From Bombay To Delhi.
Date of travel 17/1/48 Fare Rs. 154/-
Payment By Cash.

FREE BAGGAGE CHECK				
WT.	NO. OF PACKAGES	REGISTERED	UNREGISTERED	CAMERAS

IMPORTANT
Your plane departs at 1400 hrs
You will be picked up at Booking office at 1225
If you are proceeding to the Airport in your own transport you must report at our Aerodrome Traffic Office at 1330 hrs. Santa Cruz Airport

THIS PASSENGER TICKET IS ISSUED ON THE TERMS AND CONDITIONS ENDORSED ON THE BACK OF THIS TICKET. THE TERMS AND CONDITIONS CONTAINED IN THIS TICKET SHALL EXCLUSIVELY CONSTITUTE THE CONTRACT OF CARRIAGE.

PASSENGERS' COPY.

On 15 January 1948, just five days before the first appointed date for the murder, Godse and Apte visited the Tata Airlines office (Air India Ltd.) in the Fort area where they bought tickets for Delhi for the afternoon flight of 17 January. The tickets were booked under false names — Apte calling himself 'D.N. Karmakar' and Nathuram 'S. Marathe'.

that they should leave Bombay on the first train they could get on. It was arranged that they would take a room in the Hindu Mahasabha Bhavan in Delhi, where Apte and Nathuram would come and see them on the morning of 18 January.

Apte and Nathuram who, for the past three days, had gone over the details of their plot time and time again, had begun to feel that, to be sure of success, they would need one or two more revolvers. Dixitji, they knew, had supplied several revolvers and other firearms to his workers in Hyderabad state; indeed, he had bought at least three revolvers from Badge himself. Apte, who now wanted to tackle Dixitji about giving them a revolver, signalled to Nathuram, Karkare and Madanlal to leave the room, and he and Badge waited for Dixitji to return.

Hitherto Dixitji had proved an agreeably soft touch, and Apte told him a fanciful story about an expedition they were taking right into Kashmir and that they needed a revolver 'because travelling beyond Delhi had become dangerous'. But this time Dixitji refused to help. It is possible that word had been received from the big brother, Dada Maharaj, that Apte's schemes were no longer to be underwritten. After trying vainly to get at least a little money out of him 'to buy a revolver', Apte and Badge left him.

It was as they were walking out of the house and towards the others who were waiting for them in the yard of the Bhuleshwar temple that Apte, according to Badge, turned to him and invited him to come to Delhi with them.

It is difficult to believe that Badge, who had been sitting in on most of the discussions that had so far taken place, did not know their purpose. Yet he says that he asked Apte what they were going to do in Delhi and was told that Savarkar had ordered Apte and Nathuram to 'finish' Gandhi and Nehru.

At the time that Badge made this statement, he was speaking as the 'approver', the alleged offender who had earned his pardon in exchange for helping the prosecution to clinch its case. It was important to establish the fact of 'conspiracy' and also that Savarkar was behind it. But the dropping of Nehru's name seems inexplicable unless it was done to heighten the sense of shock.

But, even according to his own story, he was neither shocked nor dismayed. On the contrary, he agreed to join the plot with surprising alacrity. All he asked for was a day in Poona 'to make arrangements regarding my household affairs'.

The household affairs, it turned out were the finding of a safe place to store away the rest of his stock in trade of hand grenades and explosives. He, too, does not seem to have thought how improbable it was that he could fire a pistol at Gandhi and still return to his business in Poona as though nothing had happened.

It was thus in response to a casual question thrown at him by Apte in the courtyard of the Bhuleshwar temple in Bombay that Badge volunteered to become a member of the conspiracy to murder Gandhi. And where Badge went, Shankar went; he, too, was dragged into it even though he had absolutely no idea as to who they were going to kill and why.

It seems that the carrot that led Badge on was the prospect of ultimate payment for the material he had given the conspirators. He was desperate for money since some of his other customers had not paid him on time, and he was highly impressed by the lifestyle that Apte and Nathuram had adopted. In Bombay, Nathuram had casually paid him Rs 50, and told him that it was to cover his travelling expenses, and that the bill for his *mal* would be settled later. Since Badge, by his own admission, had not spent even Rs 10 on the journey to Bombay, he was both surprised and delighted at this largesse. These were good people to work for. Apte had assured him that all his expenses on the trip to Delhi would be similarly taken care of and, even though Badge never admitted this, Apte must have also promised him a handsome reward after their mission was accomplished.

It was all too tempting to be passed up. There was big money to be made for doing so little; meanwhile there were square meals in hotels and tots of rum and travel to distant parts, and the intoxicating glow of the soldier invited to sit at the officers' table. Badge worked hard and uncomplainingly till the last moment when his nerve failed him. The result was that he never qualified for the reward.

But nor did he get paid for the explosives and weapons he had contributed to the venture.

Such was the cast of characters. They were seven in number; the three pairs, Apte/Nathuram, Karkare/Madanlal and Badge/Shankar, and the odd man, Gopal, who of course was still in Poona worrying about his leave. The other six mingled together briefly in the temple yard and dispersed. It was decided that Badge should go to Poona for a day and put his household affairs in order, and meet them again in Bombay on the morning of the seventeenth. At this time, since their efforts to raise another revolver had failed, and since none of them knew whether Gopal really would be able to come to Delhi with *his* revolver, Nathuram thought that he, too, would go back to Poona for a day and make sure of at least Gopal's revolver.

The train by which Madanlal and Karkare had decided to leave Bombay, the Punjab Mail, left Victoria Station at five in the evening. It left without them. At the last minute, Madanlal had rushed off to Dadar, to Dr Jain's house, to see if there was a letter for him.

There was no letter. Madanlal paid Dr Jain's dues to him and then, in what could only be ascribed to a spectacular bid for self-dramatization, revealed to his host that he was on his way to Delhi, and that 'his party had plotted against the life of some leader'.

Jain was later to state that he pressed Madanlal for the name of the leader, and that Madanlal 'mentioned the name of Mahatma Gandhi'. Whereupon Jain admonished him 'not to behave like a child', and 'had a long talk with him, trying to dissuade him from what he said he intended to do'.

As a result of this talk, Madanlal, according to Jain, told him 'that he was under my obligation since I had helped him much and that he considered me like his father; and that, in case he did not listen to my advice, he would be doomed.'

Since Dr Jain, for reasons known only to himself, did not report this vital information to anyone in a position of authority for at least six days, and then, too, in an oral interview to a minister of the Bombay Government to whom he made a special request that his name be withheld from the police, it is not easy to fathom just how much of the plot Madanlal had really, revealed to him and, more, on what date he had revealed it. Dr Jain's memory is not too reliable on either point. As will be seen, when finally he reported the purport of Madanlal's talk, Madanlal had already exploded a charge of gun-cotton at Gandhi's prayer meeting, and had been arrested with a live grenade in his pocket. Jain's recollection of what Madanlal had said to him in Bombay is therefore likely to have been influenced by the actual event. For instance, Jain later stated that he knew the main ingredients of the plot as well as the names of Madanlal's accomplices as early as 10 January. Madanlal, on the other hand, swears that he himself did not know anything about the plot till the fifteenth, and all the circumstances certainly support him. And Karkare, too, bears him out. Similarly, even though Dr Jain made something of a point that Madanlal, at this meeting, had told him that Savarkar of the Hindu Mahasabha, when he heard of his exploits in Ahmednagar, had sent for him and had a long talk with him for about two hours... had patted him on the back and said, "Carry on", in his first recorded statement before a magistrate he had not even mentioned Savarkar's name.

But this much is clear. On the evening of 15 January, Dr Jain knew that Madanlal was implicated in a plot to kill or, as Jain later put it, to 'overpower' Gandhi. Beyond that he knew very little. He might have guessed that Madanlal's particular friend whom he called Karkara Seth was bound to be one of the conspirators. But he certainly did not know, as he was later to claim that he did, the names of Madanlal's other associates, and nor does he seem to have pressed Madanlal to reveal them.

Anyway, accepting Madanlal's dutiful assurance that he would never think of disobeying Jain, whom he regarded as his father, Jain did nothing. Two days later, Jain confided whatever Madanlal had told him to Angad Singh, who was a close family friend and frequent visitor to his house, and who, it will be recalled, had been introduced by Jain to Madanlal. Angad Singh, while he, too, felt that one should not take 'the tall talk of a refugee' seriously, advised Jain to report the information to the authorities all the same. Jain saw no one in a position of authority.

After leaving Jain's house, Madanlal had caught a bus to Victoria Terminus. Here Karkare was waiting for him with the tickets. They managed to find room in a third-class compartment of a train that called itself the Peshawar Express even though, because Peshawar was now deep in Pakistan, it did not go there. The train left on time, at 9.30 p.m.

An hour later, from the same station, Badge and Shankar caught the Madras Mail which, as it happens, does not accept passengers for Poona, and Badge knew it. But this was no obstacle for a man like Badge, who was something of an old hand at ticketless travelling. Instead, he bought two platform tickets and, as the train was pulling out, he and Shankar jumped into one of its carriages. At the other end, he was confident of being able to slip through by offering a small tip to the ticket collector.

All except Apte had left Bombay on the night of Thursday, 15 January, he had decided to stay on, as he told the others, to try to raise some funds for their expenses. But he had much more than money on his mind. He had no illusions that he could murder Gandhi and still return to his old life. He had to tell Manorama Salvi about what they were planning to do, and to prepare her for a final parting.

For the next two days Apte kept his room (No. 6) at the Sea Green Hotel (South). If only because, on a later occasion, he was to stay in the Sea Green Hotel (North) it is necessary to explain that both these hotels are in the same building, but are under different managements; one cannot go from one to the other without first coming out on to the road.

During the two days, Apte made no efforts to collect any funds. For much of the time, Manorama Salvi was with him, and she was desolate. 'I was quite upset and cried,' she was later to testify. 'He tried to console me. He told me that, if anything happened to him [I was] not to worry but try to be happy.'

It was a tall order. For Manorama Salvi, it was as good as the end of her life.[4] She was still in her twentieth year, and if she had not become infatuated with Apte she would have sat for her BA examination in another three months. She would thus have become the first graduate in the Salvi family and one of the first girls in the community to have gone through college. A rosy future awaited her; a well-to-do husband, or, if she preferred, a decent job. Now there would be neither graduation nor marriage. All her life she would have to live with the guilt of unchastity, the social ostracism of bearing an illegitimate child. The tight little community of mission-raised Christians in which she had grown up would treat her family like lepers.

And the man for whom she had brought all this on herself was now going off on some mysterious mission from which he was not likely to return. As it happened, Manorama belonged to a Christian family, but the life that awaited her was that of a Hindu widow, a life of renunciation and self-abnegation, a relegation to a limbo of unimaginable bleakness. Manorama played no part whatsoever in Gandhi's murder, but there can be no doubt that the punishment she received was no less severe than the sentences awarded by the judges to the conspirators.

Badge's train got into Poona at 2 a.m. on 16 January. At the barrier, Badge expertly slipped a two-rupee note into the hands of the ticket collector, and he and Shankar passed through. As soon as there was enough light to see, Shankar brought in all the stocks of explosives and weapons that had been buried in the backyard and he and Badge between them stuffed them into two bags. Badge then slept till noon and went off with the two bags. Not surprisingly it was not easy to find someone who was willing to look after them for him, or even who could be trusted not to blackmail him, and it was not till after 7 p.m. that he struck any luck. He had called at the house of Ganpat Kharat, at 148 Narayan Peth. Kharat was a member of the Bombay Legislative Assembly who had been elected on a Congress ticket, and thus, under a Congress regime, a man who wielded considerable influence.

Kharat later stated that, when Badge brought the 'bundles' to his house, he was hurrying off 'to answer the call of nature'. He only heard Badge mumble something about keeping the bags for the Hyderabad State

Congress and said yes. When, 'in 3-4 minutes' time', Kharat returned Badge had already left. Kharat later told the police that he never knew what the bags contained, and his contention was not called into question. Kharat was, nonetheless, anxious not to keep the bags in his own house. Within an hour of Badge leaving them, two of his political workers came to see him and he 'handed over one bundle to each of them for safe custody'.

Badge returned to his store just before eight, and was told by Shankar that Nathuram had been trying to get hold of him; that he had twice called at the shop, and was even then waiting for him at his office.

Nathuram had left Bombay by a fast afternoon train, the Deccan Queen, got off at Kirkee, and gone to see his brother Gopal. He was relieved to hear that Gopal was getting his leave from Saturday the seventeenth. Gopal told him that on Friday evening he would go to Uksan (his village) where he had buried the revolver, and from there catch an early train to Bombay. He would thus be in Bombay in good time to catch the Punjab Mail which left in the afternoon. It was arranged that Nathuram and Apte would meet Gopal's train at Delhi railway station on the evening of the eighteenth.

The brothers ate their evening meal together, and Nathuram went to his own room for the night. Friday morning Nathuram spent in trying to get hold of another pistol or revolver, and managed to buy a .22 bore magazine pistol. He was not at all happy with it. He wanted something of a bigger bore, and, if possible, a revolver in preference to a pistol.

When Badge came to the *Hindu Rashtra* office, the first thing that Nathuram asked him was whether he had made up his mind to go with them and Badge answered that he was ready. As Badge later recalled, 'Nathuram Godse then took out a pistol and gave it to me. He asked me to exchange it for a big revolver, but, in case I could not get hold of a big revolver, to bring the pistol with me to Bombay.'

Badge seems to have taken this last-minute commission quite calmly; certainly he did not protest that he, too, had a train to catch. He pocketed the pistol and dashed off to see a man called S.D. Sharma to whom, a few weeks earlier, he had sold a revolver which he remembered to have been bigger. Sharma readily agreed to the exchange. 'I gave him the pistol and took back the revolver,' Badge said in his testimony; 'And Sharma also gave me four cartridges with the revolver.'

This revolver was of .32 bore, but the cartridges that Sharma gave with it, even though they seemed to fit snugly enough into its chamber, happened to be of a slightly smaller bore, and possibly meant for use in a magazine pistol. But the conspirators were not to discover that they were the wrong cartridges till the morning of the day on which they had planned to kill Gandhi with them.

After giving the pistol to Badge, Nathuram had plenty of time to go and see his parents before the eleven o'clock train to Bombay. Badge was not able to finish his business with Sharma till well past midnight, and after that the only train to Bombay was at 2 a.m. As usual, the third-class compartments were crowded to capacity, and he and Shankar were unable to find room in the same compartment. The rest of the night they spent sitting up on the hard-wooden benches. They had arranged that Shankar should get out at Dadar station and go and wait for Badge at the Hindu Mahasabha office. At seven the train steamed into Victoria Station. Badge got out. Apte and Nathuram were waiting for him on the platform.

Sketch of Nathuram Godse, as drawn by Balchandra Haldipur, a member of the special cell to trace the conspiracy of the murder and arrest the co-accused. Haldipur liked making sketches and through the course of the Gandhi murder case trial made sketches of many people he met.

SIX

'Gandhi-ko?
Marne do.
Ham ko?
Makan do.'
(Let Gandhi die. Give us shelter.)

— REFUGEE SLOGAN

Nathuram Godse was an avid reader of detective novels, his favourite author being Erle Stanley Gardner. Apte, on the other hand, showed a marked preference for Agatha Christie. But their familiarity with crime in fiction had taught them nothing of the ways of criminals in real life. To the end they remained rank amateurs, shockingly incompetent in almost everything they did. Nathuram even kept an account book in which he meticulously put down all the sums of money they paid to their accomplices. Instead of trying to cover their tracks, they seemed if anything to go to special trouble to leave a well-blazed trail.

Delighted that Badge had managed to swap the fancy pistol for a more businesslike weapon, they decided to spend the morning trying to raise money for their mission. For this they engaged a taxi and shuttled all over Bombay to see people whose addresses were on their list of donors to the

Hindu cause. In between there were other trips. One to Dixitji Maharaj to make yet another bid to borrow his pistol (which he refused to part with), another to the Hindu Mahasabha office to see Shankar and give him instructions. Then back to the Fort area to the Sea Green Hotel (South) to pick up a tearful Manorama Salvi and drop her, still convulsed with sobs, near her house. If Badge is to be believed, they then went all the way back to Dadar to pick up Shankar and visit Savarkar's house to seek the great man's blessing.

Badge's amazing ability to remember every single thing that happened within his sight or hearing during those days is itself suspicious; his performance as a witness was so flawless as to resemble that of an actor who has studied his lines thoroughly and never fumbles for a word. According to him:

> We got down from the taxi and walked down to the house of Savarkar. Shankar was asked to wait outside the compound... Apte, Nathuram and I entered the compound. Apte asked me to wait in the room on the ground floor. Nathuram and Apte went up. They came down after 5-10 minutes... followed immediately by Tatyarao [Savarkar] who said to them: "Yeshaswi houn ya!" [Literally, "Come back successful!"][5]

That Nathuram and Apte should wish to see Savarkar before setting out on their mission is altogether understandable. Both venerated Savarkar as many Congressmen venerated Gandhi, as the man whose *darshan* (sight) would constitute an auspicious beginning for any venture. But to deduce from this visit, if it ever took place, that it was Savarkar who directed the two to kill Gandhi, or that he even sanctioned a killing that was proposed to be accomplished in so clumsy and so inhuman a manner, would be altogether fatuous. The taxi driver remained conveniently out of sight of the house, and Shankar, who was made to wait outside the gate, never saw Savarkar. An interesting sidelight on Badge's brilliant performance as a witness is provided by Shankar in his testimony. Even in custody, Shankar was subjected to almost incessant coaching by Badge as to what precisely he was required to say in court. He has some pertinent revelations to make about how industriously Badge himself was practising *his* lines.

By noon, when it was time for Apte and Nathuram to call at the Tata Airlines office to catch the company's coach to the airport, they had collected more than Rs 2000, and they still had to visit two more people who had asked them to call later in the day. One of the two, who had promised Rs 400, lived in the suburb of Kurla, the other was a mill-owner living in the Mahalakshmi area and, even though he had not named a definite sum, they felt sure that his contribution would be much the bigger. They gave Badge Rs 350 'for expenses', told him to collect the Rs 400 from the Kurla man later in the afternoon, and themselves went to the mill-owner.

Here they got another Rs 1000, but found that they had wasted a whole hour, so they ordered the driver to take them directly to the Santa Cruz airport, which was at least fifteen miles away. Their flight was scheduled to take off at 2 p.m. All the way they talked with great animation and Apte impressed on Badge the importance of catching the Frontier Mail that evening, and promised to meet him at New Delhi Station the following evening. But if, for some reason, they missed one another at the station Badge was to go on his own to the Hindu Mahasabha Bhavan where one of them would be waiting for him.

When, however, the taxi reached Santa Cruz they discovered that their plane was to take off from the Kalina aerodrome, about a mile further on. Apte, now worried about missing the plane, kept exhorting the driver to go like the wind, and when they got to Kalina he and Nathuram dashed off to catch their plane, yelling to Badge to pay off the taxi.

As though all this was not enough to make certain that the taxi driver would remember them well, Badge retained the same taxi to go back to Kurla to collect the Rs 400, and afterwards had himself and Shankar dropped at Kurla Station.

It was now past 3 p.m. The taxi had been engaged at seven in the morning. The meter had clocked Rs 55-10-00. The normal daily earnings of a taxi driver were then around Rs 30. Badge, who, it will be recalled, was still dressed in the flaming garb of a *sadhu,* paid the fare and, much to the driver's surprise, demanded a receipt. This the driver, Aitappa Kotian, was glad to give.

It seems that Badge had every intention of catching the Frontier Mail as Apte had enjoined him to, but, since the train did not start till 7 p.m. and he had plenty of time to get to the station, decided to call on an old friend, a Mr Navre, who ran the Asra Hotel in Dadar, which was not far from where they were. Navre, Badge later revealed, invited him to spend the night in his hotel 'as a guest of the proprietor', and Badge, who, to give him his due, had done a lot of running around for the past four days and had had hardly a full night's sleep, made up his mind to treat himself to the luxury of sleeping in a real bed. After all, he told himself, even if he left Bombay the next evening, he would still be in Delhi in good time for playing his allotted part in the plot to kill Gandhi.

With all their pre-flight publicity, there seemed little point in Apte and Nathuram having gone to the trouble of buying their tickets under false names. The service they were travelling on was scheduled to touch Ahmedabad on the way, and among the passengers to Ahmedabad, going there to attend an important religious gathering, was none other than Dada Maharaj, who had now become so cool towards them that they had not even thought of calling on him in Bombay. In the plane he managed to catch their eye and waved to them, and they waved back. At the airport building in Ahmedabad, Dada Maharaj, loaded with the garlands brought by his devotees, who now thronged around him, called out to Apte across the width of the hall: 'You had talked a lot but it does not appear that anything has been done.'

To which Apte's reply was: 'When we do the work, you will know.'

But, in the matter of blazing a clear trail, the second team, Karkare and Madanlal, had, if possible, surpassed the performance of their principals.

Karkare, who spent most of his earnings on others, had been far too well grounded in the ways of poverty to spend money on himself. Even though, because they had missed their proper train, they were now going by a very slow one requiring over forty hours for a journey that ordinarily took twenty-four, he and Madanlal still travelled third class.

Among the score or so of passengers who were crowded into their compartment was a man named Angchekar, a refugee from Pakistan, who had held a petty government job there, and who was now going to Delhi to get his services transferred to India.

This Angchekar heard one of the passengers say something to another in Marathi, which was Angchekar's mother-tongue. Angchekar got into conversation with the man, who told him that his name was Karkare, that he worked for the Hindu Mahasabha, and that he was going to Delhi for some work connected with the Mahasabha. After listening to Angchekar's troubles in turn, and finding that he was a total stranger to Delhi and had nowhere to stay, Karkare, ever willing to help a refugee, offered to take Angchekar to the Hindu Mahasabha Bhavan, which kept a few rooms for party workers, and where he and Madanlal expected to stay.

The Peshawar Express got into Delhi's main railway station at noon on Saturday. Karkare hired a tonga and in it they all drove to the Hindu Mahasabha Bhavan which, however, had none of its rooms vacant. They then proceeded to the *serai* (travellers' home) attached to the Birla temple, and drew a blank there too. In the end they went to Chandni Chowk and booked a room with three beds in one of the cheapest hotels there, the Sharif. In the hotel register, Karkare put his name down as M. Bias, but Angchekar, who signed the register after him, did not notice anything wrong; Madanlal gave his correct name.

Karkare seemed to have a lot of things to attend to in Delhi and was out most of the time, with the result that Madanlal and Angchekar were left to themselves in the hotel room. They talked at length about their experiences in the refugee columns and shared confidences, and on Sunday Madanlal even invited Angchekar to accompany him to the houses of his relatives where he was going 'to see a girl suitable for marriage'. Angchekar later revealed that at these houses they were 'treated to teas' and that 'many ladies came to see Madanlal'. That night, Sunday, Karkare quite scandalized the other two by not turning up at all, and he had still not returned on Monday morning when Angchekar left the hotel to visit the Transfer Bureau to

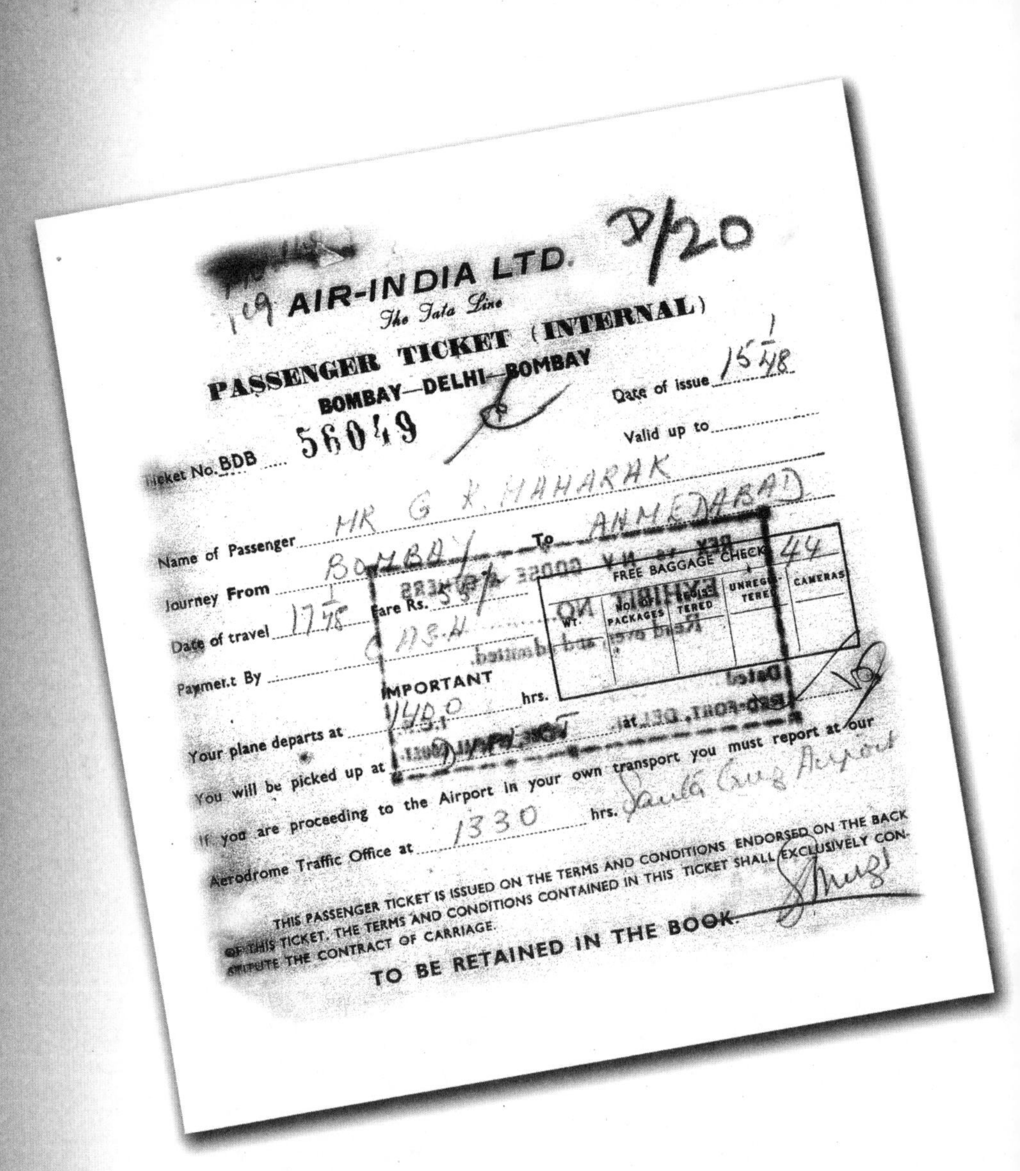

AIR-INDIA LTD.

The Tata Line

PASSENGER TICKET (INTERNAL)

BOMBAY—DELHI—BOMBAY

Date of issue 15/1/48

Ticket No. BDB 56049

Valid up to

Name of Passenger

Journey From BOMBAY To

Date of travel 17/1/48 Fare Rs.

Payment By CASH

FREE BAGGAGE CHECK				
WT.	NO. OF PACKAGES	REGISTERED	UNREGISTERED	CAMERAS

IMPORTANT

Your plane departs at 1400 hrs.

You will be picked up at ... at ...

If you are proceeding to the Airport in your own transport you must report at our Aerodrome Traffic Office at 1330 hrs. Santa Cruz Airport

THIS PASSENGER TICKET IS ISSUED ON THE TERMS AND CONDITIONS ENDORSED ON THE BACK OF THIS TICKET. THE TERMS AND CONDITIONS CONTAINED IN THIS TICKET SHALL EXCLUSIVELY CONSTITUTE THE CONTRACT OF CARRIAGE.

TO BE RETAINED IN THE BOOK.

On Godse and Apte's flight to Delhi, was another passenger they knew, Dixitji Maharaj, priest of Bhuleshwar Temple, Bombay. A firm supporter of the Hindu cause, Dixitji Maharaj had initially tried to help Apte and Godse with money, was now quiet indifferent to them, as he felt that theirs was just big talk.

Facing page: Hindu Mahasabha Bhawan, Delhi: Through different means of transport and on different days, the conspirators were collecting in Delhi. The Hindu Mahasabha Bhawan on the Mandir Marg became their place of rendezvous.

महा सभा भवन
HINDU MAHASABHA
अ. भा. राजार्य सभा
के तत्वावधान में
वेद कामधेनु विश्व विजय यज्ञ
(अश्वमेध यज्ञ)
रविवार, 9 दिसम्बर 2007 से रविवार, 16 दिसम्बर 2007 तक
आर्य समाज, दीवान हॉल, चाँदनी चौक, दिल्ली

register himself. But when he returned at about three in the afternoon he found that Karkare was back in the room and had brought another man with him. (This was Gopal Godse, but he was not introduced to Angchekar.) All three had been talking before Angchekar entered the room but stopped abruptly, and after a while Karkare somewhat brusquely told Angchekar that they were all leaving for Jullunder 'for Madanlal's marriage' within the hour and that he, Angchekar, would also have to vacate the room. Angchekar, who had finished his business in Delhi and was catching the evening train to Bombay, had no use for the room in any case. Full of gratitude towards Karkare for letting him stay with them, Angchekar asked him for his permanent address. Then Karkare said a surprising thing. He told Angchekar, 'It is not necessary for you to know my address.'

If Karkare was now trying to cover up his tracks, it was already too late. Just as Apte had made sure that he would be identified by the taxi driver Kotian, Karkare had made sure that Angchekar would remember him and Madanlal. Both would pay dearly for these indiscretions. Nathuram Godse, who actually killed Gandhi, pleaded guilty, and Madanlal was caught red-handed; but the cases against Apte and Karkare might not have been so convincingly established if both had not been so prodigal in leaving clues behind and gone repeatedly out of their way to impress their identity on total strangers, transforming bystanders into material witnesses.

Once again, Gandhi's fast unto death did not have to go on for more than five days. In that time, the country had undergone an emotional purge. Like a drunk making a good resolution in a pre-dawn moment of sobriety, the national conscience had been subjected to a jolt and perhaps even a fleeting interval of introspection.

'You have to live in the vicinity of a Gandhi fast to understand its pulling power,' wrote Alan Campbell-Johnson, who of course, had a ringside seat. The fast pushed both the Kashmir war and the communal killings off the front pages of the newspapers. Nehru and his colleagues rushed to Gandhi's bedside to try to talk him out of his decision. His answer was to impose his second condition. India must pay the Rs 55 crores to Pakistan or see Gandhi die; and never mind if the country was at war with Pakistan. Gandhi was not only demanding a change of conscience on the part of the people of Delhi, but had also served an ultimatum upon the Government of India.

Congress leaders milled around in Delhi, holding frantic consultations with groups of citizens, and worked late hours trying to hammer out a formula which they could force the groups to accept. They knew that it was not easy to bluff Gandhi that Delhi had become suddenly peaceful. For one thing there were the processions of angry refugees that came to Birla House with the sole purpose of shouting their slogans of vengeance within his hearing. Also there was what Gandhi called his private intelligence system. Every day he received hundreds of letters from all sorts of people telling him of their sufferings as they would to a close relative, and many people even came to see him to demand redress.

'I would beg of all my friends not to rush to Birla House, nor try to dissuade me or be anxious for me,' Gandhi had said at his prayer meeting on the twelfth. 'I am in God's hands.'

This was one prohibition that even Gandhi must have known would never be obeyed. People came to Birla House in droves and took their places around the tight inner circle of the men and women of Gandhi's entourage. The lawns of Birla House resembled a fairground. Newsmen from the great papers of the world gathered around like birds of prey scenting death, set up their typewriters under convenient trees and recorded the comings and goings of great men and wisely interpreted the signs. One of the wisest was to ascribe a boil that had suddenly erupted on the palm of his hand to his own involvement in Gandhi's ordeal.

Birla House, not Government House where Mountbatten lived, nor No. 13 York Road where Nehru lived, was now the centre of the capital, and Nehru acknowledged the shift by calling a meeting of his cabinet on the lawn of Birla House 'to consider afresh the issue of Pakistan's share of the cash balances.'

At that meeting, the government capitulated to Gandhi. They would be good boys and pay up the Rs 55 crores to Pakistan. Now only the other

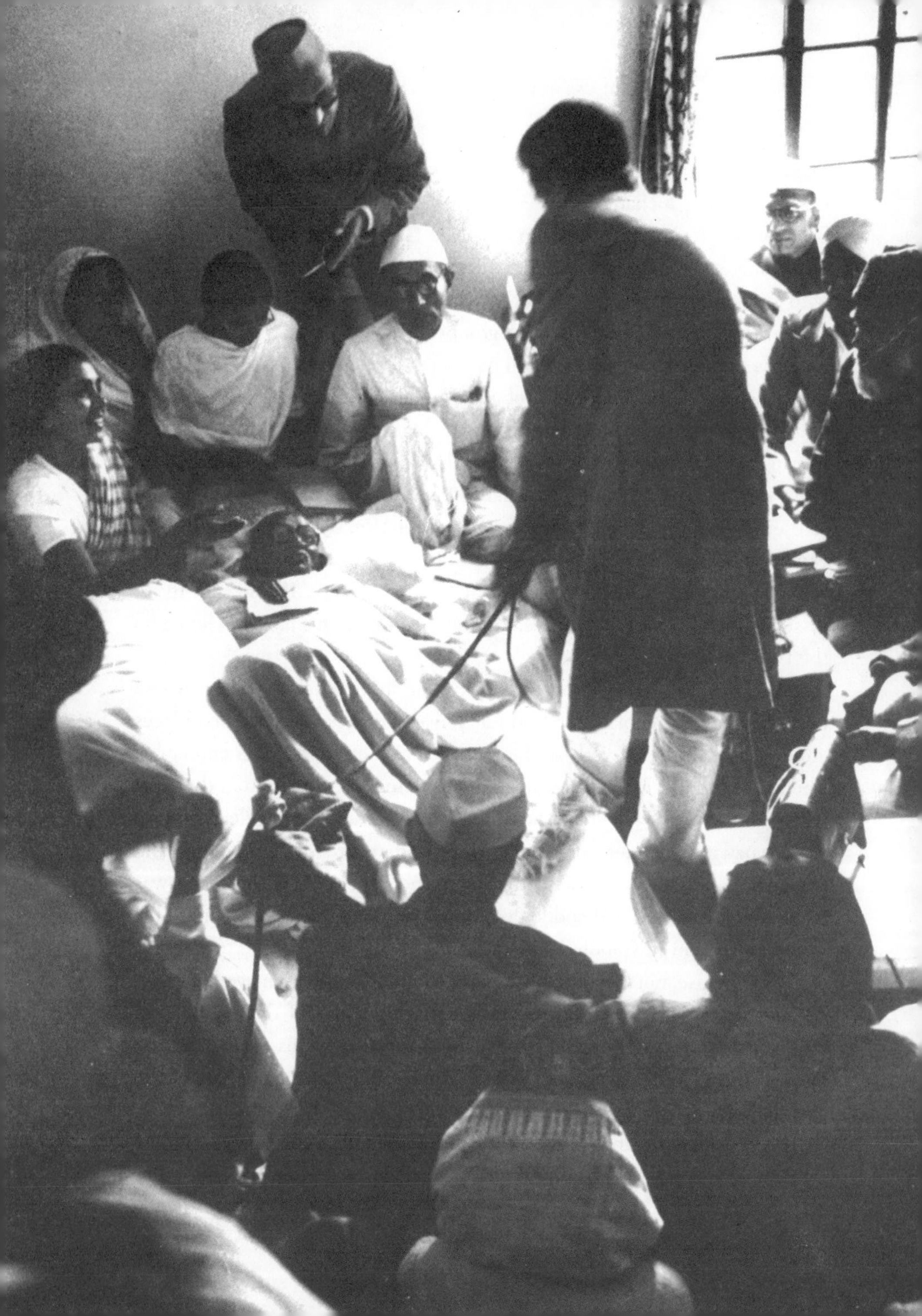

Birla House: Gandhi spent the last 144 days of his life here. Birla House, not Governor-General's residence, nor No. 13 York Road where Nehru lived, was now the centre of the capital.
Facing page: 'You have to live in the vicinity of a Gandhi fast to understand its pulling power,' wrote Alan Campbell-Johnson, the Press Secretary of Mountbatten. Gandhi's earlier fasts had given results, and this time too when he decided to go on a fast on 13 January 1948 for communal harmony and payment of Rs 55 crores to Pakistan, he hoped he would be able to demand a change of conscience.

condition remained to be fulfilled. To be sure it was not a decision that a dozen men sitting around Gandhi's bedside could be called upon by their leader to endorse. It was something that had to be established by visible proof of the slaughter of Muslims begin halted, by the intended victims of that slaughter coming out and testifying that they now felt safe, by the opposing communities mingling together to celebrate one another's festivals as they once had.

But even this now seemed possible. The tide was definitely turning. In the words of Pyarelal, Gandhi's private secretary: 'The people woke up to their full sense of responsibility and set out organizing an all-out campaign to bring about a real change of heart.'

But, if the fast was turning the tide, it was also creating discernible swell on the opposite shore. The local leaders could reason with the citizens of Delhi, but the refugees from Pakistan, who were now as numerous as the citizens, had no loyalty to or regard for the local leaders. The refugees had suffered directly at the hands of the Muslims, and they longed for revenge. They felt outraged that Gandhi should have staked his own life to save the Muslims from their due retribution. And the paying of a vast sum of money to Pakistan was, in their eyes, nothing short of an act of national sabotage.

They marched to Birla House to voice their protest. Inevitably, they were stopped by the guards at the gate. Placidly, exchanging obscenities with the guards, they squatted by the roadside and settled down for a long vigil. Every now and then they shouted slogans: 'MARTA HAI TO MARNE DO!' ('If he wants to die; let him die!') and 'KHOONKA BADLA KHOONSE LENGE!' ('We want blood in return for blood!') A few stones were hurled at the windows of Birla House. Whenever their demonstrations got a little out of hand, the police made a lathi charge and dispersed them. But within minutes they gathered again.

Whenever a ministerial car passed in or out of the gate, their shouting would rise in a deafening crescendo. The other ministers sat slumped in their cars as though they did not hear the yells, but Nehru had his car stopped and jumped out.

'Who dares shout "Let Gandhi die"?' he demanded. 'Let him who dares repeat the words in my presence. He will have to kill me first!'

Nehru's tirade stopped the shouting, but only while he was in the vicinity. Lying in bed and trying to sleep, Gandhi must have been woken up again and again by the roar from Albuquerque Road, 'MARTA HAI TO MARNE DO! KHOONKA BADLA KHOONSE LENGE!' And at time he must have wondered to himself if this time he would be able to bring it off.

He did bring it off. On the night of 15 January, and thus within three days of going on his fast, a government communique announced that it had reversed its decision to withhold the share of Pakistan's cash balances in order to 'remove the one cause of suspicion and friction'. This decision, the communique added, 'is the Government's contribution, to the best of their ability, to the non-violent and noble effort made by Gandhiji... for peace and goodwill.'

Gandhi in a message from his bedside complimented the government on 'the promptness with which they had unsettled their settled fact'.

Meanwhile, by a heavy-handed use of the carrot as well as the stick, the protest marches of the refugees had been stopped; at least, they were stopped before they reached within a mile of Birla House. From the sixteenth, Gandhi was not disturbed by anyone shouting slogans that exhorted him to die.

The Congress President, Rajendra Prasad, who was soon to become the President of India, had evolved a seven-point formula that would meet the requirements laid down by Gandhi for ending his fast. It was in the form of a pledge to be taken by the Hindus and Sikhs that they would not molest the Muslims, and it had to be endorsed by the leaders of the various political parties, of the refugee organizations, of religious institutions, and even of citizens' committees in the predominantly Muslim areas of the city. It must have been something of a problem to prevent some of these leaders, gathered in one room, from flying at each other's throats, but like wild animals facing a common danger they were tamed by a sense of impending calamity – the threat of Gandhi's death. Even so there must have been a good deal of finger-crossing or its Indian equivalent, tongue-biting, at the time of the actual signing. After an all-night sitting on the night of the seventeenth, Rajendra Prasad succeeded in obtaining all the signatures he wanted. In the morning, the signatories carried the document in triumph to Gandhi.

The people of Delhi had pledged themselves 'to protect the life, property and faith of the Muslims, and [promised] that the incidents which have taken place in Delhi will not happen again.'

Gandhi, in a voice that was charged with emotion, began to tell them how deeply touched he was, and then broke down. A little later there was 'a ceremony of prayer,' at which 'texts from the Japanese, Muslim and Parsi scriptures were recited, followed by the mantra:

Lead me from untruth to truth,
From darkness to light,
From death to immortality.

Then he broke his fast, by taking a glass of fruit juice which was handed to him by a Muslim friend, Abul Kalam Azad.

The airline coach took Apte and Nathuram into the centre of New Delhi, and by 8.30 on the evening of 17 January they were installed in a room (No. 40) in the Marina Hotel in Connaught Place. The Marina in New Delhi was the exact counterpart of the two Sea Greens in Bombay, a middle-class hotel for westernized tastes, but patronized almost entirely by Indians. In the hotel's register, they put their names down as M. Deshpande and S. Deshpande. It never became clear which was which; nor did it matter. They had dinner and went to the Hindu Mahasabha Bhavan where Karkare was waiting for them. They had a brief chat with him and returned to their hotel. The next morning, Karkare joined them for breakfast, and afterwards all three went in a tonga to take a look at Birla House where Gandhi was staying.

In India, the name Birla has the same ring of power, influence and wealth that is generated by that of the Rockefellers in the USA, or the Mitsubishis in Japan; Birla House in Delhi was then the residence of the head of the family, Ghanashyam Das Birla. Today Birla House is a national monument and the road on which it is situated, then called Albuquerque

Road, has been renamed Thirtieth January Marg (Tees January Marg) to commemorate the date of Gandhi's assassination.

Even though anyone who wanted to attend Gandhi's five o'clock prayer meetings could freely enter the compound of Birla House, for the rest of the day it was not easy to get past the police guard at the gate. But, to get a general idea of the layout of the garden and the place where the prayers were held, it was not necessary to enter the gate. There were service lanes on both sides of the house and at the back, and a separate entrance to the numerous servants' quarters and garages situated at the rear. Much of the garden could be overlooked from these lanes and, even from the main road, in the mornings Gandhi could often be seen beyond the low brick wall, sitting in the sun in a cane chair and with a towel draped over his shoulder, bending over his papers or dictating to a secretary.[6]

It will be recalled that, in case they missed one another at the railway station, they had arranged to rendezvous at the Hindu Mahasabha Bhavan, where Karkare and Madanlal expected to stay. Nathuram, who had been a prominent and influential party worker and had attended many of its conventions in Delhi, knew the secretary of the Party, Ashutosh Lahiri, well. He gave Karkare a letter of introduction to Lahiri, and as a result of this Room No. 3 was allotted to Karkare from the afternoon of the eighteenth.

That afternoon, while Madanlal, accompanied by Angchekar, was taking a look at marriageable girls in the Chandni Chowk area, Apte, Nathuram and Karkare went to attend Gandhi's prayer meeting. Gandhi did not appear, because he was in bed; but he had sent a message to be read out over the public address system. This was the day on which Gandhi had decided to give up his fast and, according to his biographer, D.G. Tendulkar, 'it was a happy day for him and all of them'. The crowd at the meeting was a little larger than usual, and everyone milled around like excited schoolchildren at an unscheduled holiday. The three conspirators wandered all over the garden and finalized their plan of action. Now that the fast was over, they were confident that Gandhi would come out and begin to conduct prayers himself within a day or two.

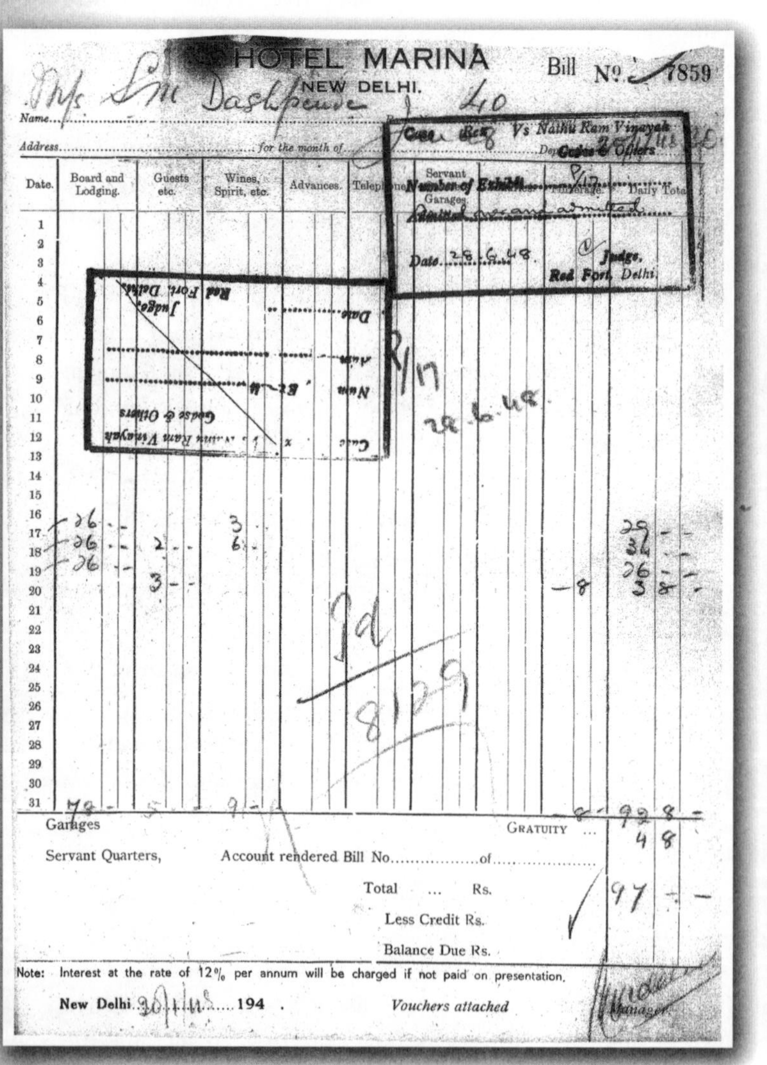

HOTEL MARINA
NEW DELHI.

Bill No. 7859

Name M/s S.M. Deshpande 40

Address .... for the month of ....

Case Vs Nathu Ram Vinayak Godse & Others

Number of Exhibit P/17

Admitted

Date 28.6.48 Judge, Red Fort, Delhi.

Date.	Board and Lodging.	Guests etc.	Wines, Spirit, etc.	Advances.	Telephone		Daily Total
16	26						
17	26		3				29
18	26	2	6				34
19	26						26
20		3				8	3 8
31	78	5	9			8	92 8

Garages

Gratuity ... 4 8

Servant Quarters, Account rendered Bill No........of........

Total ... Rs. 97

Less Credit Rs.

Balance Due Rs.

Note: Interest at the rate of 12% per annum will be charged if not paid on presentation.

New Delhi 20.1.48 194 . Vouchers attached

Manager.

On January 17, 1948, when Nathuram Godse and Narayan Apte reached Delhi, they took a room in Hotel Marina (Room No. 40), situated in Connaught Place and checked in with another set of new names – M. Deshpande and S. Deshpande.

HOTEL MARINA

VISITORS' INDEX

Name (IN BLOCK CAPITAL)	[Nati]onality	Permanent Address in India	Arrived from	Purpose of Visit	Visitor's Signature	Full Address of the place to which [departing]	Police Signature
[illegible]	British	A.S.I. New Delhi	Bombay	Business	[illegible]		
[illegible]	Do	Do	Do	Do	[illegible]		
A. MERCHANT	Indian	Do	Do	Do	[illegible]		
[illegible] STRINGER	English	[illegible] N.D.	Calcutta	"	[illegible]		
[illegible]	Indian		Ferozepur	Business	[illegible]	Business	
[illegible] J.R.F.	British	A.S.I. Bombay	Bombay	Duty	[illegible]	Pilot	
[illegible]	Indian	"	"	"	[illegible]	"	
[illegible] P.M.	English	Lloyds Bank Delhi	[illegible]		[illegible]	Transit	
B. B. Sethi	Indian	Sethi [illegible] 12 [illegible]	B'bay	[illegible]	[illegible]		
[AL]EXANDER LANE	AMERICAN	7991 Prospect Ave. LA JOLLA, CALIF. U.S.A.	CALCUTTA	ROUTE CAIRO	Alex. Lane	GRAND HOTEL CALCUTTA	
[illegible] J.E. GIBSON	Indian	[illegible]		Business [illegible]	[illegible]		
[illegible]	Indian	[illegible]	Ferozepur	Pleasure			
[illegible] DEATKER	Indian	Gorton Castle	Simla	official	[illegible]	14 [illegible] Rd. N.D.	
P. [illegible]	Indian	Paper Mills Simla	Ahmednagar	Business	[illegible]		
[illegible]	"	Ahmednagar					
DESHPANDE	Hindu	[illegible] Bombay	Bombay	Business	S DESHPANDE	checked	
DESHPANDE	"	P/15. 28.6.48		"	M DESHPANDE	[illegible]	
[S]ANGHVI	IND	BOMBAY	"	Business	[illegible]	20/1/48 [illegible]	
[illegible] FOREGARDRIA	IND.	River View Cottage SIMLA	LONDON	Visit GHQ	[illegible]		
[illegible] M. HILTON	British	[illegible]	Karachi	Business	H. M. Hilton		
[illegible] JANSINGH	Hindu	[illegible] Estate N.T.	Nainital	do	[illegible]		
[V]AUGHAN-FOWLER	BRITISH	RAJKOT	RAJKOT	BUSINESS	[illegible]		
[illegible]AZRILENKO	British	Bombay	Bombay	Business	[illegible]		
[R]ANGANATHA [R]AO SAHIB & Mrs	Indian	[illegible] Nal View [illegible] Bombay	Bombay	Business	[illegible]		

Case Rex Vs Nathu Ram Vinayak Godse & Others

Num Exh. P/15

Read over and admitted

Dat 28.6.48 [illegible] Judge, Red Fort, Delhi

While Godse and Apte stayed in Hotel Marina, Vishnu Karkare, who had reached Delhi by train went to the Hindu Mahasabha Bhawan with a letter of introduction from Nathuram Godse for the secretary of the Party, Ashutosh Lahiri. Karkare was allotted a room, which later became the place for their secret consultations where they ironed out the final role each of them had to play.

Pleased with the way everything was going, they went to the New Delhi Railway Station where both the fast trains from Bombay, the Punjab Mail and the Frontier Mail, were due to arrive within an hour of one another. Badge and Shankar were to come by the Frontier Mail, and Gopal by the Punjab Mail. Both trains arrived on time but, even though they tramped up and down their entire lengths several times, they did not see either Badge and Shankar or Gopal. Of course, Badge and Shankar, who had stayed on an extra day in Bombay, were not on their train, but Gopal had travelled by the Punjab Mail and had arrived. What had happened was that he had jumped out even before the train had come to a halt and, instead of waiting in one place, had gone walking up and down the platform looking for *them* in the milling crowd. They concluded that he too had missed the train. They went back to the Marina, feeling for the first time depressed and jittery because, even though Madanlal had brought over their stock of explosives, neither of their revolvers had arrived. Apte, normally a one-drink man, treated himself to two double Scotches.

That night, Karkare did not go back to the Sharif Hotel but slept in the room that had been given to him in the Hindu Mahasabha Bhavan. He knew that, if they had somehow missed Gopal and the other two at the railway station, they were bound to show up at the Bhavan, and did not want to miss them. But Badge and Shankar did not come, and neither did Gopal. After waiting on the platform till the next train from Bombay had come and gone, he had curled up on a bench and gone to sleep in case his brother or one of the others came looking for him during the night.

Early on the morning of the nineteenth Apte and Nathuram drove in a taxi to the Hindu Mahasabha Bhavan and were greatly perturbed to learn that their three missing companions had still not shown up.

But there was nothing they could do, Nathuram and Apte walked across to the Secretary's office in the adjoining building and sat for a few minutes talking to Mr Ashutosh Lahiri, or at least listening to him; he was holding forth indignantly against the Peace Committee, which had stated that his party had also signed the seven-point pledge that had persuaded Gandhi to end his fast.

According to Lahiri, the Mahasabha had done nothing of the kind; nor had it authorized any of its members to do so. He had prepared a press statement clarifying the position. He gave his callers an advance copy of his statement.

No one knows exactly at what time Nathuram and Apte went to see Lahiri, nor how long they stayed with him. The question assumed importance later on because that morning someone booked a trunk call to Bombay from Lahiri's office number.

In the India of those days a trunk call entailed all the tiresome paperwork that is normally associated with making an insurance claim. The call had to be 'booked' at the telephone exchange where the number of the caller, the time of booking the call, the number of the person called, the names of the particular persons with whom the caller wished to speak, the priority (ordinary or, at double rates, urgent) that was to be accorded to the call, the time of the call coming through, the duration of the conversation, and the cost of the call were meticulously recorded in a register.

And because long-distance telephone calls were important transactions, there was, of course, no question of any outsider making one without the knowledge and permission of the subscriber. It was thus most improbable that Lahiri or someone in a position of authority in his organization should not know who had booked the call.

This call, an urgent one, was booked at 9.20 a.m. The number called in Bombay was that of Savarkar's house. The names of the people to whom the caller wished to speak were given as G. Damle, Savarkar's secretary; or Appa Kasar, Savarkar's bodyguard.

Later the investigators sought to make capital out of this call by contending that it was made by Nathuram to discover from Savarkar's house whether Gopal had passed through Bombay. This was all of a piece with their general belief that all the conspirators received instructions or at least blessings from Savarkar before they proceeded to Delhi. Gopal maintained stoutly to the author that he did not even know where Savarkar's house was. On the other hand, there were dozens of perfectly good reasons why the Hindu Mahasabha's Secretary in Delhi might have wanted to speak to

Savarkar or at least to pass on a message to him through one of his lieutenants. After all, Savarkar was to the Mahasabha what Gandhi was to the Congress, the top man in the party irrespective of who happened to be its elected president. And Lahiri, it must be remembered, was on the point of making an announcement that was bound to bring on a storm of protests from the public as well as the government.

But, in the face of the witch-hunting zeal that suddenly overtook officials and politicians alike in the wake of Gandhi's murder, no one wanted to confess to having called up Savarkar's house, so that the mystery of who made the call was never solved. The police contention that it was Nathuram who had made it could not be sustained. But, even if it had been, it would still not have served their purpose, because the call never came through. After waiting till 11.30, whoever had booked it cancelled it. The only purpose the call served was to plant a glaringly conspicuous clue for the investigators to connect Savarkar's name with the plot to kill Gandhi.

But, according to Karkare; at least an hour before that time, while all of them were anxiously waiting in his room wondering what to do, they heard a tonga driving up and went out to see who its passengers might be. There was only one passenger – Gopal.

They pulled him into the room and the first thing they asked him was whether he had brought the revolver. He had. After that, Apte, Nathuram and Karkare left him in the room to have a bath and rest, and themselves once again hurried off to Birla House for another tour of the grounds.

In the afternoon, Karkare returned to the Hindu Mahasabha Bhavan, picked up Gopal, and went to his room in the Sharif Hotel. Here Madanlal and Gopal met for the first time. All three sat on the hard steel hotel beds and waited for Angchekar to return, to tell him that they were leaving Delhi and going on to Jullunder to see about a bride for Madanlal. After getting rid of Angchekar, all three went back to Karkare's room in the Hindu Mahasabha Bhavan. Badge and Shankar had still not turned up.

In the evening, while Madanlal and Gopal stayed in the room, Karkare went and saw Apte and Nathuram at the Marina Hotel, from where all three proceeded to the New Delhi Railway Station to meet the train on which Badge and Shankar should have travelled on the previous day, the Frontier Mail. Once again they drew a blank. Thinking that they had perhaps missed Badge and Shankar as they had missed Gopal, they went on to the Hindu Mahasabha Bhavan and discovered that the two had indeed arrived. They had missed them on the station because they had come by the Punjab Mail and not the Frontier Mail.

There was no separate room for the new arrivals, and nor was it considered necessary to bother about one. Apte just told them to 'sleep in the hall' and that's where the two dossed down for the night.

The Asra Hotel in Dadar is no Taj, and indeed it is doubtful if in the whole of Bombay you could find a cheaper place to stay. But its restaurant prides itself on its vegetarian delicacies and Indian sweets and, as the guests of the proprietor, Badge and Shankar were given a room to themselves. They had slept till late and eaten a hearty breakfast and then gone for a leisurely stroll through the Dadar Bazaar. Badge bought a cap for Shankar and some blankets for himself against the cold nights of Delhi. Around noon they went back to the Asra to partake of what the hotel called its Sunday 'Feast', and also collected from Mr Navre a basket of *laddoos* (a popular Indian sweet) to take with them for eating on the train.

Early in the afternoon, they took a local train to Victoria Terminus and hung about on the platform for hours before the Punjab Mail, an earlier train than the Frontier Mail which Badge had promised to take the previous evening, was due to leave. This time Badge bought himself and Shankar 'intermediate'-class tickets, which were a little more expensive than third-class ones but entitled them to padded seats. They reached Delhi on the evening of Monday, 19 January. The time set for killing Gandhi was less than twenty-four hours away, and all the others had already gathered in the capital.

There was no one to meet them on the platform, nor was Badge expecting to be met. Resourceful as ever, he hired a tonga and drove to the Hindu Mahasabha Bhavan. It was a bitterly cold evening and a steady winter drizzle was falling. They had not eaten their evening meal, either, but luckily the basket of *laddoos* was still more than half full. As Badge and Shankar entered the hall of the Hindu Mahasabha Bhavan, they saw 'Madanlal with one person', who it turned out, was Nathuram's brother Gopal.

The .32 revolver which Badge had managed to get from Sharma was still in Badge's or rather, Shankar's charge, the service revolver had been brought by Gopal, and the explosives had come in Madanlal's bedroll. The two principals, Apte and Nathuram, had travelled 'clean'.

The Delhi they had come to was a city becalmed after a storm, a city that was said to have been purified of its sins. The morning papers of the nineteenth described how its Muslim citizens were moving about freely and how some of them had even formed a procession and had been greeted by the Hindus and Sikhs with gifts of fruit and sweets.

This was a little too theatrical to ring true, and gave rise to the suspicion that things were being stage-managed by the party in power. By now, too, the tremendous pressure built up by the popular wave to save Gandhi's life had subsided, and many people were taking a closer look at the peace pledge and discovering that it was not as unanimous as it was made out to be. The extremists in the Hindu Mahasabha in particular were clamouring to know how their local spokesmen had allowed themselves to be browbeaten by the Congress leaders into subscribing to the peace pledge in the face of the declared policy of the party to the contrary. This charge was stoutly denied by the party's secretary, Mr Ashutosh Lahiri. He announced that neither he nor anyone authorized by him had signed the seven-point pledge.

But, even if they had not actually signed the pledge, the Mahasabha's local leaders had not remained unaffected by the mood of the moment and, by allowing themselves to be persuaded to remain present in Gandhi's room while the others signed the pledge, had given the impression that they, too, had signed it. To the Congress leaders, that was all that mattered. The crisis had been surmounted, Gandhi's life saved. Now they were directing their energies to a massive follow-up operation to make sure that, wherever Gandhi went, Hindus and Muslims and Sikhs would be sharing fruit and sweets.

But the Mahasabha leaders were conscious that they had been made to look silly, and Lahiri was desperate to eradicate the impression that his party had subscribed to the peace pledge.

Meanwhile, to stop the Hindu and Sikh leaders from inciting their followers again, the government had issued a ban on all communal processions and meetings, and Lahiri had to content himself with issuing a press statement. In this, after sharing the general feeling of relief that Gandhi had given up his fast, he pointed out that the representatives of his party had never signed the seven-point pledge, and that the party would never consent to the implementation of the pledge. He charged that 'the fast had only succeeded in weakening the position of the Hindu in their own lands as well as in Pakistan,' and concluded by reiterating 'with all emphasis, that we dissociate ourselves completely from this suicidal policy'.

This statement was issued on the nineteenth; and Nathuram and Apte, who were given a copy of it by Lahiri himself, were intensely gratified. It was good to see that their party still stood by its pledges and refused to bend in answer to the call to save Gandhi's life. Now that the moment of action was drawing closer, they were looking all around them for such signs to help strengthen their resolve.

The evening-papers contained another item of welcome news: Gandhi, whose health had been causing some anxiety during the last two days of his fast, was said to be making good progress, and it was confidently hoped that he would be able to attend the prayer meeting on the following day and say a few words to his congregation.

Thus, a practical difficulty was being resolved. They had come to murder Gandhi, but, so long as Gandhi remained in his bed and did not come out of his room, it was not going to be easy to carry out their plan. He was always surrounded by his favourite disciples, and only his regular visitors could enter the room. It was good to know that he was going to come out; it would be so much easier to kill him in the open.

Room No. 3, Servant's Quarters, Birla House. On January 20, Apte took Badge and Shankar to Birla House and showed them this room, just four or five paces from the place where Gandhi used to sit during the prayer meeting. The plan was to shoot him from the rear window of this room. But it failed when Badge, who was to shoot him from the window, saw a one-eyed man sitting outside the room. Paralysed with fear, he abandoned any thoughts of killing the Mahatma.

SEVEN

Gandhi was the man most responsible for the terrible events culminating in the creation of Pakistan.

— NATHURAM GODSE

On the night of the nineteenth, Madanlal and Gopal slept in the room in the Hindu Mahasabha Bhavan, and Badge and Shankar in the entrance hall outside. Karkare spent the night with Apte and Nathuram in the Marina Hotel room.

The drizzle had continued throughout the night, but had abated towards the morning, and by 7.30 the sky had cleared. It had been arranged that they would meet in the Hindu Mahasabha Bhavan early the next morning. But, at about 8.30, only Apte and Karkare turned up. They explained that Nathuram was laid up with one of the severe attacks of migraine from which he periodically suffered, but that he had promised to join them later in the day. Apte then asked Badge and Shankar to go with him to Birla House so that he could show them on the spot exactly what he wanted them to do. Even though Madanlal and Gopal, who had been assigned equally important roles in the murder plot, had never been to Birla House, they did not go with Apte even this time because they were waiting for water to be heated for their baths. Karkare, who had already familiarized himself with his working-ground, thought it a waste of time to go over it yet once more, and stayed on at the Mahasabha Bhavan.

Apte found a taxi and took Badge and Shankar to Birla House. After hanging about in front of the main gate for a few minutes Apte led them to the servants' quarters at the back of the house, and they made their way into the grounds through the service entrance. Part of the garden at Birla House was what was termed 'sunken', and the wide lawn that led from the main house to a small summer house was on two levels. Apte pointed out to Badge the place where Gandhi sat during the prayer meeting, which was on the raised portion of the lawn, and explained how this spot was 'within four or five paces' of the rear window of one of the servants' rooms at the back.

This room, No. 3 was occupied by one of the Birla family's chauffeurs, Chotu Ram, and the window in it was actually a decorative ventilation-grille in the wall formed by 'leaving out bits of masonry'. An excellent description of this grille is given in the testimony of Sardar Jaswant Singh, Deputy Superintendent of the Delhi Police, who actually 'measured the dimensions of the trellis work.'

> It is not a straight trellis work... the various openings are not of the same size and shape... none of the openings is rectangular in shape... the size of the biggest holes is 6" x 3". There are eight such holes. There are in all 26 holes in the trellis work.

Apte sauntered close to this grille and, according to Badge, 'took measurements of the opening with a piece of string.'

Apte himself had never thrown a grenade in his life. Indeed, he still believed that the only way to extract the pin holding the striker in position was to pull it out with one's teeth. It is also doubtful whether he had ever actually fired a revolver. All the same, he now pronounced that through a hole in a grille 'a revolver could be fired and also a hand grenade could be thrown.'

After that he guided the other two back to the servants' quarters and pointed out the room with the grille which they had seen from the other side. He told Badge that all he had to do was to enter the room on the pretext of wanting to take a photograph, shoot Gandhi through the grille and follow this up by shoving a grenade through the hole and into the congregation.

Neither Apte nor Badge had entered the room itself, but both seemed satisfied that it would serve their purpose. And as to Shankar, since Apte had been explaining things to Badge in an undertone and in Marathi, which Shankar hardly understood, he still had no idea why he had been taken on a tour of the Birla House garden or what he was required to do later in the day. Apte, now feeling no doubt that he had given his men a commando-type dry run of a daringly conceived raid, took them back to the Mahasabha Bhavan for the next step in the indoctrination of his team.

When they got there, it was already past eleven, and only Gopal was in the room, bathed and ready; the other two, Karkare and Madanlal, had gone to lunch. But Apte decided to put his team through another practice exercise even though three of its seven members were absent. 'We're going into the wood at the back to try out the two revolvers,' he told the others.

What happened at this firing practice bordered on farce, though the actors themselves were so desperately serious about their roles. As Badge recalls it, 'On reaching the jungle, Apte asked Gopal to take out his revolver. It was taken out and, on pressing the catch, it was found that the revolver chamber did not come out.'

The .38 Webley Scott which Gopal had brought back to India had lain buried in the ground for nearly four years and had become encrusted with mud and rust.

Apte thereupon asked Badge for his revolver; and Badge, who never carried anything incriminating on himself if he could get Shankar to do it, in turn ordered Shankar' to produce it. Apte then loaded the revolver with the four cartridges that Sharma had given with it and, handing it back to Shankar, asked him to fire it at a tree. Shankar said that he would not be able

Occupied by one of the Birla family's chauffeurs, Chotu Ram, Room No. 3, as planned became the 'Site of action'. The window was actually a decorative trelliswork ventilation-grille, with 26 openings in all. Neither Apte nor Badge had actually entered the room to see this window from inside, but they were confident that it would serve their purpose.

Though the day – January 20 – had arrived and the place was fixed, the weapon was something they had to still decide on. A .38 Webley Scott and a .32 revolver were the two weapons they had. During target practice in the jungle behind Hindu Mahasabha Bhawan they found that the revolver was a 'useless weapon', and they could only rely on the .38 Webley Scott, which needed to be repaired urgently.

to fire a shot, but Apte told him to 'Just press the trigger'. Then 'Shankar fired a shot. The bullet did not reach the tree but fell down in between.'

Badge's revolver was a .32 and in perfect order. The trouble was that the ammunition that Sharma had supplied was either of the wrong caliber or defective.

Apte cursed and pronounced the smaller revolver to be 'a useless weapon'. Everything now depended on Gopal's revolver being repaired in time. Gopal, who remembered that he had a bottle of coconut hair-oil and a penknife in his room at the Bhavan, sent Shankar to fetch them, as well as a blanket to sit on so that the cleaned parts should not collect more dirt. Shankar ran all the way there and back. They spread the blanket under a tree and Gopal began to scrape off the rust from the mechanism of his revolver while the others watched anxiously.

But soon there was a moment of sheer panic. They heard voices and had just pushed the two revolvers under the blanket when they saw three uniformed men approaching. The ruse they thought of on account for their presence in the forest was characteristic. Badge was made to lie down on the blanket as though in pain and Shankar rubbed the oil from the bottle on his ankle. Only when the men came close did they realize that they must be forest guards on their rounds. One of the guards demanded to know what they were doing; and Gopal, who had learned to speak Punjabi well during his time with the Army, told them that they had come out for a quiet walk and were resting for a few minutes because one of them had twisted his ankle. The guards appeared satisfied with this explanation and went on their way, but the panic had been too much for Apte. He told them it was no use trying to repair the revolver in the open and that they should go back and do it indoors. Thereupon all four went back to the room in the Bhavan, and found that Karkare and Madanlal had returned.

It was already noon, with zero hour barely five hours away. Apte bundled his men and their hand luggage into two taxis and took them to the Marina. He then told Badge and Shankar to go down to the restaurant and eat their lunch and, while they were away carried out an experiment to discover how long the blasting fuse they had brought with them took to burn. They shut the door and ignited a length of the fuse. According to Karkare:

> There was a blinding flash and a hissing sound. When we opened our eyes, the room was thick with black smoke which made us cough. We picked up a mattress from one of the beds and stamped out the still smouldering bits and pieces. A hotel servant had come rushing to the door to find out what was happening, but Apte managed to fob him off with a story about a mattress having caught fire while he was lighting a cigarette.

When, after their leisurely lunch, Badge and Shankar returned to the room upstairs, they found everyone in a jubilant mood, Gopal had succeeded in repairing his revolver. At least, he had managed to put its moving parts in working order. Whether it would actually fire could not be tested since it was now too late for more target practice.

They locked themselves in and during the next half-hour carefully primed the hand grenades and fitted firing charges and fuses into the gun-cotton slabs. After that, they sat down to a council of war.

Their armoury now consisted of Gopal's .38 revolver, which they hoped had become serviceable; Badge's .32 revolver, which they knew to be useless; five 36 hand grenades fitted with seven-second fuses; and two one-pound slabs of gun-cotton with ninety-second fuses. They had, or at least Madanlal had, handled explosives before, but none of them had fired a revolver or thrown a 36 grenade, and they had very little idea of the capabilities or limitations of either weapon. For instance, Badge (according to an altered plan) confidently hoped to shoot Gandhi with his revolver at a range of some thirty feet, when, at that sort of distance, it would take a practised shot to make certain of hitting a man. And, as to the hand grenades, their idea was to get close to Gandhi and hurl them into the crowd at random from all sides, little realizing that they risked committing hara-kiri along with their gruesome mass murder. Nathuram, a little trembly after a bout of migraine, opened the proceedings with an exhortation that all of them must work with the absolute conviction of the rightness of their cause and the fullest faith in victory, since 'this was their last effort'. Apte then took over and got down to practicalities. The first thing to do, he told them, was to 'create a commotion', and then finish off Gandhi and whoever happened to be in his vicinity with revolver shots and grenades. The commotion was to be created by exploding their two charges of gun-cotton. Madanlal would set off one. Who would fire the other one?

He was met with a stony silence. The fact was that none of the others had ever set off a charge of explosive and had no idea how to do it. Badge, despite the fact that he ran a business selling explosives and firearms, was later to confess, 'I had taken no lessons as to how to use hand grenades, gun-cotton slabs, revolvers, pistols, etc... I have myself thrown no hand grenades or exploded gun-cotton slabs.'

'Why not', Badge now suggested to Apte, 'do with just one blast? We don't really need two.'

And so it was decided. Only one of the gun-cotton slabs would be exploded by Madanlal, who, after lighting the ninety-second fuse, would go and join the others around Gandhi, ready to throw a grenade at him.

When the report of the blast was heard, Badge would fire Gopal's service revolver at Gandhi through the ventilation-grille that he had been shown in the morning and Shankar, who would have managed to worm his way close to Gandhi, would, at point-blank range, pump into him the remaining three bullets in the chamber of Badge's .32. Immediately after emptying his revolver, Badge would push a hand grenade through the ventilation-grille with the barrel of his revolver. The revolver shots would be the signal for the other grenade-throwers to hurl their grenades in the general direction of Gandhi. For this purpose, the five grenades that they had brought with them would be distributed one each to Badge, Shankar, Karkare, Madanlal and Gopal. Neither Apte himself nor Nathuram would carry any arms, but it would be their business to guide the operation by 'giving signals'.

Any questions?

There were no questions. The plan was perfect. Nothing could conceivably go wrong. The gun-cotton charge would explode and create panic; Badge would be able to make his way into the room that overlooked Gandhi's seat; Gopal's revolver would go off; the bullets of the smaller revolver which had performed so miserably earlier in the morning would miraculously achieve velocity. All of them would then hurl hand grenades from all sides like boys throwing stones into a pool and, after it was all over, walk away from the scene of carnage, undetected and unhurt. They would saunter back to their respective rooms and lie low for a day or two and then catch their trains and planes back to wherever they were headed for. And it would not be long before the nation recognized them for what they were: heroes and public benefactors, true patriots who had rid their motherland of the evil genius who had assisted in her ravishment.

If Apte knew that Shankar had not understood most of what he had been told, or indeed that he did not even know what Gandhi looked like, he was not worried. Shankar was merely an appendage of Badge's, and it was Badge's business to explain things to him. And Badge's method of explaining the plan was to tell him 'to throw his hand grenade at the person at whom I threw mine; that he was to fire his revolver at the person at whom I fired mine – an old man called Gandhiji who was to be "finished".'

There was nothing more to discuss. If it occurred to the others that the two leaders had given themselves no active roles, and that they would not even be carrying a weapon, it could not have seemed odd to them.

They still had a whole hour to while away before setting out on their mission; they spent the hour in tacking small refinements onto their flawless plan.

And this again plummeted into farce. It was as though the approach of zero hour had not only dispelled their tension, but had also retarded their mental capacities.

Apte decreed that they should all adopt false names for the occasion. So Nathuram became 'Deshpande'; Apte 'Karmarkar'; Karkare 'Bias' (or 'Vyas');

Badge, 'Bandopant'; and Shankar 'Tukaram'. No one now remembers what names Gopal and Madanlal were given; no one considered that it would be impossible in the confusion of the moment for all seven of them to remember everyone else's false name.

Karkare then made the suggestion that they should all assume disguises, and everyone agreed that it was an excellent idea. They rigged themselves out with one another's clothes, everyone trying to put on something that he did not normally wear. Badge discarded his saffron robes and wore a white knee-length 'Nehru' shirt and white dhoti and a towel draped over his shoulders like a scarf. Nathuram put on khaki shorts and a shirt as though he were a policeman, Apte a dark suit with a black scarf; Madanlal wore the jacket of Apte's Air Force blue suit, and Karkare 'painted false moustaches, darkened his eyebrows, and made a red mark on his forehead'.

And thus, made up like a troupe of village fun-men, they set out to murder the Mahatma.

They were hypnotized by their own thoughts. They would kill Gandhi (to say nothing of the dozens of others who happened to be in his vicinity) and still go on as though nothing had happened. So sure were they that they would not even be suspected of the deed that they had made no preparations whatsoever to leave Delhi in a hurry in case anything went wrong. That very morning, both Nathuram and Apte had given clothes to be washed by the hotel *dhobi* (washerman) which they confidently expected to collect on the twenty-second.

Surjit Singh, an unlettered young Sikh who had fled from Pakistan, had managed by some miracle to bring out his car with him. He now made a living in New Delhi by running the car as a 'private' taxi (which meant that he did not have a licence to run it as a taxi). He was proud of the fact that his car was of a distinctive yellow-green colour which he called *moongia* (the colour of gram) and that it was perhaps the only 'taxi' in Delhi, private or licensed, which had a luggage-carrier fitted on its top. On the afternoon of 20 January, Surjit was waiting for a fare near the Regal Cinema when four people came up and, since the taxi had no meter, settled the fare in advance for taking them to Birla House, waiting there for half an hour, and bringing them back.

His four passengers were Apte, Gopal, Badge and Shankar. Apte directed Surjit to take his car to the back of Birla House, and they all got out near the servants' quarters. Surjit saw them go through the gate and into the garden. He waited near his car for a few minutes, and then thought he would go and attend Gandhi's prayer meeting; so he too went through the gate.

Nathuram, Madanlal and Karkare had preceded the others to Birla House. All three now came up and reported that everything was going according to plan. Madanlal had placed the explosive charge in position and would set it off as soon as Apte gave him the signal, and Karkare had arranged that the occupant of the room with the ventilator-grille should let Badge go in and take a photograph.

Nathuram and Apte walked with Badge towards the room and, as they approached it, Badge saw 'a one-eyed man sitting on a cot near its door'.

This was a bad omen. To see a one-eyed man at the start of any venture was to invite certain failure. Badge turned and told Apte that nothing would make him go into the room now.

Badge was paralysed with fear. He had convinced himself that the room was like a trap; that, if he once passed the one-eyed man at the door and entered the room, he would never come out of it alive. He begged his two companions to 'let him strike Gandhi from the front', and in the open meeting. Nathuram and Apte kept telling him that there was nothing to fear, that their plans of escape were foolproof. But nothing would make Badge change his mind. Meanwhile time was running out. Gandhi had already arrived, and the hum of the opening prayers chanted by the dozen or so young girls could be heard from where they were. The prayer meeting seldom lasted for more than twenty-five minutes. It was the hour of sunset, and within half an hour it would be too dark to see properly.

There was nothing for it but to give in. Yes, Badge could shoot Gandhi in the open meeting.

But Badge had already abandoned any thought of killing Gandhi. Just as he had agreed to join the plot of assassination as another man might agree to make a fourth at bridge, now, with the countdown about to begin, he was throwing in his hand. A mental process was reversing itself. A quirk of bravado had sparked it; a fit of panic had put out the fire. However, one should not suppose that the one-eyed man sitting in front of Chotu Ram's room No. 3 had given Gandhi an extra ten days of life. As will be seen, even if Badge had agreed to go through with the plan he would never have been able to fire his revolver from one of the openings in the room.

On the pretext of explaining the changed plan to Shankar, Badge took him back to the waiting taxi while the other conspirators strolled nervously in the garden. By coincidence, the taxi driver wasn't there, and Badge had plenty of time to roll up his own and Shankar's revolvers in the towel which he had draped around his shoulders. He placed the bundle on the rear seat of the taxi. After that he gave his hand grenade to Shankar to keep and warned him that he was not to 'do anything with it' till he, Badge, gave him the word. Then, balling both his fists and thrusting them deep inside the pockets of his Nehru shirt so as to create the impression that he was carrying both the revolver and the hand grenade in them, he and Shankar went back to rejoin the others.

Despite the fact that he was now unarmed, Badge went up to Apte, who asked him if he was ready. Badge said later: 'I told him I was ready and started walking towards the prayer ground. I saw Apte placing a hand on Madanlal's shoulder and heard him say, "Chalo" ['OK' or 'Go ahead'].'

Thus was Madanlal sacrificed.

But thus, too, was prevented the mass slaughter of innocent bystanders; the simple-minded men and women who came to the prayer meetings as they would go to a temple, intent on getting the Mahatma's *darshan* [sight] and nothing else. That day the crowd was small, perhaps no more than 200 people in all; but there can be no doubt that at least half of them would have found themselves caught in the killing-ground of one or the other of the five hand grenades that were to be thrown in their midst. That Apte and

Nathuram should have thought that this slaughter was justified in their bid to kill one man shows how sick their minds were. Their victims would have been mainly Hindus, and thus their act would have been every bit as callous as the worst of the Muslim atrocities they were seeking to avenge.

Nearly a hundred yards from the Birla House servants' quarters, were the servants' quarters of No. 9 Albuquerque Road, and in one of these lived Nanak Chand and his young wife Sulochana. Their three-year-old son, Mohinder, was always straying away to play with the children of the Birla House servants. On the evening of 20 January, when Sulochana had gone to the back of Birla House to look for her son, she saw 'a person placing a bomb and then lighting a match-stick. I forcibly picked up my child... saw sparks coming out of the string or the thing attached to the bomb.'

Madanlal, too, saw Sulochana. In fact, he told her to pick up her child and run. Then he hurried off to the meeting to tell Apte.

'I told Apte that the gun-cotton would explode any moment. Apte assured me that everything was under control.'

Apte could see both his front-line soldiers, Badge and Shankar, who had managed to take positions on both sides of Gandhi, and they were so obviously ready to empty their revolvers into him the moment the 'bomb' went off. Then the second line would go into action; Karkare, Madanlal and Gopal, as well as Badge and Shankar, would hurl their grenades at Gandhi and those around him.

The explosion was heard. Everyone in the crowd heard it. No one fired a shot; no one hurled a grenade. Madanlal, who happened to be looking at Shankar, saw him 'take to his heels', and then saw that Badge, too, was running. At that time, Apte tapped him on the shoulder and whispered that the plan had miscarried.

Madanlal had never been to Birla House before, and had no idea of where to go. He took off in the direction of what he thought would be an exit and found himself in the imposing porch of Birla House. He whirled about and dashed through the bushes and across a drive and found himself approaching the main entrance to the building and a group of agitated-looking policemen. The one thing he could not now afford to submit to was a search of his person, for he still had the grenade in his pocket. He doubled back and managed to find the servants' gate through which he had come, and this brought him close to the spot where he had placed the explosive charge. The woman with her child was still there, saying something to a policeman with a rifle and two other men. She turned to Madanlal and pointed a finger. 'That's the man!' she screamed.

Surjit Singh, the taxi-driver, had never seen Gandhi before. Today he saw him being carried to the meeting in a chair. This was Gandhi's first public appearance after his fast had ended, and he was still too weak to walk. From his place in the outer circle of the crowd, Surjit heard the chanting of the verses from the Gita, and then Gandhi addressed the meeting. But all Surjit heard was an indistinct murmur. It was nearly twenty minutes before someone told him that the microphone had broken down. Disappointed, he sauntered back to where he had left his car. He heard an explosion, but is not certain whether it occurred while he was still at the meeting or after he had returned to his taxi. From what Gopal Godse states, Surjit must have returned to his taxi a couple of minutes *after the* bomb had exploded.

'The explosion was loud enough to be heard at a far-off distance', writes Tendulkar, Gandhi's biographer, but 'Gandhi remained unruffled'. He went on with his address as though nothing had happened, and soon the restive crowd settled down. The prayer meeting went through its prescribed routine of opening chorus, speech, recitations from the Koran, the Bible and the Gita, and finally the *Ramdhun* with its bi-religious invocation to Ishwar (Hindu) and Allah (Muslim) to 'give wisdom to all'.

The Mahatma's own reaction to the incident was utterly true to character. In talking about it later in the evening, he was, if anything, full of praise for Madanlal. 'The boy is a *bahadur* [brave warrior],' he declared, and compared him to Bhagat Singh, the leader of a terrorist gang whom the British had executed and who had become something of a national hero. Gandhi went on: '*Bachhe hain, Ahbi yeh samajhte nahin. Maroonga tab yaad karenge, ke boodha theek kehta tha.*' ('They're like children. They don't understand. After I'm gone they'll realize that what the old man used to say was right.')

When Gopal Godse saw Shankar and Badge running away, his first instinct was to bolt. But, as he got to the waiting taxi, saw the white bundle on the rear seat, realized what it was, and discovered that the driver was absent, the thought suddenly struck him that this was his one chance of finishing the job on his own. He grabbed the bundle, thrust it into the cloth bag in which he was carrying the grenade and dashed in the direction of the servants' quarter. Since everyone was running about at this time, no one took any notice of him. All the servants' quarter were suddenly empty and their doors wide open. He boldly walked into Chotu Ram's room, shut the door behind him and fastened it with the chain with which it was meant to be secured from inside, and took out the .38 revolver.

A glance at the grille made him realize that it was set too high in the wall to provide a view of the prayer ground. He jumped and managed to grab hold of a ledge and heaved himself up. But he needed both his hands to keep in this position. For a few seconds he struggled frantically to hold himself up with one hand and use the other to grip the revolver. It was impossible. He let go, ran back to the door and tried to release the chain. He broke into a cold sweat when he realized that he couldn't pull it out. For a few seconds he struggled desperately, terrified that he had locked himself in. Then he put down the bag he was carrying and, applying both hands, prised the chain off its hook. The door opened with a startling bang. He ran out and made for the waiting taxi. Nathuram, Apte and Karkare had already come there, and so had their taxi driver. They piled into the car and, according to the driver, told him urgently to 'start the car - start the car!' He drove them back to Connaught Place.

Almost unbelievably, the floor of Chotu Ram's room was at a lower level than the ground at the back from where, it will be recalled, Apte had measured the openings in the grille without much difficulty. In fact, from inside the room the height of the grille was a little more than seven feet.

And, if Gopal could not fire a revolver through one of the holes, there was no question of Badge being able to do so, either. Gopal was not a tall man – perhaps five-feet eight inches – but Badge is barely five-feet.

In the car Karkare told them in Marathi how he had seen Madanlal being led by the police to the tent they had pitched outside the gate of Birla House, and how he had caught Madanlal's eye and signalled to him that his friends would stand by him.

After the taxi dropped them, they strolled across into the open field in front of the Regal Cinema, and stood under the trees. Their minds were numbed by the realization of failure, and the only thing they could talk about was their immediate plans. Karkare, who regarded Madanlal as his special responsibility, was anxious to stay on in Delhi for another day and see if he could do something to help him. Then he would make his way to Bombay and lie low. Gopal was keen to go back to Poona and resume duty, and decided to catch the Punjab Mail the next morning. Apte and Nathuram were leaving Delhi that night, but in some direction other than that of Bombay.

They shook hands as though to encourage one another and parted. The bundle which contained both the revolvers was still in Gopal's hands, and Gopal took it away with him. This was something they would soon come to regret.

Apte and Nathuram walked the short distance to the Marina and checked out, preferring not to make any inquiries about their laundry. Karkare and Gopal sat in a coffee shop for a few minutes and then took a tonga to the Hindu Mahasabha Bhavan. They found that Badge had already removed his things from their room and had gone. They, too, collected their belongings and went to Old Delhi, where close to the railway station they found a cheap hotel, the Frontier Hindu Hotel. Here they took a room for a day, Gopal giving his name as 'Rajagopalan' and Karkare as 'G.M. Joshi'.

Once outside Birla House, Badge hired a tonga, and he and Shankar went to Karkare's room in the Hindu Mahasabha Bhavan in which they had left their luggage. While he busied himself 'tying up his bedding,' he sent

Shankar off to bury the two cloth bags full of grenades and explosives which they still possessed somewhere in the woods at the back of the Bhavan. After Shankar had gone on this errand, Apte and Nathuram turned up in a taxi and demanded to know why Badge had not carried out his part of the operation. Badge thereupon 'abused them and asked them to get out. And they got out.'

As soon as Shankar came back Badge sent him to fetch a tonga, and in it they were driven to New Delhi railway station. But the station platform was bristling with policemen, so they drove on to the Old Delhi station. Here they did not see too many policemen, and a train for Bombay was ready to leave within half an hour. They got into a crowded compartment. Two days later they were back in Poona.

Badge did not know it then, but Apte and Nathuram also happened to be at the Old Delhi railway station at the time, but on a different platform. They were in a first-class compartment of the overnight train to Kanpur, which left only a few minutes after Badge's train. Since they were by themselves in a four-berth sleeping compartment, they could talk to one another freely.

As Apte later recounted to Karkare:

> To be sure, we were greatly distressed by our failure, but we had by no means lost our determination, and there was no question of packing in – of going back to the routine of business and family life. I kept telling Nathuram.
>
> "We can't turn back now; not at this stage. We'll have another try, recruit a new lot of men, collect more money. But we just can't drop the whole thing now."
>
> Nathuram didn't say much, but somehow I could sense that he was not altogether in agreement. It was not till the next morning that I discovered what he was thinking about. It must have been past midnight when I dozed off. I had a disturbed sleep and, at about six the next morning, I was only half-awake when I heard Nathuram say:
>
> "Nana, did you sleep well?"
>
> I mumbled something and stretched my limbs and sleepily answered:
>
> "Urn-hum, and you?"

He did not answer my question, Instead he said:

"I'm going to do it. I don't need any help, not another man. No recruiting people, no depending on any one else."

My eyes were still closed, and I swear that, in that instant, I saw Gandhi dead.

Their train reached Kanpur a little before noon on Wednesday, the twenty-first. By this time, the Delhi Police had succeeded in extracting enough information from Madanlal to put them on the trail of a 'Kirkree Seth' from Ahmednagar, and 'the Manager of a Rashtriya paper in Poona'. They also had good descriptions of the others, such as 'a man who called himself Deshpande and was staying at the Marina Hotel [Apte]. A man with a beard [Badge], and his servant, aged twenty years.' That same evening, Wednesday, two inspectors of the Delhi Police flew to Bombay.

In Kanpur, Nathuram went into the railway station office and, in his own name, booked a retiring-room with two beds. That day they spent on the station itself. At 11.30 the next morning they caught the Lucknow-Jhansi Mail which, at Jhansi, gave them a connection with the Delhi-Bombay Punjab Mail. They reached Bombay's Victoria Terminus at noon on 23 January, and proceeded to a cheap mid-town hotel where Apte had stayed several times before with his mistress. It was the Arya Pathikashram on Sandhurst Road; and its Manager, Gaya Pershad Dube, regarded Apte, who always demanded and paid for a whole room to himself, as a favoured client. This time, however, Dube could not oblige Apte and his friend with a separate room; in fact, the best he could do was to give them two beds in a room that had six other lodgers, but promised to do something better for them the next morning.

Apte and Nathuram left their luggage in the hotel and hurried off to Thana, to the house of Mr G.M. Joshi, were Karkare normally stayed whenever he was in Bombay. But Joshi had not seen anything of Karkare since he had left for Delhi, so they went to the two or three other people whom Karkare was known to visit. Considering that the new plan was to be a one-man effort, their anxiety to get in touch with Karkare seems strange, but they had been out of touch since Madanlal's arrest and did not even know whether any of the others were still free. Nor were they sure whether they were going to stay on in Bombay or proceed to Poona, and thus did not leave any instructions for Karkare at these houses as to how he was to contact them when he finally did come.

In the evening they sent a friend to Poona to pass word to Gopal that they had arrived in Bombay and that Miss Salvi would know where they were staying.

They did not return to the hotel till late at night. Next morning the manager came and told Apte that they would have a double room to themselves, which Apte accepted. They then went to a nearby hotel, the Elphinstone Annexe in Carnac Road, and booked another room there. Nathuram registered here as 'N. Vinayakrao and friend'. According to the Arya Pathikashram's manager, Apte returned before noon with 'a lady who stayed with him throughout the day of 24 January and the night between 24 and 25'. On the morning of the twenty-fifth, Sunday, Apte shifted to the room in the other hotel, and the 'lady', Manorama Salvi, went with him, and stayed with him through most of the next two days, while Nathuram saw movies and otherwise managed to leave the two as much to themselves as possible.

EIGHT

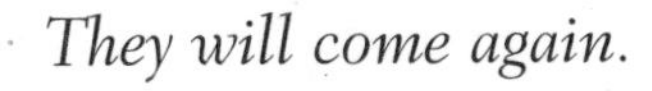

They will come again.

— MADANLAL PAHWA

At his prayer meeting on the evening after Madanlal's arrest, Gandhi again spoke of him with kindness.

> No one should look down upon the misguided young man who had thrown the bomb. He probably looked upon me as an enemy of Hinduism. After all, had not the Gita said that, whenever there was an evil-minded person damaging religion, God sent someone to end his life?

And, as though knowing something about the methods of interrogation practised by the police in India, Gandhi also made a special appeal to the Inspector-General of Police 'not to harass the youth in any way'.

According to Madanlal, he was not only harassed, but also subjected to some revoltingly sadistic tortures. He was pounded on the soles of his feet with a twist of hard rope while questions were fired at him; made to lie on the floor with two legs of a *charpoy* [string bed] resting on his hands and on which a policeman jumped up and down; his sexual organs were played with, abused, prodded and beaten with sticks; and – something he came to dread most – he was treated to what he believes was a local speciality, 'the ordeal by ants'. They would hold big red ants in their fingers, infuriate them by spitting on them, and then release them on his naked body.

He screamed, he howled like an animal, but he talked too – and what he said went down in the records as a confession made voluntarily because his companions 'had deserted him and run away and he considered it his duty to get them arrested'.

He believes to this day that no one could have withstood the sort of interrogation that he was put through, but he is also proud of the fact that he did not tell them everything he knew. By making distorted statements and pretending that he did not understand any Marathi he was able to camouflage the identities of his colleagues.

By screaming louder than he need have, by ranting incoherently and whispering meekly in turns, and revealing too many irrelevant details which went down into the 'case-diaries' as they were uttered he was able to throw the police off the right trial for just long enough to prevent them from arresting the ringleaders before they were able to strike again.

But, if Madanlal had not told them everything he knew, he certainly had told them enough. If the police had acted with more than routine zeal, it is doubtful if Nathuram Godse or any of the other conspirators would still have been free on 30 January, the day on which Gandhi was murdered.

Chotu Ram, the occupant of room No. 3 in the Birla House servants' quarters, had told the police how some men had come to ask him to be allowed to take a photograph of Gandhi from his room, and his description of them tallied with that given by Madanlal. Within three hours of Madanlal's arrest, the police knew that what he had done was intended to serve as a signal for an attempt on Gandhi's life, that the final preparations for a concerted assault had been made, and the final instructions given in a room in the Marina Hotel. Late at night, they took Madanlal to the Marina. As Mr C. Pacheco, the manager of the Marina Hotel later testified: 'He was brought handcuffed and with his face covered. The covering was removed and he was asked to lead them to the room where his friends were staying. He led them to room No. 40.'

The police called in witnesses and searched the room. In a drawer of a table they came upon a typewritten sheet. It was the statement issued by Ashutosh Lahiri, the General Secretary of the Hindu Mahasabha, declaring that his party had not signed the seven-point pledge that had been instrumental in making Gandhi give up his fast

Later, the judge who tried the case, Mr Atma Charan, declared this bit of evidence to be inadmissible and 'altogether discarded [it] for the purpose of arriving at any conclusion, one way or the other'. But at the time it led the police to suspect that the Hindu Mahasabha was connected with the plot to murder Gandhi; and the Hindu Mahasabha, by projection, led them to Savarkar.

By the time they had finished the search of room No. 40 and gone through the procedure of recording the discoveries in the presence of witnesses it was long past midnight. All the same, Madanlal's interrogation continued. It was important to prevent him from dropping off to sleep. The case-diary of one of the interrogating officers records that he 'was talking in whispers'. Early the next morning, he was led to the Old Delhi railway station.

Two trains leave Delhi for Bombay in the morning; the Frontier Mail at eight, and the Punjab Mail at nine. Gopal Godse was leaving by the second, and Karkare had come to see him off. Gopal had already found a seat in a third-class compartment, and had deposited his cloth bag which contained both the revolvers as well as his unused hand grenade under his bunk, and he and Karkare had gone into the tea-room on the platform for breakfast. As Gopal later admitted to the author:

> We had just sat down when we saw a police party arriving with a man whose head and shoulders were covered with a brown blanket. Even before the blanket was removed, we knew that the man was Madanlal. We were quite certain that he had revealed our names and that he had been brought to the station to identify us.

The tea-room is large, perhaps forty feet by thirty and it was not crowded. Madanlal was made to take a good look all around while two policeman watched his eyes for signs of recognition. After he had turned the full circle, he shook his head. His escort again covered his head with the brown blanket and he was marched out. 'It was just our good luck that he did not look in our direction,' Gopal added.

But Gopal was wrong. Madanlal had seen Gopal as well as his good friend Karkara Seth the moment the hood was removed from his head, but had managed to stare straight through them. Only after he had completed his inspection did he shake his head. They took him out and began to search the carriages of the train. When they had gone to the other end of the train, Gopal sauntered back to his compartment and took his seat.

One of the people who had got himself into a state over Madanlal's arrest was his professor friend in Bombay, Dr J.C. Jain. Several of Jain's friends knew that he knew Madanlal, and at least one, Angad Singh, knew that Madanlal had hinted to him that he was involved in a plot to murder Gandhi. Jain had done nothing whatsoever to report this information to the police, and must have realized that, if Madanlal said anything about it in his statement, there was a possibility that his own silence might land him into trouble.

Jain was in his fortieth year. He held a Ph.D. degree in Hindi and was a professor in a college. He was thus a man of education and social background who was well aware of his duties and responsibilities as a citizen. That he should have originally passed off Madanlal's revelations as refugee bombast is altogether understandable. But now, after Madanlal had been caught, Jain knew that it was his clear duty to report what he had heard to someone in authority.

His normal course would have been to rush to the nearest police station to make a report. Instead, for reasons which were never satisfactorily explained, he sought interviews with the Deputy Prime Minister of India and the Chief of Bombay's Congress Party and, when he failed to make contact with either, descended, as it were, to Bombay's Chief Minister, B. G. Kher. (The approximate analogy for this sort of behaviour would be for a professor in Columbia University who had discovered that President Kennedy was to be murdered during his Dallas visit insisting on passing on the information only to the Vice-President or, failing him, to no one of less than cabinet rank.)

It was not till four o'clock in the afternoon of the twenty-first that Jain was admitted into Mr Kher's room. But, before Jain could come to the point, Kher had to go somewhere else, and he passed him on to his Home Minister, Morarji Desai.

Morarji, as it happens, also held the police portfolio and, if only in fairness to his department, should have ordered Jain to go to the police with his story; at least he should have taken the precaution of getting someone to make a record of what Jain had to say. Instead, he gave Jain what amounted to a confidential hearing and, incredibly, he even agreed to Jain's request not to 'disclose even to the police' the source of his information. One result of this was that both Jain and Morarji had later to rely entirely on their memories to recall exactly what had been said at this interview. Morarji believes that the only name Jain mentioned as a conspirator of Madanlal was that of Karkare, whereas Jain 'claimed to have disclosed the names of Madanlal's confederates [as given by him in his interrogation] and made a grievance of their not having been arrested.'

After Gandhi was murdered, what Jain claims to have told Morarji and what Morarji believes he heard was to spark a bout of caustic histrionics between the two men. Morarji, according to Jain,

> flared up and said to him [Jain] that he was a conspirator and could be put into jail and he asked why information had not been given to him earlier. He shouted at Jain and Jain went on listening and ... said to Morarji Desai, "If I was a conspirator, you are a murderer," and that is what he would repeat to the world, "you're guilty, you're guilty!"

Following pages: 194-97: Copy of Dr J.C. Jain's statement to the court. A close friend and mentor of Madanlal Pahwa, Dr Jain from Bombay had some inkling about Madanlal's trip to Delhi, which he had passed off earlier as refugee bombast. If what Mr Jain told to Bombay Home Minister, Morarji Desai, on 21 January had been taken cognizance of at an appropriate time, maybe the tragedy could have been averted.

Z. P. Poona. 1947 Civ. A 27

Exhibit No. 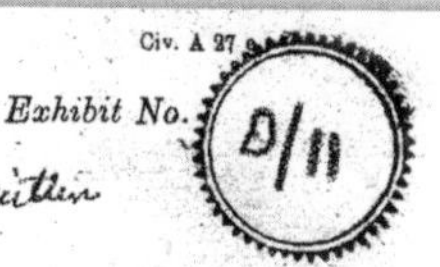

~~Deposition~~ Statement OF WITNESS No. 9 FOR THE Prosecution

I do hereby on solemn affirmation state that—

My name is Jagdish Chandra Jain Father's name Kengimal

Religion Hindu Caste Bania Agarwal Vaishya

Age about 39. Occupation Professor of Ardha Magadi & Hindi

Residence 28 Shivaji Park District Dadar Bombay 28

~~Examination-in-Chief~~

I am a Professor of Ardha Magdi & Hindi at the Ramnarain Ruia College Matunga. In October 1947 I met Madanlal. He was a refugee from the Punjab. He was introduced to me by Mr. Gupta of Amir Masjid Mahim. Madanlal was looking for a job & for a short time sold my books. He said he was doing some fruit business with Ahmednagar. He told me that through the generosity of a Gujarati lady he also had an interest in a fire cracker business. Madanlal introduced me to a [illegible] Madanlal told me of a meeting which he attended at Ahmednagar & in which he opposed Rao Saheb Patwardhan who had

an intelligent young man & was merely being
made a scapegoat by his party. Madanlal
listened to me and thanked me for my advice.
Madanlal met me on the following day. He said
he was proceeding to Delhi & would return
in a few days. ~~Bepore~~ I wanted to bring this to
the notice of Jai Prakash Narain but merely
told him that there would be a great conspiracy
in Delhi but as he was in a great hurry
to leave I could not tell him the details.

4 On 21/1/48 after reading the news
of the explosion of a bomb at the Prayer meeting
of Gandhiji I tried to contact Vallabhai Patel.
I failed to do so as he had already left for the
Aerodrome on his way to Delhi. I also tried
to contact Mr S.K. Patil. He also had accom
panied the Sardar. I rang up the Premier Mr B.G.
Kher. He gave me an appointment for 4 P.M. at
the Secretariat. Mr Morarji Desai Home Minister
was present. I gave the Prime Minister the
whole statement as set out above. I also
offered my services to unearth this conspiracy.
I requested them to take such action as they
considered necessary. I will be able to identify

spoke of Hindus & Muslims living peaceably together. Madanlal told me that the person who accompanied him was one Karkare, a big Seth of Ahmednagar.

2. Madanlal said that a group had been formed at Ahmednagar & that Karkare was financing the group. Madanlal stated that the party to which he belonged had ~~plan~~ plotted to do away with some great leader. Madanlal mentioned the name of Mahatma Gandhi.

3. I was horrified at such a suggestion ~~& tried to dissuade him~~ I tried to dissuade him for about 2 hours & said that he was making unnecessary trouble for himself & for others. I reminded him of all the repercussions & said that he was

Madanlal I think I shall be able to identify Karkare also.

[This statement was made voluntarily by the deponent & was recorded by me under sec 164 of the Criminal Procedure Code. While this was being done the Police were excluded from the Court room.]

I accept this statement:- Jagdishchandra Jain

Read over to the witness & accepted as correct

Oscar H Brown
Chief Presidency Magistrate,
Bombay.
26/3/48

REX vs. N.V. GODSE & OTHERS
EXHIBIT NO. 2/11
Read over, and admitted.
Dated 5.8.48
I.C.S.
RED-FORT, DELHI. JUDGE, SPECIAL COURT.

Neither was guilty of murder or conspiracy. Justice K.L. Kapur, who headed the one-man commission (known as the Kapur Commission), which was later appointed to investigate the allegations that several people had advance information of the plot to murder Gandhi, questioned Professor Jain at length. He was led to conclude that he could not be 'clear about what exactly Jain had told the Home Minister', and in his report calls attention to the more obvious discrepancies between Jain's first and subsequent versions of what he had reported. But this much is certain. On 21 January, Jain told the Home Minister of Bombay that there was a plot to murder Gandhi and that, other than Madanlal, a man called Karkare who lived in Ahmednagar was involved in it.

Jain left Morarji's office at about 5 p.m. and Morarji immediately sent for Mr J.D. Nagarvala, Bombay's Deputy Commissioner in charge of the Intelligence Branch. But Nagarvala happened to be busy, so Morarji told him to see him at the Bombay Central railway station from where he was going to catch the Gujarat Mail at 8.30 p.m.

Jamshed Dorab Nagarvala – 'Jimmy' to his numerous friends – had most of the sterling virtues of his calling as well as most of its blind spots. He was thirty-four years old, tall and well-built, with large round eyes in a round face which was thus not constructed for displaying sternness or for intimidating criminals. And yet he came close to Hollywood's concept of an ideal police officer. He was altogether wedded to his profession and revelled in the power it gave him; bluff, jovial, a devoted friend and a terrifying enemy, he was worshipped by his subordinates and trusted by his superiors.

He was also utterly loyal to Morarji Desai, who, for his part, treated him as his special favourite, or at least thought of him as his star policeman. At the railway station Morarji told Nagarvala what Jain had reported to him, without of course revealing Jain's name. It will be recalled that, according to Jain, Madanlal had been taken by his friend Karkare to see Savarkar who, after listening to Madanlal's exploits for two hours, had patted him on the back and told him to 'carry on'.

Whether Morarji Desai, by his manner more than by his words, indicated to his subordinate that this complaint would serve as a useful handle to discipline Savarkar, who had been as much a thorn in the flesh of the Congress Raj as of the British Raj, will never be known; but whatever he said seems to have been enough for Nagarvala to discern Savarkar's hand in whatever conspiracy was being hatched even if, as will be apparent, he had still no idea of the nature of the conspiracy. The result was that, in addition to the routine measures Nagarvala initiated to prevent the murder of Mahatma Gandhi, he also 'organized an unobtrusive watch on Savarkar's house'.

'We already had a dossier on Savarkar,' Nagarvala later explained. Of course they did. But, then, they must also have had dossiers on Morarji Desai and Nehru as well, and a monster one on Gandhi himself. During the British days all these men were seditionists.

Long after Savarkar had been cleared of any complicity in the plot, and at least two years after Nagarvala, who, having duly reached the pinnacle of a policeman's career and served as the Inspector-General of Police, had retired, Nagarvala was still to insist to the author, 'To my dying day I shall believe that Savarkar was the man who organized Gandhi's murder.'

But similarly, long after they had served their terms of imprisonment, Vishnu Karkare, Gopal Godse and Madanlal Pahwa, who were separately questioned by the author, as to whether they thought that Gandhi's murder had served the national interest, were unanimous in insisting that it had.

Such are the convictions of the truly committed.

In the train, Gopal Godse had plenty of time to think. The sight of Madanlal, handcuffed and hooded and being led around by his captors to hunt out his erstwhile companions, kept tormenting him. But for a chance the prisoner might have been himself. He longed to get back to Poona and be with his wife and little daughters and to submerge himself deeply in the blissful routine that had governed his life before the past week. He would gladly have given a whole year of his life to be able to undo whatever had happened in that week. In the event, he was to give seventeen years of his life to atone for the brief seizure of insanity that had overtaken him.

And, as though to drive home the lesson that his repentance was already too late, towards the end of his journey, Gopal received yet another jolt of panic.

He had alighted at the Dadar junction and was waiting on the platform for his Poona connection when a railway policeman came up and demanded to inspect his baggage. Aside from the cloth bag in which he was carrying the two revolvers and the unused grenade, Gopal also had a bed-roll. Trying to gulp down his fear, be dutifully opened the bed-roll with alacrity. The policeman prodded and probed among the bedclothes and sauntered off. Apparently he was on the lookout for some stolen goods which could not have been contained in a small cloth bag. Gopal never discovered what they were.

His train reached Kirkee station at 5 p.m. on the twenty-second. He went home and shut himself in a room and brooded. His first concern was to get his revolvers stored somewhere safely. Frugal to the last, it does not seem to have occurred to him to fling them out of the window of the train during the night or while it was crossing a river, and both weapons and their ammunition were still with him. By nine o'clock he had decided to find a home for at least one of them. He took out his .38 and wrapped it, together with its spare cartridges, in Badge's towel and placed the bundle in a cloth bag. An hour later he was in Poona and knocking at the door of a family friend who lived in Sadashiv Peth. The friend, Pandurang Godbole, later testified: 'I opened the door. Gopal was alone. He told me he wanted to keep with me an article. The article was a revolver with some cartridges... wrapped in a towel and placed in a bag. The bag was then placed in a box by me.'

So at least one of the weapons had been safely stored away, or so Gopal thought. He still had the .32 which, it will be recalled, Badge had taken in exchange from a man called Sharma who lived in Poona. Gopal had some vague idea of returning it to its rightful owner through Badge and getting back his brother's .22 pistol which Sharma had been given in exchange. He still had three days of his leave left, and thus plenty of time in which to get rid of the other revolver.

After Gopal's train had pulled out, Karkare had gone on sitting in the tea-room at Delhi railway station till he felt sure that the police party had gone away. Then he walked across to the Frontier Hindu Hotel, paid his bill and brought his luggage to the railway station waiting-room. In the afternoon he went to see one or two of his Hindu Mahasabha friends.

Karkare was desperate to do something to help Madanlal, such as engaging a good lawyer who would try to get him released on bail or at least to advise him about his best defence. But his friends had no wish to get mixed up in anything so dangerous and refused to help. Karkare spent the whole of Wednesday and Thursday tramping the streets of Delhi like a lost soul and coming to the waiting-room to sleep. With the help of some of Madanlal's relatives, he was able to enlist the services of an advocate, Mehta Puran Chand, to act for him.

On 23 January, he left Delhi, filled with an overpowering sense of guilt that he was abandoning his friend. In the story-book tradition of a hunted criminal trying to shake off pursuit, he got off the train at Mathura, then took a bus to Agra where he caught another train, changed trains twice during the night at a junction called Itarsi and again at Kalyan, and in the early hours of the morning of the twenty-fifth, which was a Sunday, alighted on the Thana railway station.

At 5 a.m. he reached Mr Joshi's house, Shanta Sadan, in the Navpada enclave and called up to him from the street. Despite the early hour the Joshi family welcomed Karkare. One of the first things they told him was that Apte and Nathuram had come looking for him two days earlier. Karkare was thrilled to get news of his colleagues and wanted to get in touch with them at once, but his host had no idea where they were staying in Bombay or indeed whether they were still in Bombay. Karkare decided to send a telegram to Apte's house in Poona but, knowing that the police might be watching Apte's house, and not wishing to reveal his own whereabouts, did not want to send it from Thana. Joshi's eighteen-year-old son, Vasant, was sent to the Central Telegraph Office in Bombay, which is all of twenty miles from Thana, to send the telegram which, because it was a Sunday, had to be sent express.

APTE
ANANDASHARAM
POONA
BOTH COME IMMEDIATELY – VYAS

'Vyas' (which is also spelt as 'Bias') it will be recalled, was the code name Karkare had been given.

When the guards at Birla House had overpowered Madanlal and handcuffed him and marched him off in triumph to their tent outside the gate, he had turned on them with a snarl of contempt and told them: '*Phir ayega*!' ('They will come again!')

The threat had given the police a jolt. So this was not just a case of a demented refugee registering his protest in a startlingly novel manner. He had companions. They would come again. Who? When?

Mr T.G. Sanjevi, the Chief of Delhi Police, at once gave orders to increase the strength of the guard at Birla House from five men to twenty-six, of whom seven were to be in plain clothes, and he detailed some of his best officers to find out from Madanlal who his companions were, and what they were going to do.

Nearly a dozen officers of the Delhi Police took it in turns to interrogate Madanlal. The questioning went on almost continuously over the next ten days; in fact, right up to the evening of 30 January, when suddenly from being the star criminal Madanlal, much to his own relief, found himself relegated to a position of minor importance.

But, during those ten days, the investigating officers in Delhi were so totally absorbed in grilling their solitary captive that they overlooked what might have proved a far less un-cooperative and more reliable source of information – the Hindu Mahasabha office in New Delhi. After all, within hours of Madanlal's arrest, they had discovered in the Marina Hotel room a copy of Ashutosh Lahiri's statement of the previous day. If, instead of jumping to the conclusion that the discovery of this statement showed that the Mahasabha had had a hand in the murder plot, they had used it to seek a clarification from its author, he would at the very least have told them that the Editor mentioned by Madanlal was none other than Nathuram Godse of the *Hindu Rashtra*.

The Kapur Commission observes that 'the investigation was not of a high order', and that it gave one 'the impression that the Delhi Police was entirely paralysed'. In particular, Justice Kapur points out: 'No investigation was made of the Hindu Mahasabha Bhavan where a majority of the conspirators had stayed... (nor of) Mr Ashutosh Lahiri, who knew Nathuram Godse well and also Apte.'

Nor, as it turned out did Madanlal tell them much.

The case-diaries of the officers who conducted his interrogation make pointed reference to his intransigence, that he made *mukhtalif* or contradictory statements, and that he 'did not disclose information about his accomplices,' for which, the diary observes, he was 'instructed accordingly'. Another diary has a more ominous comment, that he was 'taken to the civil lines and advised to state true facts and not indulge in incorrect statements.'

Madanlal, too, confirms that, once he got his second wind, he did not give away much information. But, on the day of his arrest, he had told the police that he had six other accomplices and had furnished descriptions of them, given particulars of the taxi in which they had driven to Birla House, had named Karkara Seth from Ahmednagar as one of the accomplices and also revealed that another was 'the Editor of the *Hindu Rashtra* or the *Agrani* which was the Marathi language newspaper published either in Bombay or Poona'.

On the afternoon of the twenty-first, within twenty-four hours of Madanlal's arrest, two officers of the Delhi Police, Deputy Superintendent Jaswant Singh and Inspector Balkishen, were on the plane to Bombay. Their orders were to see Mr J. D. Nagarvala, the Deputy Commissioner of Police in Bombay, and apprise him of the facts, and then proceed to Poona to see Raosaheb Gurtu, the Deputy Assistant Inspector-General of Police, CID. They were also to assist the Bombay Police in the investigation of the case. They later said that they had carried with them a copy of Madanlal's statement. This statement was, in conformity with the police procedure then in practice all over northern India, written in the Urdu script which hardly any of the senior police officials in Bombay could read.

Early on the morning of 22 January the two officers saw Deputy Commissioner Nagarvala and, according to them, gave him a copy of Madanlal's statements 'together with an English note containing its precis,' and also verbally told him everything they knew and, in particular, that Madanlal had mentioned the editor of the *Hindu Rashtra* or the *Agrani* as being one of his principal accomplices. Nagarvala, for his part, denies that they ever mentioned anyone other than Karkare.

Their request was for arresting Karkare, even whose name they did not know properly ... they had no documents excepting a small piece of paper on which they had something written in Urdu – one or two words in Urdu.

Much fuss was later made about whether or not the Delhi Police had asked the Bombay Police to trace the man who was the 'Editor of the *Hindu Rashtra*'. The whole controversy acquires a strangely Alice in Wonderland quality when one, remembers that any police officer in Delhi – or, indeed, any private individual – by merely making a telephone call to Bombay could have found out that the Editor's name was Nathuram Vinayak Godse. Under the Press Act, every provincial government maintained a register of all the newspapers published within its jurisdiction, showing the names of their editors and proprietors.

If Nagarvala had been given this information, he might possibly have succeeded in apprehending Nathuram in time to prevent Gandhi's murder, or at least arranged to post a few Poona policemen who knew Nathuram by sight among the guards at Birla House. But, having mentioned this as a fairly reasonable possibility, it must be pointed out that at the time Nagarvala, too, was obsessed by an equally Alice in Wonderland type of hunch of his own, and was not particularly receptive to such facts, opinions or inferences that did not fit in with his pet theories.

As Nagarvala told a fellow police officer at the time, 'The conspiracy was to kidnap Mahatma Gandhi. It was a very big organization, with about twenty principal conspirators, each assisted by twenty persons and in possession of considerable quantities of firearms and other lethal weapons.'

So convinced was Nagarvala of the genuineness of his theory that in spite of the information that was later fed to him by the Delhi Police, and even after reading a copy of Madanlal's statement, he went on pressing for its acceptance and, in fact, blandly suggested that 'the Delhi Police had been won over by the gang of kidnappers.' As late as 30 January, Nagarvala wrote to the Chief of Delhi Police two letters which 'highlight the theory of kidnapping'.

It was only after Gandhi was murdered that Nagarvala gave up working to the scenario that he had himself dreamed up.

Also, and this is hardly likely to be admitted, there existed between the Bombay and Delhi police departments the sort of rivalry and areas of sensitivity that commonly afflict the different branches of the civil authority in every country. From the point of view of Bombay, it was hardly seemly on the part of the Delhi Police to offer to assist in the detection of Bombay's own bad men. And, to be sure, over the next few days, there were instances of one network conveniently failing to pass on to the other some vital piece of evidence that it had managed to unearth. After Gandhi was murdered, some inspired person in Delhi (who is believed to have been the Deputy Prime Minister, Sardar Patel), being mindful of these crosscurrents, took steps to modify their effect by deputing one man, Nagarvala, as the special officer in charge of the investigation, thus forming under that officer what amounted to a separate police team that did not belong exclusively to either network.

It was therefore hardly surprising that the two Delhi policemen felt that their reception in Bombay was far from cordial. During the twenty-second and twenty-third, they had at least three interviews with Mr Nagarvala, who outranked them, and who brusquely told them to get out of their uniforms, to leave their hotel room because he did not want their presence to be advertised in Bombay, and to refrain from conducting any inquiries on their own. If, while in Bombay, they had somhow kept in touch with their own

10½ بجے دن - نمبر 3 - اِس وقت معہ انسپکٹر صاحب دفتر پولیس
سی - آئی - ڈی بواری ٹیکسی پہنچے - مسٹر نگروالا صاحب کی خدمت میں
پیش ہوئے - جن کو پھر دوبارہ جملہ حالات مقدمہ ھذا بتلائے گئے - ایک یادداشت
انگریزی جس میں مختصر بیان مدن لال ملزم انگریزی میں درج ہے - اور
اِس کے نیچے یادداشت S. P. صاحب نیو دھلی کی درج ہے - جناب نگروالا
صاحب کی خدمت میں پیش کی گئی - جنہوں نے اِس یادداشت کو بغور پڑھا
اور اپنے پاس یادداشت رکھی - تحریری نوٹ متعلقہ مقدمہ ھذا واپس دی - جو کہ
نقل ھذا ہے - جناب نگروالا صاحب کو Karkra کے متعلق تمام حالات واضح کئے
گئے اور مزید یہ بھی عرض کیا گیا کہ مدن لال ملزم نے یہ بھی بتلایا تھا
کہ ھمراھی ملزمان میں سے ایک ملزم جس کا نام نہیں جانتا - ھندو راشٹریہ
یا اگرنی اخبار کا ایڈیٹر تھا - جس کا رنگ سانولہ ، عمر 33/34 سال - قد تقریباً
5'6" بیان کرتا تھا - یہ معلوم نہیں کہ وہ ایڈیٹر بمبئی یا پونہ کا ہے - اِس کے
علاوہ دیگر تین مرھٹہ و راجہ صاحب جو کہ اپنے ھمراھی ملزم بیان کرتا تھا- کے
حلیئے بتلائے گئے - ایڈیٹر ھندو راشٹریہ یا اگرنی اخبار اور Karkra ساکن احمدنگر
کے متعلق مسٹر نگروالا صاحب کی خدمت میں خاص طور پر زور دیا گیا - کہ
اِن کا ذکر ملزم کے بیان میں صاف طور پر آ چکا ہے - اِن کی گرفتاری کی
پہلے کوشش کی جاوے - تاکہ اِن سے دریافت عمل میں لائی جا سکے -

The attempt on Gandhi's life on January 20 had failed. Though all the other six conspirators were able to flee the spot, it was Madanlal who was arrested by the Delhi Police. Through his distorted statements and pretending that he did not understand any Marathi, in which the others were proficient, he was able to hide the identities of his partners in crime. Recorded in Urdu, his statement to the Delhi Police was of no use to the police in Bombay as a copy of the same was taken for them without being translated. **Facing page:** Translation of Madanlal's statement.

1086-A

Madan Lal s/o Pishori Lal ~~Caste~~ Pahwa of Pakpattan Dist Montgomery West Punjab aged 20/21

Refugee went to Bombay in Middle of November

Contacted Mahasabha worker for employment

Met Karkare who appeared to be active worker or president of the Sabha. Karkare also proprietor of a hotel – Deccan Guest House. Karkare having come to know that the accused was a member of RSS unfolded a plan to train to kill Mahatma Gandhi who ~~was~~ is enemy of hindus

Came to ~~Dehi~~ Delhi with Karkare reaching here about 17.1.48

Stayed at Hindu Sharif Hotel Room No 2 Servant Ram Singh took his and Karkare's clothes for washing to a laundry. The accused gave Rs 15/– for sewing charges of pant and for washing charges

Left the hotel on 19.1.48 in the evening. Karkare met Sham Deshpande ~~and~~ in the Hindu Mahasabha Bhawan and got Room No 3 where they placed their luggage.

headquarters, they would have learned that the *dhobi* at the Marina had produced the laundry left behind by the inmates of room No. 40, and that it contained three pieces of clothing which were clearly marked with the initials 'NVG'. This detail, coupled with Madanlal's mention of an Editor of the *Hindu Rashtra,* should have led them a step further in the process of discovering the identity of Nathuram. But the information was not divulged by the Delhi Police to their men in Bombay; and Nagarvala, the man who had the means to make use of it, knew nothing about it. According to the Kapur Commission, 'There is no indication of any importance having been attached to the discovery of "NVG" or of any use having been made of it.'

In the event, the police did not cotton on to it till after the murder, when Nathuram gave himself up and himself gave his name to the police. Justice Kapur observes, 'As a matter of fact the police had not been able to establish the identity of the conspirators till after the murder.'

On the afternoon of 23 January, the two Delhi policemen were admitted into Nagarvala's presence again. It will be recalled that their orders had been to proceed to Poona to see Raosaheb Gurtu, the Assistant Deputy Inspector-General of the CID, who could have almost instantly cleared up the mystery about the editor's identity, and the two men were all ready to go on to Poona. But Nagarvala 'ordered them in plain words that they should return to Delhi'.

They took a train the same evening, and were back in the capital twenty-four hours later. From the station they took a taxi directly to their headquarters and reported how they had fared in Bombay: they had not been able to secure the arrest of Karkare, nor had they discovered the editor's identity. They also told their departmental superiors how cavalierly they had been treated in Bombay. 'We were actually put under some sort of "Nazar quaid" [house arrest],' they complained.

But when, the next morning, the report of his two emissaries reached the desk of the Inspector-General and Director of the Intelligence Bureau, Mr T.G. Sanjevi, he was in no mood to make an issue of their grievances against the Bombay Police. The conspirators were believed to belong to the

Bombay province, and in order to trace them it was vitally important for him to obtain the fullest cooperation from the Bombay Police. He decided to try a fresh tack.

Mr U.G. Rana, the Deputy Inspector-General of Bombay's CID, happened to be in Delhi for some routine work. Sanjevi sent for Rana, gave him a copy of Madanlal's full statement together with an English translation of it, and told him to take it personally to the Bombay Police and to get them working on trying to find and arrest the people mentioned in it.

Rana was given his order on the twenty-fifth, in good time for him to catch the afternoon plane to Bombay, which would have got him there at 9 p.m. There was no question of his not being able to find a seat on it, because every aeroplane in India has a minimum of four seats set apart of government personnel, and allotted to other passengers at the last minute only if they are not claimed by government officers travelling on duty.

But Rana did not take the plane. He caught a train – and not a train to Bombay, either, but to Allahabad. In fact, he went in the same general direction Nathuram and Apte had gone when they ran away from Delhi. Only Rana went farther away than they.

Mr Rana later said that he was forbidden by his doctor to fly in aeroplanes and that he could find no accommodation in any of the several Bombay trains, and those who were in a position to call for this explanation seem not to have been surprised by it. At least, no one censured Rana for what Justice Kapur describes as his snail's pace.

But there was another explanation. Rana was close to retirement and had come to Delhi on official business. As a good Hindu, there would have been nothing unusual in his wanting to take advantage of his nearness to Allahabad to visit the place and indulge in a ritualistic bath at Triveni, the holy waters where the Ganges, the Jumna and the Saraswati rivers meet. All that Rana needed was a couple of hours in Allahabad, which could be squeezed in between the Delhi-Calcutta Mail getting into Allahabad station and the next Calcutta-Bombay train. It had been done before; it will be done again. A dip in the waters of Triveni confers great spiritual virtue.

So Rana went to Allahabad, at least three hundred miles out of his way, and reached Bombay on the afternoon of the twenty-seventh, two days later than if he had taken a plane, and a whole day later than if he had caught a direct train.

From the railway station he went directly to see Nagarvala. In fact, he stayed with Nagarvala as his guest, and gave him the full report on Madanlal's interrogation, which contained the reference to the editor of the *Hindu Rashtra* being one of the conspirators.

But Nagarvala was still riding hard on his runaway theory that the plot was not for murdering Gandhi but for kidnapping him, and even managed to persuade his guest that the Delhi Police were on the wrong track. He and Rana thereupon telephoned Sanjevi. Sanjevi may well have been flabbergasted by the audacity of the supposed plot and the numbers thought to be involved in it, but, according to Justice Kapur, 'is not shown to have found fault with the kidnapping theory, or rejected it, nor did he violently react against it'.

When Sanjevi did do was to ask Nagarvala to send him a report the following day. 'Nagarvala sent the report three days later, and Sanjevi received it on the day after Gandhi was murdered. In any case, this report 'contained no information about the assassins.'

NINE

Don't you see I am mounted
on my funeral pyre?

— M.K. GANDHI

As compared with the cops, the villains were, after the fiasco of their first attempt, showing themselves to be vastly more businesslike. Gopal Godse, who was still on leave, visited Apte's house every morning and evening to find out if Apte's wife had heard anything from her husband; and when, on the morning of the twenty-fourth, he himself received a message from Nathuram that he and Apte had come to Bombay, he promptly went and told Apte's wife about it. He also impressed upon her that, the moment she heard anything from her husband, she was to pass on the message to him.

Early in the afternoon of Sunday, 25 January, Champa Apte received a telegram. It was from a man called 'Vyas' in Bombay, and she could not make head or tail of it. She dutifully sent it on to Gopal.

To Gopal the telegram made a lot of sense. It told him that Karkare, too, had arrived in Bombay but had not been able to get in touch with Nathuram and Apte. It was up to him, Gopal, to bring the three together again.

Gopal rushed to the railway station and caught the first train to Bombay. He had to get there and back before the next morning, when he was due to report for duty at the Ammunition Depot, and thus had no time to go to Poona and retrieve his .38 revolver, which he had given to his friend Godbole for safe keeping. Badge's revolver was still with him, for even though he and Badge had met he had been so put off by the hatred with which Badge spoke of Nathuram and Apte that he had changed his mind about returning the revolver. Now he took it with him to Bombay for what it was worth.

On Sunday, Apte and Nathuram were in a position to move a step forward in the pursuit of their new plan. They went to the house of a wealthy sympathizer of the Hindu cause, a Mr Paranjpe, who was a partner in the Silver Bank Company, and asked him for a 'loan' for their paper. Paranjpe promised them Rs 10,000, but told them to collect the money from his office the next morning, Monday. Having thus made sure of plenty of spare cash, they went to the Air India office, and booked two tickets for the morning flight to Delhi two days later, on Tuesday. At the booking-counter, Apte gave his name as 'D. Narayan Rao', and Nathuram as 'N. Vinayaka Rao'; and, though they were actually staying at the Elphinstone Annex Hotel, they gave their address as the Sea Green Hotel.

Gopal got into Thana a little after six in the evening. The first thing he did was to ring the Northcote police hospital where he left a message for Miss Salvi to tell Apte that 'Vyas' had arrived. Then he went on to the Navpada area and to G.M. Joshi's house to see 'Vyas' (Karkare) himself.

It was not till three hours later that the two principals joined them. The plan did not take long to explain. Nathuram told them that he was going to find a reliable pistol or revolver, get as close to Gandhi as possible, shoot him, and then give himself up.

According to Karkare, a silence followed this statement. He and Gopal stared at Apte to see what he had to say. Apte said nothing. The leadership had already passed out of his hands. When Karkare asked him what he was going to do, Apte told him: I'm going to Delhi too. I am going to be there, with Nathuram.'

'Then I'm coming too,' Karkare announced. 'I, too, want to be there, even if it means certain death.'

And so it was decided, within a matter of minutes. Gopal took out the revolver and passed it to his brother. The action signified that he did not want to go with them. In fact, he soon called out to Joshi and asked when the next train for Poona was due. There was plenty of time. According to Joshi's son, Vasant, Gopal Godse was still in the house after he had gone to sleep, at about 10 p.m., but left some time during the night.

The striking force had been reduced from seven to three but, for the plan they had in mind, even that number was not really necessary. It was just that Apte and Karkare had decided to stand by Nathuram even if it meant sacrificing themselves.

How much Karkare's host Joshi heard of this talk never became clear. As will be seen, Karkare and Apte came to his house again and again even after Gandhi's murder and when Joshi must have known that they were hiding from the police. But, as in the case of Manorama Salvi, who was not called to give evidence because she would prove 'a hostile witness', the police must have decided that G.M. Joshi was far too friendly with Karkare and Apte to give evidence that was sure to send them to the gallows. He was never called upon.

Monday, 26 January 1948. The day began with a mist and a bracing mountain breeze that Bombay experiences perhaps only a dozen time during what it calls its winter season; the sort of day, in fact, on which nothing could go wrong. Apte and Nathuram decided to risk breaking cover to get hold of a dependable revolver. They knew that both the brothers of the Bhuleshwar temple possessed licensed revolvers, either one of which would have suited Nathuram's purpose admirably. Both brothers also possessed the resources to produce such a weapon from somewhere else. After all, the elder one, Dada Maharaj, had once promised to give Apte a good revolver in exchange for the pistol that Apte had given him in Poona.

They had an early breakfast and took a taxi to the Bhuleshwar temple. They saw Dada Maharaj first, who later testified:

Back in Bombay, after the January 20 debacle, Godse decided, 'he was going to find a reliable pistol or revolver, get as close to Gandhi as possible, shoot him, and give himself up'. Staying in Bombay's Elphinstone Annexe Hotel, Godse and Apte booked themselves Air India tickets for Delhi. Again this time the names were different – N. Vinayak Rao and D. Narain Rao.

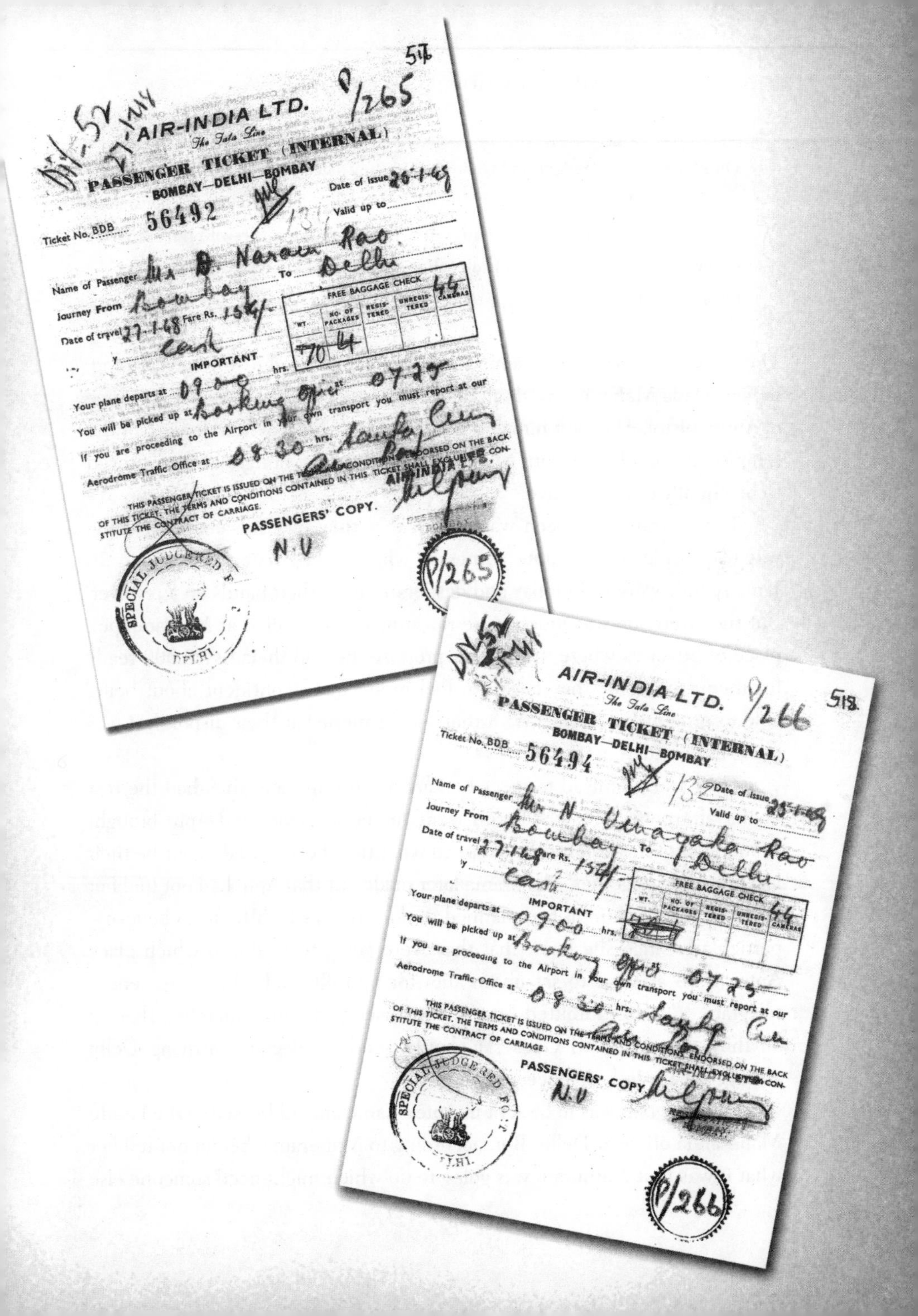

517

P/265

AIR-INDIA LTD.

The Tata Line

PASSENGER TICKET (INTERNAL)

BOMBAY—DELHI—BOMBAY

Date of issue 25-1-49

Ticket No. BDB 56492

Valid up to

Name of Passenger Mr D. Narain Rao

Journey From Bombay To Delhi

Date of travel 27-1-48 Fare Rs. 154/-

y cash

FREE BAGGAGE CHECK				
WT.	NO. OF PACKAGES	REGISTERED	UNREGISTERED	CAMERAS
70	4			

IMPORTANT

Your plane departs at 0900 hrs.

You will be picked up at Booking Office at 07.25

If you are proceeding to the Airport in your own transport you must report at our Aerodrome Traffic Office at 08.30 hrs. Santa Cruz Air Port

THIS PASSENGER TICKET IS ISSUED ON THE TERMS AND CONDITIONS ENDORSED ON THE BACK OF THIS TICKET. THE TERMS AND CONDITIONS CONTAINED IN THIS TICKET SHALL EXCLUSIVELY CONSTITUTE THE CONTRACT OF CARRIAGE.

AIR-INDIA LTD.

PASSENGERS' COPY.

N.V

SPECIAL JUDGE RED FORT DELHI

P/265

518

AIR-INDIA LTD. P/266

The Tata Line

PASSENGER TICKET (INTERNAL)

BOMBAY—DELHI—BOMBAY

Ticket No. BDB 56494

132

Name of Passenger Mr N. Vinayaka Rao

Date of issue 25-1-49

Valid up to

Journey From Bombay To Delhi

Date of travel 27-1-48 Fare Rs. 154/-

y cash

FREE BAGGAGE CHECK				
WT.	NO. OF PACKAGES	REGISTERED	UNREGISTERED	CAMERAS

IMPORTANT

Your plane departs at 0900 hrs.

You will be picked up at Booking Office 07.25

If you are proceeding to the Airport in your own transport you must report at our Aerodrome Traffic Office at 08.30 hrs. Santa Cruz Air Port

THIS PASSENGER TICKET IS ISSUED ON THE TERMS AND CONDITIONS ENDORSED ON THE BACK OF THIS TICKET. THE TERMS AND CONDITIONS CONTAINED IN THIS TICKET SHALL EXCLUSIVELY CONSTITUTE THE CONTRACT OF CARRIAGE.

PASSENGERS' COPY

N.V

BOMBAY

SPECIAL JUDGE RED FORT DELHI

P/266

> On 26 January 1948, Apte and Godse came to my place and demanded from me the revolver which I had promised to them, or its equivalent in money. I considered myself morally bound either to return Apte's pistol, give him a revolver in exchange, or give him the price of his pistol... they appeared to be more anxious to get the revolver than the price of the pistol.

The money meant little to them just then, the promised revolver everything; in fact, Dada Maharaj gave them neither a serviceable revolver nor the price of Apte's pistol. They left him and walked across the cool marble floor of the temple yard to where Dixitji Maharaj lived. But the younger brother proved to be equally uncooperative.

The morning had been wasted. All that they had succeeded in doing was to provide two separate witnesses who would swear to it that on 26 January they were in Bombay and desperate to lay their hands on a revolver. But the afternoon was much more rewarding. They called at Mr Paranjpe's place of business where, true to his promise, he had their Rs 10,000 ready for them. Suddenly they began to feel much more confident about being able to procure a revolver. With that sort of money at their disposal, it was going to be much easier.

They had promised to meet Karkare at 10 p.m., and thus had the rest of the afternoon free. Nathuram went to see a movie, and Apte brought Manorama to the hotel room to spend what they both feared might be their last few hours together. Manorama later made out that Apte had not told her what he and Nathuram had planned to do. But this is difficult to believe – particularly since she knew that they were going to Delhi, to which place Apte, in an attempt to set up an alibi for himself, had told her to send a telegram. As she admitted later: 'Apte asked me to remember that, if anything happened to Godse, I should send a telegram "arriving Delhi arrange for Godse's defence".'

The telegram was to be sent in Apte's name and addressed to the Hindu Mahasabha office at Delhi. But, according to Manorama, he did not tell her what it was that Nathuram was going to do which might need someone else to arrange for his defence, or why it was so important for Apte to establish that he was in Bombay while Nathuram was doing it.

After an early dinner, Nathuram and Apte went by train to Thana. Karkare met them on the platform, and all three of them walked across the lines and squatted down under a lamp in a lonely part of the goods yard. Nathuram briefed Karkare about their future plans. He and Apte were flying to Delhi the next morning, from where they would go straight to Gwalior where Nathuram knew someone who, he felt sure, would be able to procure for him a reliable weapon. They hoped to be back in Delhi on the morning of the twenty-ninth, which was a Thursday. If Karkare left Bombay by train on the twenty-seventh, he would get into Delhi on the night of the twenty-eighth. On the twenty-ninth he was to wait for them near the stone fountain in the middle of the Queen's Gardens just outside the entrance to the Old Delhi railway station.

'I'll wait there all throughout Thursday,' Karkare promised.

Karkare had run out of money, so Apte gave him Rs 300 for expenses. After that they strolled back to the main platform and sat in the tea stall till the last local train to Bombay came in. Karkare saw the other two off and then walked back to Joshi's house.

The next morning, Nathuram and Apte flew to Delhi.

Three weeks after their journey to Delhi, their air hostess, Miss Lorna Woodbridge, stated on oath that she remembered the two passengers who had given their names as 'D. Narayan Rao' and 'N. Vinayaka Rao', that they had occupied one of the last rows of double seats, and even that Nathuram had sat near the window and Apte away from the window. She explained that she had special reason to remember one of the two – Apte – because he had asked her 'for coffee or sweets more often than what people normally did'. At an identity parade held in Bombay late in February 1948, Miss Woodbridge unhesitatingly picked out not only this passenger, but even the man who had sat next to him.

Lorna Woodbridge's gift of total recall may seem as unlikely as Manorama Salvi's lack of curiosity, but it had the effect of destroying Apte's carefully worked out plan to set up an alibi for himself. If Apte and Nathuram had not visited the two brothers of the Bhuleshwar temple and not been spotted by Miss Woodbridge, it might have been a little more difficult for the prosecution to prove that Apte had travelled to Delhi with Nathuram and was standing beside him when he shot Gandhi dead.

From the airport, Apte and Nathuram went straight to Old Delhi railway station, which they reached in good time to catch the Delhi-Bombay express. This train got into Gwalior just before midnight. At this hour, they were among the few passengers to go out of the first-and second-class exit. Outside in the yard, each behind a manure-fire smoking in the bright moonlight, a dozen or so tongas were waiting for fares, their drivers muffled up in layers of blankets against the cold. They approached the rank and asked if any of the drivers knew the house of Dr Parchure. Apparently they all did, and one of them – Gariba – agreed to take them there for one rupee.

Karkare, the third member of their reduced striking force, was at this hour sitting up in a packed third-class compartment of the Bombay-Delhi Frontier Mail. He had spent the morning in Joshi's house, writing some letters. Just before noon, he had taken his luggage and gone to the Central Station, at least three hours before his train was due to start. He had no role to play other than that of onlooker to the murder – a role for which he had himself volunteered. And, for the privilege of being able to see Gandhi being struck down, this mild-mannered, essentially kind-hearted and generous man was as good as sacrificing his life.

Dr Dattatray Sadashiv Parchure who, along with his wife and children and the wives and children of his several brothers, lived in an enormous family mansion on the Station Road in the Lashkar, or the Cantonment area of Gwalior, was the sort of character whom the late Ian Fleming might have been proud to have invented. He was forty-seven and he was, at best, only a moderately successful medical practitioner, but he was by far the most controversial political figure in Gwalior, with many powerful friends and some deadly enemies. A round face in which large black eyes stared dully from behind spectacles that were thick enough to be opaque, a full black flowing beard under a luxurious growth of hair that cascaded over powerful shoulders, he looked both saintly and sinister, more like a guru than most gurus manage to look, and yet someone endowed with the capacity for anger, venom, and fanaticism.

As a background to whatever Parchure stood for in Gwalior's politics, it is necessary to explain that, under the Raj, Gwalior was, like Hyderabad and Kashmir, a large princely state. It had not gone under Congress rule automatically upon the transfer of power. The Maharaja still remained its ruler, and all he had done was to sign what was called a 'standstill agreement' with Nehru's government. The Congress, desperately anxious to merge the princely states into India, was doing everything in its power to foster and support democratic movements in the princely domains – a process which many princes believed was merely a device for sabotaging their rule. And, since the Congress's idea of democratic rule was rule by the Congress Party, it was keen to set up a Congress ministry in the Gwalior State.

The claim of the Congress to represent public opinion in Gwalior was fiercely contested by the Hindu Mahasabha. Since no popular elections had been held, there was no means of assessing whose was the more realistic claim; but, judging by the subsequent course of politics in these parts, it seems that the Hindu Mahasabha had good grounds to feel that it represented the majority party in the state.

And the Gwalior Hindu Mahasabha had been built up from scratch almost entirely by Dr Parchure. He was its secretary as well as its principal organizer. He was also the 'dictator' of the militant wing of the Gwalior unit of the Mahasabha, which called itself the 'Hindu Rashtra Sena' (Indian National Army). The Sena was thus the Gwalior counterpart of Savarkar's Dal, in whose activities Nathuram and Apte had taken such prominent parts. The Sena claimed to have a strength of three thousand.

Parchure and Nathuram had met several times before in the course of their work for the Hindu Mahasabha; and, a year or so earlier, when Parchure had gone to Poona to deliver a series of political lectures, he had

STATEMENT OF WITNESS NO. 1.

I do hereby on solemn affirmation state that :—

My Name is Manorama — Father's name Daulatrao Salvi.

Religion christian — Caste Anglican Church of India, Burma and Ceylon.

Age about 20 — Occupation Student.

Residence Northcote Police Hospital District Bycalla.

[*Note* :—I have been asked to record the statement of this witness under Section 164 Criminal Procedure Code. For this purpose I have proceeded to record the statement of this witness in open Court after excluding the Police officers and constables.

OSCAR H. BROWN,

20-2-48.

1. I am making this statement voluntarily and without any suggestion or pressure from the Police or anybody else. I have been asked by the Chief Presidency Magistrate if I wish to make a full and free disclosure of the information which I have and I state that I wish to make a statement.

2. I am a native of Ahmednagar. At present I am studying in the Wilson College, Bombay. I am in the Senior B.A. Class. I was educated prior to this at the Ahmednagar American Mission Girls' School. I used to reside in the Hostel for girls at Ahmednagar. My father is a Medical Officer at the Northcote Police Hospital at Bycalla.

3. I know Narayan Dattatraya Apte. He used to teach Mathematics in the American Mission High School at Ahmednagar. I was in the 3rd standard when I first met him. I was then about 12 years old. He was a B. Sc., when I was in the fifth standard Apte went to Poona to get a B.T. diploma. He returned to our school when I was in the sixth standard. When I was in the seventh standard Apte obtained a Kings Commission and left our school.

4. I passed my Matriculation in 1944 from Sholapur centre as the examination was not then held at Ahmednagar. I then came to Bombay and joined Wilson College. I resided in the Pandita Ramabai Hostel at Alexandra Road Gamdevi. This Hostel is reserved for women students of Wilson College.

5. When Apte left our school at Ahmednagar he gave his address to some of the pupils including me and I wrote to him at Poona. In that letter I gave him my address in Bombay. In or about July 1944 I got a letter from Apte in which he said he was coming to Bombay and would visit me at the Pandita Ramabai Hostel. A few days later he called at the Hostel to see me and 2 other former students of his *viz.*, Shakuntala Viswas Shri Sunder and Saraswati K. Ujagore. He took all 3 of us at about 2 p.m. to see a cinema show at the Rosey Cinema. The film was "Kadam Bari". The show began at 3-30 p.m.

40

6. After the show Apte took all 3 of us for a walk to chowpatty sea shore. At 7-30 p.m. Apte left us and we went home alone. A week later Apte came to Bombay again from Poona straight to the Hostel to see me. He invited me to accompany him to a late show at a cinema but I declined. I saw him off as far as Chowpatty. He invited me to lunch with him on the following day at 1 p.m. He came for me at about 11-30 a.m. and took me to Arya Nivas on Sandhurst Road. After lunch I accompanied him to V. T. and he left by the Deccan Queen for Poona. I returned to the Hostel by tram.

10

7. After this Apte came to see me 2 or 3 times a times(?) a month and and he used to take me out to lunch and to cinemas. I became very friendly with Apte as a result of this. In October 1944 I went to Sheogaon for my vacation, to my father who was serving there. I wrote two or three letters to Apte from Sheogaon. He replied to them under the name Nirmala implying that my correspondent was a girl and thus disarming any suspicion on the part of my father. I had asked Apte to adopt the petname Nirmala as our warden Dr. Miss Hewat had reported to my father that Apte was corresponding with me. My father had requested me not to meet Apte.

8. I returned to Bombay in November 1944 after the vacation. Apte came to see me in the Hostel and I went to him at Arya Niwas or Arya Pathik Ashram. After my previous examination I visited Apte at Arya Pathik Ashram and I spent the night with him at Gujarat Niwas. The next morning I returned to the Hostel and Apte left for Poona. Before he left for Poona he wanted me to meet Barrister Savarkar. Apte said he was a disciple of Savarkar and held him in high esteem. I declined to meet Savarkar. Later I went to Sheogaon to my father for my vacation. While there Apte and I corresponded with each other. He signed all his letters as Nirmala.

20

9. On or about 17th June, 1945, I returned to Bombay. Apte met me at Poona Railway Station. He made an appointment with me to meet him at Tilak's statue at Chowpatty. He took me to Arya Niwas where I spent the night with him. Apte again referred to Savarkar and his remarkable exploits.

30

He said Savarkar was the only man who could shape or mould the destiny of India. I was not interested in Savarkar or his doings. I have stayed with Apte in all about 10 or 12 times at various hotels in Bombay. Once in 1945 I received a letter from Apte from the Mahasabha Bhawan, Delhi. Apte had gone to Delhi for some Sabha work. He told me he wished to see the paper controller in connection with the paper " Agrani ". He always gave me a copy of it to read whenever we met.

40 10. Thereafter I stayed with Apte at the Poona Hotel for 2 days on my way to Sheogaon. Savarkar was staying at the same Hotel. Godse once came to the hotel to speak to Apte. I saw Godse for the first time. Apte pointed him out to me as Godse. Apte and Godse were very friendly. I spent part of my October Vacation in 1945 with my uncle Revd Mr. Wanjara at Ahmednagar. From there I went to Sheogaon and returned to Bombay for the new college term. I once wrote to Apte a letter against Savarkar and Apte got intensely annoyed and wrote me a scolding letter. Later he told me he was going to Bilaspur for a meeting of the Mahasabha.

Read over by me and accepted as correct.

(Sd.) MISS M. D. SALVI,

20-2-48.

Before me.

(Sd.) OSCAR H. BROWN,
Chief Presidency Magistrate,
Bombay.

Whenever Apte and I stayed at any hotel he gave for the hotel register our names as Mr. and Mrs. Apte. During the October vacation 1946 I saw Apte in Poona and he told me he would come to Bombay and then fly to Delhi. He gave me his address as Mahasabha Bhawan, New Delhi. He later told me that he had met Gandhiji at Delhi. He said that he had put some questions to Gandhiji and was pleased to find that Gandhiji could not answer him. Apte came to Bombay again and appeared to be restless. He appeared to be making some plans. His thought was to destroy the Muslim localities in Bombay by fire. I tried to dissuade him from such plans but he had made up his mind. He was arrested and afterwards discharged. 10

About the middle of January 1948 Apte went again to Delhi. Before he left I was quite upset and cried. He tried to console me. He told me that if any thing happened to him not to worry but to try to be happy. 20

On or about 20-1-48 Apte asked me to remember that if any thing happened to Godse I should send a telegram " Arriving Delhi arrange for

Godse's defence." I did so. Later I was shocked to find that Godse had shot Mahatma Ganhdi. I sent the telegram as desired. On or about 3rd February 1948 Apte mentioned to me that he had an appointment with one Karkare.

Read over and found correct.

(Sd.) M. D. SALVI, 30

21-2-48.

Recorded by me.

(Sd.) OSCAR H. BROWN,

21-2-48.

Chief Presidency Magistrate,

Bombay.

Note :—When this statement was recorded in Court the Police were excluded and the deponent made her statement freely and voluntarily as recorded by me.

(Sd.) OSCAR H. BROWN,

21-2-48. 40

Chief Presidency Magistrate,

Bombay.

Copy of Manorama Salvi's statement in court wherein she acknowledged her relationship with Narayan Apte and stated that he used to write to her regularly and sign off as her friend Nirmala.

held talks with Nathuram about the desirability of merging the Sena and the Dal together. These talks had failed, but while they had lasted they had brought out the fact that both men felt equally intensely about many aspects of their mission in life. It was this man whom Nathuram had decided to visit to ask for a weapon with which to kill Gandhi.

At this particular time, Parchure had a very special reason for feeling enraged against the Congress Party and, by projection, against its superstar, Mahatma Gandhi. Parchure and his colleagues of the Mahasabha had tried to convince the Maharaja of Gwalior, Jayajirao Scindia, that theirs was the majority party in the state and thus, when the time came for the Maharaja to hand over the administration to the people's representatives, it should be handed over to the Mahasabha. It seems that the Maharaja was himself convinced of the validity of this claim, but it soon became clear to him that the Government in Delhi would never have tolerated his handing over power to a non-Congress ministry. The result was that, on 24 January, and thus only four days before Nathuram and Apte were dropped at Dr Parchure's doorstep by the tonga-driver Gariba, a Congress ministry had been formed in what had been the princely State of Gwalior.

Parchure was furious.

In his confession given before Mr R.B. Atal, the First Class Magistrate of Gwalior, three weeks later, which he later repudiated as having been extracted under duress, Parchure stated: 'I had just gone to bed. My eldest son, Nilkant, came to my room and told me that two guests have come. I told my son to open the door... and came down immediately... and found Nathuram Godse and Narayan Apte.'

Parchure offered them tea, which Apte gratefully accepted but Nathuram, a confirmed coffee-drinker, declined. Upon Parchure expressing surprise that they should have turned up at his house 'without any previous intimation' Nathuram explained that they had decided to 'do a terrible feat', which was to kill Gandhi. He then produced a revolver which he told Parchure did not work properly, and asked him to try to get them 'a better revolver from someone in Gwalior'. Parchure promised to see what he could do in the morning, and went back to sleep, taking it for granted that his two midnight visitors would become his house guests.

The next morning Parchure sent off his son Nilkant and his 'bodyguard' Roopa to fetch a man called G.S. Dandvate and after telling his guests that they could trust him completely, went off to his dispensary in the Patankar Bazaar. At midday, when he returned, he found that Dandvate had arrived and he and his two guests were examining a 'country-made' revolver that he had brought. This weapon, after firing a shot with it in the enclosed garden on one side of Parchure's house, Nathuram and Apte rejected.

They had hoped to return to Delhi by the Punjab Mail which passed Gwalior in the afternoon but, upon Parchure protesting that it would not be possible for him to 'arrange' for a revolver in such a hurry, agreed to stay till evening. They joined their host for lunch and afterwards 'had a talk on the current political developments'. Parchure goes on:

> In the evening Dandvate came to my house with a pistol with about 10-12 rounds... Godse and Apte examined its automatic arrangement and approved of this pistol. Dandvate said the price of the pistol was Rs 500. Apte paid him Rs 300 and promised to pay the rest later on.

The pistol, an automatic 9 mm Beretta in excellent working order, would have made the mouth of any would-be assassin water; in fact, for the manner in which Nathuram had planned to kill Gandhi, it would have been difficult to find a more perfect weapon.

The Beretta had travelled halfway across the world to serve its fateful destiny. Manufactured in Italy in 1934, it had been taken to Abyssinia by one of Mussolini's officers. From him it was 'liberated' by an officer of the 4th Gwalior Infantry, which regiment had been sent to Abyssinia as part of the force which accepted the surrender of the Italians. But since the Battalion's return to India the pistol had changed hands several times. In any case, in Gwalior itself there was nothing wrong with anyone possessing a pistol, because even though the Gwalior State had an Arms Registration Act,

SECRET.

D/3

From

Inspector-General of Police,
Delhi Province, Delhi.

To

The Director Scientific Laboratory,
East Punjab, C.I.D. at Phillaur.

97
7.5.48

Subject:- F.I.R. No. 68, U/Ss 302/120-B, I.P.C., dated 30.1.48, P.S. Tughlaq Road, New Delhi.

No. 228-S.P.S. Dated Delhi, the 6th of May, 1948.

Sir,

I am sending herewith the automatic pistol No.606824 which was seized from the accused Nathu Ram V. - Godse on 30th January, 1948 in connection with the assassination of Mahatma Gandhi Ji, along with a spent bullet ~~xx~~ enclosed in sealed cover bearing five seals of Dy. Com Police, Special Branch II C.I.D. Bombay, recovered at Gwalior from the courtyard of one of the accused for expert opinion as to whether this bullet could have been fired and had been fired from this very automatic pistol. I am also sending automatic pistol No. 719791, P. Berretta, CAL 9 Cortz-M.C. 1934-Brevettato Gurdone-VT 1938 XVI along with five cartridges for favour of examination on the point as to whether the spent bullet mentioned above could be and had been fired from this automatic pistol. Both the pistols, the cartridges and the spent bullet are being sent per hand of Inspector Malik Bal Kishan of the Delhi C.I.D.

Reply per bearer is requested.

Replied 16/5
DAG

I HAVE ETC., ETC.

[signature]
For Inspector-General of Police,
Delhi Province, Delhi.
6/5/48.

The past experience of 20 January had taught them to be careful with the weapon. After careful deliberation they zeroed in on an automatic pistol — 9 mm Beretta. Manufactured in Italy in 1934, the Beretta had travelled from Abyssinia to Gwalior, from where it was procured for the crime with the help of Dr Sadashiv Parchure. **Facing page:** Copy of the Inspector-General of Delhi Police's letter to the Director Scientific Laboratory, where the automatic pistol was sent with the spent bullet for examination.

it had never been seriously enforced, and the mere possession of a firearm was not, as it was in British India, a serious criminal offence. Dandvate, who sold the pistol to Nathuram, said in his statement that he had bought it from a man called Jagdish Prasad Goel, and during the course of the trial this Goel admitted that he had sold it to Dandvate. But Goel did not explain how he himself had come by it. Of course, once it became known that the Beretta had been used to kill Gandhi, no one wanted to own up that it had, at one time or another, belonged to him; and it is possible that Goel, by refusing to mention the name of the person who had sold it to him, was shielding him from trouble. In any case, since Nathuram had admitted his guilt, the question of establishing the chain of ownership of the pistol before Dandvate sold it to him was of little importance.

To continue with Dr Parchure's subsequently repudiated confession:

> At 10.30p.m. on 28 January, Dandvate got a tonga and Nathuram Godse and Apte left my house for the railway station ... I went to my bedroom and slept. Dandvate also went to his house. The next day, i.e. 29 January 1948, I mentioned to my eldest brother Krishnarao Parchure that two gentlemen had come to me with a plan to kill Gandhi at Delhi and that I had arranged a pistol for them.[7]

By 11 p.m. the 'two gentlemen' were back in the yard of the railway station where the tongas waited behind the manure-fires throwing up slender columns of smoke in the light of the full moon. The Bombay-Amritsar Express was due in another thirty minutes. But the train was late by nearly three hours, and they did not leave Gwalior till well past two in the morning – the morning of the twenty-ninth.

TEN

Every condition laid down by Gandhi for giving up his fast is ... against the Hindus.

— NATHURAM GODSE

Ever since the advent of Independence, the nation's capital had been put under one of the most pernicious enactments of the Indian Penal Code – section 144, which, among other things, empowers the authorities to disallow such public meetings as might, in their opinion, disrupt peace. This, in the charged atmosphere of the times, virtually meant that all public meetings had been banned. Nevertheless, during the hectic week of Gandhi's fast, section 144 had not been enforced by the Delhi Police with their customary strictness because so many groups of citizens had come forward to demonstrate their zeal for communal harmony by making public pronouncements. To ban their meetings would have made the police look as though they were in league with the anti-Gandhi/anti-Muslim faction of the population.

Since public meetings of one kind had been allowed to take place, the Delhi unit of the Hindu Mahasabha thought of taking advantage of the laxness on the part of the authorities to sneak in a meeting of their own, and make known to the people of Delhi that their organization had never subscribed to the seven-point Peace Pledge that had been devised to persuade Gandhi to give up his fast.

At four o'clock on the afternoon of 27 January, they gathered in strength in, of all places, the great open space in the middle of the capital's shopping-centre, Connaught Place. And, even before the few policemen on duty realized that this was not just another meeting called by some civic group to preach communal harmony, speaker after speaker had got up and denounced Gandhi for 'coercing' the Government into paying Rs 55 crores to a country that was at war with India, and the government for letting Gandhi dictate terms to it. One speaker likened Gandhi to Hitler and predicted that he would meet Hitler's fate. The meeting passed a resolution rejecting the Peace Pledge and denouncing the government for the payment of the cash balances to Pakistan. It ended with rousing cries of 'Long live Hindu Unity! Turn out the Muslims! Long live Madanlal!'

Long live Madanlal! It was heresy. Even the refugees from the Punjab must have flinched when they found themselves called upon to join in that cry.

The government, of course, was horrified. How could such a meeting have taken place in the teeth of section 144? Congressmen thundered, officials squirmed and looked for scapegoats ; explanations were called for, reprimands doled out. It was sheepishly admitted that, on the part of the administration, there had been a 'deplorable slip-up'.

That the meeting was allowed to take place at all may have been the result of an administrative slip-up, but the Delhi Police were perfectly aware that the meeting reflected the mood and sentiments of a large section of the city's population, and who can say how many in their own ranks were not in sympathy. The truth was that the effect of the Peace Pledge was wearing off. The people of Delhi had heeded the Mahatma's counsel and stopped killing the Muslims or driving them out of their houses. In all good faith they had waited for a similar halt in the atrocities across the border. There was no such halt.

Gandhi's fast, which Mountbatten had hoped would serve as 'the great gesture for Pakistan to act in the same way', had affected Pakistan not at all. If anything, there had been a renewed frenzy of communal massacres in Pakistan, and every day the papers carried properly watered-down reports of whatever had happened in the past day or two in Bhawalpur, Gujarath, Okha and a dozen other places. After the first horrifying impact, one could only think of these incidents in generalities, as a number killed, wounded, abducted.

What came to be called 'the Parachinar Tragedy' is put down by Justice Kapur is his report in twenty-three words: 'On the night of 22 January Parachinar camp was attacked by tribesmen. 130 non-Muslims were killed, 30 wounded and 50 abducted.'

But in describing the fate of those who were 'abducted' Justice Kapur cannot confine himself to cold judicial prose.

The kidnapping of young women and the treatment to which they were subjected was a sordid chapter in the history of human relations. They were taken, molested, raped, passed on from man to man, bartered, sold like cattle, and those who were subsequently rescued gave an account which would be, to put it mildly, hair-raising.

What a Supreme Court Judge, a man trained to look upon the passions of mankind with god-like detachment, found to be 'hair-raising' was enough to make many Hindus and Sikhs blind with rage. To them a week of life under the lash of the Peace Pledge had been like a penance. Their brethren were being driven out of Pakistan; they themselves had no houses to live in; the Muslims of Delhi had their houses. The answer was clear: 'Turn out the Muslims!'

To Gandhi, the Parachinar tragedy was a challenge, 'a test of his faith'. It did not deflect him from his immediate objective, which was to make the capital of India safe for its Muslims. On 25 January, he told his prayer audience how 'it gladdened his heart to be told by Hindu and Muslim friends that a reunion of hearts was in the course of being established.'

And then he went on to tell his audience what a wonderful thing it was that the annual Mehrauli *urs* was going to be held from the next day.

Mehrauli is a village where the cowherds who supplied milk to the imperial city had lived from times immemorial. It is close to the

Palam airfield, and passengers looking down from planes see it as a vast anthill cut away from the top, its buildings no higher than its heaps of manure.

Mehrauli came into its own but once a year, when it held a fair to honour its holy man, Qutb-ud-din Mazar, who had lived and died there. During the wave of the communal riots in and ground Delhi that had caused Gandhi to go on a fast, Mehrauli, too, had been sacked by crowds of Hindus and Sikhs. They had driven out its Muslim population and had smashed the screens and lights of the divine's tomb. When the wave of violence had subsided, many of the Muslim families who had fled from Mehrauli had been prevailed upon to go back and live in their houses. But those that had gone back still lived in terror, and they had given up all thought of holding the *urs,* or fair, which that year was due to begin from 26 January.

Gandhi had come forward as their champion. One of the conditions that he had laid down upon the Hindus and Sikhs of Delhi for giving up his fast was that they must make it possible for the Muslims of Mehrauli to hold their annual fair.

The fair thus constituted a major point in the seven-point Pledge. Its signatories had assured Gandhi that 'the annual fair of Khwaja Qutb-ud-din Mazar will be held this year, as in previous years.'

For Gandhi, the fair was altogether symbolic; that it could be held at all represented to him the change of heart that he had been endeavouring to bring about. And it was entirely fitting that when, on 27 January, he visited the fair the Mullas led him right inside the shrine as though he was one of themselves. He told them how deeply he was moved to see the 'wanton damage to the marble screens enclosing the inner shrines'.

Gandhi has been called a saint, a villain, a politician, a statesman, a fool, a knave, a charlatan, an astute tradesman, a naked fakir and many other things, but the few words he now said at the urging of the Mullas of the Mehrauli shrine are enough to show that, whatever else he might have been, he was, above all, a truly civilized man.

> I have never known what it is to be communal. To unite all sections and all communities that people this vast land of ours has been my dream ever since my childhood, and till that dream is realized my spirit can know no rest.

The Amritsar Express got into Old Delhi station a little before noon. Nathuram walked up to the ticket window, showed his second-class tickets and asked to book a retiring-room with two beds. The clerk on duty, Sundarilal, told them a room would be vacant in an hour. They whiled away the hour at the station itself and, soon after one o'clock, got into the room, No. 6. Nathuram gave his name as 'N. Venaik Rao'.

Some of the bigger railway stations were provided with these retiring-rooms for the use of first- or second-class passengers who, instead of going to some hotel in town, could stay at the station itself in reasonable comfort. The rooms were large and high-ceilinged and provided with their own bathrooms. They could be occupied only for twenty-four hours, and the charge for a double room was Rs 5. Old Delhi station had seven such retiring-rooms,

Nathuram and Apte, who had had a pretty strenuous and tense time for the past three days, bathed and changed their clothes and then, calling the shoeshine boy who was attached to the retiring-rooms, arranged to have their soiled clothes washed. Then they went to one of the station restaurants, treated themselves to a good lunch, went back to their room and settled down to a long siesta.

All this while, the third man, Karkare, had been waiting for them in the park across the road barely two hundred yards away.

He had got into Delhi the previous evening, and he, too, was camping in the station, but not in a retiring-room. He had spread his blanket on the platform itself and gone to sleep among the hundreds of refugees who had made the railway station their temporary home till someone came and drove them away. In the morning he had queued up for one of the public lavatories, washed himself at one of the public taps and eaten his breakfast in the tea shop. Then, asking one of the refugees with whom he had struck up a friendship to mind his bed-roll, he had gone across to the park to start his vigil.

It was a raw, cloudy morning, and Karkare shivered as he sat perched on the side of the fountain and smoked cigarettes. After a couple of hours, he had begun to walk slowly round the park, turning every few seconds to look in the direction of the entrance. He was by no means alone, because many of the refugees had overflowed from the station into the Queen's Garden and settled down under the great trees, converting the park into a grubby gypsy encampment.

On one of his rounds, Karkare passed a man lighting a kerosene stove and brewing tea. Then, from a gunny bag the man took out a few cups and saucers and set them out in the dust. When Karkare came round again, he saw that four or five men and women from among the inhabitants of the garden had gathered round and were drinking tea. Karkare stopped and asked the man if he was selling tea.

'Yes, Babuji. Just set up my tea shop,' the man said, waving a hand at the array of cups.

'Shop?' Karkare could not help asking.

'What more does one need to support oneself?' the man answered. 'No one to support, see! Both my sons were killed even as I looked on, the wife clubbed to death.'

Karkare had nothing to do. After the other customers had gone away, he squatted down and paid for another cup while the man talked; and, oddly enough, what he was saying made Karkare believe that what they were about to do was somehow going to be the answer to all that the Hindus and Sikhs had gone through.

It was just another refugee saga, with only slight variations, told without bitterness or anger but with a sense of resignation. Chased out of his home... rescued by soldiers ... the trek to India ... no food and water for a whole day and then a dry biscuit ... the time thousands of them fell like wolves on a man carrying a few loaves of bread ... Delhi at last and a release from purgatory. In Delhi he was able to find a place ... just a lean-to with barely enough room for a man to stretch out.

'I set up my tea shop there; and then I was driven out.' He had lost his composure. He uttered a foul word and betrayed the first sign of hatred, anger.

'Driven out?'

'*Ji-han* – by our own soldiers, with bayonets – the great man had gone on a fast because I had occupied a Muslim house. Hah! So they threw me out – bodily.'

Karkare wished him luck and got up. Then he said, 'You know, I too began with no more than what you have now. Yes, I too started a tea shop. I prospered.'

'Babuji, I have no wish to prosper – merely to live out my days.'

Karkare went back to his post near the fountain. The stone was now warmed by the sun. He sat down, smoking. Soon after five, the sun went down and a cold wind sprang up. The refugees had started cow-dung fires for cooking their evening rotis. Then through the smoke he saw them. He had been waiting for more than seven hours.

Nathuram and Apte came; from the way they walked he knew that they had got the revolver. '*Chalo*!' Nathuram said, 'Come! And all three walked towards the Old Delhi railway station.

Karkare followed the other two into the retiring-room and, as Apte shut and bolted the door, Nathuram rummaged in his little steel trunk. 'Look!' he said to Karkare.

Cradled in his hands was a shiny blue-black weapon such as he had never seen before. Karkare goggled. 'But it has no wheel,' he said

'It's an automatic. You just keep pressing the trigger and it'll go on firing.'

'And ammunition?'

In answer, Nathuram held up a package done up in a handkerchief.

Like a trophy won by a team, the Beretta was passed from hand to hand before Nathuram put it away again. 'We'll try it out in the morning,' he said.

After that they walked towards Chandni Chowk, aware of a heightened sense of perception, taking in the sights and sounds and smells as though they were tourists in a strange town; and, like tourists, they stopped in front of a cheap roadside photographer's stall, and Nathuram had his picture taken. The photographer promised three copies within an hour. They spent the time eating dinner in a nearby vegetarian restaurant, and then separated. Karkare and Apte went to see a film, Nathuram to collect his photographs.

All that Karkare later remembered of the film was that it was in Hindi, that it was based on a story of Rabindranath Tagore, and that it was very long because it was past midnight when it finished. The traffic on Queen's Road had all but ceased as they walked back towards the railway station. At the entrance, Apte suddenly stopped and told Karkare that he was not going up to the room. 'He might be sleeping and I'd never forgive myself if I were to disturb his sleep on his last night as a free man.'

Karkare saw Apte walk back towards Chandni Chowk; he never discovered where he spent the night. He himself slept among the refugees on the platform. In the morning, when he went up to the retiring-room, he found that Apte had already arrived. Nathuram, Karkare discovered, had slept well.

All three then walked across to the non-vegetarian restaurant on the first floor for breakfast. As they were about to order, the waiter gave Nathuram and Apte a sweeping *salaam* and a friendly grin and piped up in Marathi, 'Sahibs you've come a long way from home, haven't you?'

They stared at him in panic. Then Nathuram said: 'So have you. The last time I saw you, you were in the Poona station restaurant.'

'That's right, and I've served both of you many times there. Transferred here only a couple of weeks ago.'

The European-style railway restaurants were, in those days, given under contract to one company, Brandon and Co., and waiters were constantly being shunted about from one railway restaurant to another. But it was worrying to be recognized, on this of all days.

The waiter took their orders. Buttered toast, tea, coffee. After he had gone, Nathuram silently joined his wrists together as though they had been handcuffed, and shook his head at the coincidence. As soon as they had finished breakfast, they went back to their room and locked themselves in.

'Nathuram wrote some letters,' Karkare later recalled to the author. 'And we watched in silence. We felt already separated from him and ashamed of ourselves that we could not do more for him. All that we could do was to stay with him, till the end, to show him that he was not alone, that I and Apte were with him.'

Nathuram wrote three letters. Together with the telegram that Manorama Salvi had been told to send from Bombay, he hoped that these letters would provide Apte and Karkare with adequate alibis, and also explain away their joint effort of 20 January as 'a peaceful demonstration that had been spoilt by the rash act of a friend'.

The letters were dated that day, Friday, 30 January. Two of them were addressed to Apte at his home and office address respectively in Poona, and the third to Karkare in Ahmednagar. They were written in Marathi and the substance of all three letters was the same. It was that the recipient was bound to be shocked by whatever Nathuram had done; but he had been driven to do it because he had found that to register protests by holding demonstrations in Delhi was an altogether futile method. Then he had said:

> My mind is inflamed in the extreme because I see no solution to the political iniquities. I have therefore decided on my own to take a last and extreme step of which you are bound to hear in a day or two. I am convinced that the peaceful demonstrations such as the ones we staged at Panchgani or Delhi will serve no useful purpose in the present circumstances. I have therefore decided to do what I want to do, without depending on anyone else. The enclosed photograph should be carefully preserved.

Each letter contained a copy of Nathuram's photograph, taken the previous night.

After that they discussed the best way for Nathuram to get within pistol range of Gandhi. They had heard reports that the guard at Birla House had been doubled and that many plain-clothes men had been detailed to move about among the prayer-meeting audience. Thinking a step ahead of both the Delhi and Bombay police chiefs, they feared that some of these plain-clothes men might be from Poona and might know them by sight.

Apte then came out with a suggestion which deserves mention if only to show how juvenile his mind was – that Nathuram should pretend to be an old-fashioned photographer and enter the grounds with a camera and tripod and with a black cloth draped over his head.

And when Nathuram turned it down Apte came out with something equally preposterous. 'What about a *burqua*? Many women go to the prayer meeting wearing *burquas*.'

A *burqua* is like a walking tent with slits for the eyes, and is commonly worn by orthodox Muslim women all over the world.

'And they're permitted to sit right in the first circle,' Karkare added. It was quite true that the women who came to the prayer meetings sat closest to Gandhi, within eight or ten feet, which would bring Nathuram close enough to make sure of killing him.

All three thought it was an excellent idea, and Apte and Karkare dashed off to try to get hold of a *burqua*. They knew two or three shopkeepers in Chandni Chowk who might help. But the shopkeepers were Hindus and had no idea as to where to buy *burquas*, which only Muslim women wore, But, seeing how disappointed they looked, one of them offered to get a *burqua* from somewhere in half an hour's time. 'For what size of woman?' he asked.

'Oh, a very tall one,' Karkare told him. 'Not too fat.'

Within half an hour they were back at the man's shop, and right enough he had a *burqua* ready.

It cost them fifty rupees. They carried it in triumph to their room where Nathuram wriggled into it and, according to Karkare, looked no different from a rather strapping Muslim lady. Then Nathuram tried to walk and found himself stumbling at every step; nor could he move his arms freely. He peeled the thing off and flung it on the bed. 'No use,' he pronounced.

'If you only knew how much it cost,' Karkare complained. 'What a day to start worrying about expenses,' Nathuram remarked. With the question of disguise still unsettled, they took a taxi to the Birla temple and walked half a mile into the wooded country at the back, almost to the same spot where, ten days earlier, some of them had held their first target practice. Here, according to Karkare:

> We selected a tree roughly as broad as a man's trunk. On it we drew circles to indicate the head, the chest and stomach. Nathuram stood about 20 to 25 feet away

and began firing. He was able to get his bullets into the circles. After that he fired more shots from varying distances, from fifteen feet, then ten, and in the end five. He was fully satisfied with the performance of the Beretta. He put on the safety catch and slipped the automatic in his pocket.

It was while they were walking back from the woods behind the Birla temple that Nathuram told the others that he had given up the idea of wearing any kind of disguise. Instead, he would wear clothes that would resemble a uniform. In a wayside store they chose a grey militia-cloth shirt with deep pockets and shoulder flaps and a khaki forage cap such as some regiments wore and which could be tucked under a shoulder flap. Afterwards they went and had lunch in a Punjabi restaurant close to the railway station and went back to the room. Here Nathuram tried on the shirt. It fitted well.

By now it was nearing 1 p.m., which was the hour at which they had to leave their retiring-room. Nathuram and Apte went down to the ticket counter. The same clerk who had given them the room, Sundarilal, was on duty. Nathuram asked if he could have the room for another day. To ask an Indian railway clerk to book a retiring-room at a busy station for more than twenty-four hours is like asking a policeman if you could double park in a shopping-area – guaranteed to provoke a reaction. Sundarilal bristled with authority and not only told Nathuram that he could not have the room for another day, but also went upstairs and stood around to see that they cleared out at the proper time; and, as they were taking their belongings out, he loudly ordered the attendant to put a lock on the door.

It was typical of their methods that, after taking all the trouble to set up alibis for his colleagues, Nathuram had succeeded in making sure that Sundarilal and the attendant would both remember him and his two companions only too well.

They carried their luggage to the common waiting-room for second-class passengers – an enormous hall strewn with cane-bottomed benches and a few tables – that was occupied, at any given moment of the night or day, by at least twenty passengers with their families and luggage. Children bawled, waiters brought trays of food, and porters trotted in and out with more luggage. It was certainly no place to discuss anything secret.

They found an empty bench for Nathuram to rest on, and the two others crouched on the floor beside him ready to jump at his slightest bidding and talking in undertones. Did he feel like anything special to eat or drink? they kept asking him.

Yes, he did. He felt a craving for salted peanuts.

Karkare and Apte hopped up. 'We'll go down and get you some,' they told him. But none of the shops in the station itself or its vicinity had salted peanuts. Sheepishly they went back to the waiting room. Nathuram, who was reading a paperback copy *of Night in Glenzyle* by John Ferguson, grinned as they approached. 'I knew you wouldn't get any here,' he told them. 'I've known that from previous visits.'

For a few minutes they sat near him, feeling like relatives sitting near a man's deathbed. Apte got up and beckoned to Karkare. 'We'll be back in an hour,' he told Nathuram, who merely smiled but did not ask them where they were going.

Out in the corridor, Apte explained to Karkare that they might as well use the time to find out if the guard at Birla House contained any policemen who looked as though they might be from Poona.

They took a taxi and had themselves dropped at the corner of Akbar Road where it meets Albuquerque Road. From there they walked along Albuquerque Road to Aurangzeb Road and back again, and thus had a good look at the gate of Birla House. There were certainly more policemen at the gate, but all of them looked like north Indians. They turned back and at the cab rank near the Edward Road Officers' Mess got a taxi. As they were passing India Gate, Karkare, in an agitated voice, told the driver to stop.

'What's the matter?' Apte asked in alarm.

'Look!' He was pointing a finger at the food barrows around India Gate and, right enough, there was one selling salted peanuts.

The big clock on the tower of Delhi station was showing three o'clock when they returned. When Karkare presented the packet of peanuts to

Nathuram his eyes opened wide. 'Did you have to go to Poona for them?' he asked.

He shared out the peanuts and, as they munched, Apte told Nathuram in whispers that, though there were more policemen at the gate of Birla House, they hadn't seen anyone who looked as though he might be from their own parts.

They still had an hour to kill. Suddenly there was nothing more they had to say to one another. Every time Karkare tried to say something his voice would choke, and Apte kept giving him warning looks.

Somehow the time passed. Nathuram glanced at his watch and rose. 'Quarter-past four,' he said. 'I'd better get going. I have posted those letters.'

'Do you want us to be there?' Apte asked. 'Why not?' Nathuram said, 'After coming so far.' He tapped the pockets of his uniform shirt as though to make sure that the Beretta was there. Then he went out.

The other two sat on the bench on which he had lain. After ten minutes Apte said: '*Chalo*.' They went down and got a tonga. As the tonga started, Karkare could not stop himself from crying.

'Steady, Vishnupant, steady,' Apte kept telling him. 'You don't want to spoil everything for him now, do you.'

At Connaught Place they dismissed their tonga and got into another, and had themselves dropped while they were still a couple of hundred yards away from Birla House.

At this stage, the police had ample evidence to suspect the existence of a plot to kill Gandhi. Apart from Madanlal's initial threat of *'Phir Ayega'* (*'They will* come again!'), they now possessed his detailed statement, which was also supported by the revelations made by Dr Jain in Bombay. But if the Bombay Police, in whose jurisdiction literally all the suspects lived, had made little use of the information than to initiate a watch on the movements of a favourite bugbear of Kiplings' India, Savarkar, the Delhi Police, whose duty it was to protect Gandhi's person, had done little more than to double the strength of the guard at the gate of Birla House and to plant a few plain-clothes men among the Birla House servants.

But the Delhi Police at least had a valid excuse for their arthritic action. It was Gandhi's own resistance to any measures to protect his life.

Aside from the murder threat, the Delhi Police were worried about the rising truculence among the refugees. They could see that the effects of the shock treatment of Gandhi's fast were wearing off rapidly, and many refugees were openly shouting slogans in praise of Madanlal, whom they regarded as one of themselves, as a man who had registered their protest in such a daring manner. Supposing another refugee fanatic thought of emulating Madanlal?

One way of making sure that no person who came for the prayer meeting carried a lethal weapon was to subject everyone to a personal search. But when someone mentioned the idea to Gandhi he was horrified. 'Would you search people who go to a church or a temple or a mosque?' he demanded.

The fact was that of late Gandhi had tended to live more and more in a world of his own making, and which bore no relationship to the world in which people who had to run the government, or administer the laws of the country, lived – or, indeed, to any conceivable social order of the past or present. He spoke in all seriousness of an army which should be non-violent, of a majority party, which should voluntarily withdraw from the business of governing, of an economy which should reject all technological advances, of a society that should abide by his own standards of austerity as well as humanitarian ideals.

The lot of the policemen charged with guarding him was not easy. In his vicinity, you had to creep on tiptoe as though afraid to cause harm to wrongdoers. The idea of subjecting all comers to a personal search was quickly dropped. Anyone could come and go.

So on 30 January, when a man wearing a grey shirt and a forage cap tucked in his left shoulder flap walked in through the service gate, no one checked him. Nor did anyone accost the two men who came half an hour later, swathed in grey shawls against the cold and wearing flat woollen caps.

Even on the previous evening, 29 January, there had been a little unpleasantness at Birla House. A batch of refugees from Bannu had come to see Gandhi. They complained to him that, after all the agonies they had endured, they had now been evicted from the houses they had occupied.

They were embittered and angry and in no mood to be fobbed off by explanations of the duties and responsibilities of a secular government. But still less were they prepared to put up with Gandhi's philosophical flourishes.

'I want to reach peace through agony', Gandhi told them.

'We owe all our miseries to you,' one of the refugees shouted back. 'Why don't you just leave us to our own devices and go and retire in the Himalayas?'

'My Himalayas are here,' Gandhi had countered.

Before the man could come out with anything more offensive, he had been hustled out of Gandhi's presence by a couple of plain-clothes policemen.

30 January. If Gandhi himself had a feeling that it was not just any other day, it was because he believed that he had accomplished what he had come to Delhi to do – to make life safe for its Muslim inhabitants. Now he was free to go on his way, to other places and other problems. And he was anxious to go; but he still had to grapple with two more questions before he left. He had been working on them for the past two days. Today he had the answers ready, or nearly ready.

One concerned the party, the other the government. He had been appalled by the 'ungainly skirmish for power' indulged in by Congress stalwarts, giving the impression that their struggle for Independence from Britain was motivated primarily by greed for power and personal gains. The other was the question of choosing between Nehru and Patel to head the Government of India.

He had decided the first question all on his own, exactly as if the Indian National Congress, with a membership running into millions, was under his personal command. The party, he declared, had 'outlived its use'. He had therefore changed its role and drafted for it a new constitution in which he had charged it to withdraw from active politics and serve the people as a kind of mammoth Moral Rearmament Army.

The other question was not so easily decided. He had to make up his mind between the two men whose friendship he most cherished.

The rivalry of Nehru and Patel had been a long-standing affair; but so long as both had remained in Gandhi's shadow there was no question of one taking precedence over the other. Now that they were both members of the government, if only because a country could not have two prime ministers, one had to outrank the other; and, indeed, the post of the deputy prime minister had been specially created as a sop to Patel's self-esteem. But this at best was a makeshift solution, and Patel certainly had not resigned himself to playing No. 2 to Nehru. What was more to the point, in the five months since their taking office Patel, in the departments he headed, had shown some spectacular achievements. As Patel had grown more confident of his ability to get things done, he had begun to show increasing resentment of Nehru's dominance, and in private conversation lost no opportunity to debunk Nehru's idealism and his reluctance to make difficult decisions. The relationship between them, which had never been really friendly, had steadily worsened. Each, in his all but daily interview with Gandhi, had some complaint to make about the other, and they wrote waspish little notes to one another on their office files.

If Nehru shied away from difficult decisions, Gandhi, who took pride in his ability not to let sentiment come in the way of the national good or at least of political expediency, could be brutally pragmatic. Many years ago he had declared Nehru to be his 'chosen son'. Now, according to the diary maintained by Patel's daughter Maniben, he was having second thoughts about that choice. Gandhi is quoted as saying to Patel: 'You both are unable to get on and it will ever be so. One of you should withdraw. Looking to your popularity [record?] at present, you should be raised.'

But, upon this question on which his own future revolved as on most others, Patel was far more clear-sighted than Gandhi or Nehru. Arguing that Jawaharlal was younger and far more popular than himself, and also that he was internationally known, Patel sent a letter to Gandhi asking that he 'should be relieved'.

Unable to agree with him, Gandhi had told Patel to come and talk to him again on the afternoon of the thirtieth.

With his mind almost totally absorbed by these two problems, Gandhi could not have given much thought to himself. The stir caused by the incident days ago had passed off. But, even at the time, Gandhi had not even bothered by the explosion because he had thought it was some kind of 'military practice'. And when Lady Mountbatten, who had come to see him soon afterwards, had congratulated him on his coolness he had explained to her that he had not even realized that something had been exploded in the grounds of Birla House. 'If somebody fired at me point blank and I faced his bullet with a smile, repeating the name of Rama in my heart, I should be deserving of congratulations.'

That moment and that test had arrived.

Gandhi had risen at his usual hour, at 3.30 in the morning, said his prayers, done three hours' work at his desk, and gone to sleep again before most other men were awake. He was up again at eight, had glanced over the day's papers, and had his body massage and bath. He had taken breakfast at 9.30, and as usual it consisted of goat's milk, cooked and raw vegetables, oranges and a decoction of ginger and sour limes. Another two hours of work had been followed by another nap. By two o'clock he was ready for the twenty or so daily visitors who were privileged to come into his room: refugee leaders, favoured reporters, hangers-on, a few devotees come for his *darshan,* and those who had friends among the members of his entourage, senior government officials and, of course, ministers. Birla House was still the place where the highest decisions of the government were made or could be set aside.

At four o'clock came Sardar Patel, accompanied by his daughter. Even though Patel stayed with Gandhi for the next hour, nothing definite seems to have been decided about his letter of resignation. Miss Patel's diary contains a maddeningly meaningless entry which purports to be the substance of what her father told her Gandhi had said to him.

> I had talks with Gandhiji even on the last day. At the time [he] told me that it is not possible to pull on with [sic] either of you. Both of you should remain. Tomorrow we shall clarify everything when we meet.

	Manu Ben Gandhi daughter of J. Kar ? Dalal Gandi, resident of Parmandal Gujrat Kathiawar, now residing in Birla House New Delhi.	~~Manu Ben Gandhi, daughter of J. Kar Dalal Gandhi~~ At about 5-10 I ~~left~~ started in the company of Mahatma ji from his residential room for the prayer ground. Shrimati Abha Ben Gandhi, Shri Brij Kishore Chandiwala, Mehta Nand Lal and Sardar Gurbachan Singh also accompanied us. Mahatmaji had placed his hands on my and Abha Ben's shoulders. Besides the above named persons Shrimati Sharla Mehta and other women of the Birla House
8 (concld)	Manu Ben Gandhi (concld)	also accompanied us. When Mahatma ji reached the prayer ground he greeted the people with folded hands. When he reached a short distance away from the steps a man who was caught on the spot and whose name was subsequently known as ~~f~~ Narayan Vinayak Godse, resident of Poona fired three pistol shots at him from a close distance. Mahatmaji got wounded. We supported him. The culprit was caught on the spot by the Police and the public. Mahatmaji expired shortly after.

The Last Walk: Gandhi walking towards the lawn for his last prayer meeting on 30 January 1948 with his grandniece Abha, his 'living walking stick'.
Facing page: Statement of Manubehn Gandhi given to the Delhi Police.

On 30 January 1948, Gandhi left his room at ten past five for the prayer meeting. As usual, Manu and Abha, his grandnieces, walked on either side. He walked briskly across the lawn and climbed the five shallow semi-circular steps that led to the raised portion of the lawn where people were waiting for him. Godse, Apte and Karkare pushed their way forward. With the pistol in his hand, Godse folded his hands to say 'Namaste'. And then, as he testified later, '... the shots went off, almost on their own.'

That tomorrow never came. But surely what Gandhi had said was that Patel and Nehru should both remain because it was not possible to 'pull on' *without* either of them?

A little before five, Gandhi's two teenaged grand-nieces, Manu and Abha, came into the room. Gandhi consulted the big watch he wore dangling from his waist by a cord and told Patel that it was time to go for his prayers. At ten past five he left the room. As usual Manu and Abha walked on each side so that he could lean on their shoulders. In her hands Manu carried Gandhi's spittoon and rosary. Gandhi walked briskly across the lawn and climbed the five shallow semi-circular steps that led to the raised portion of the lawn where the prayer-meeting audience awaited him. He folded his hands to return their greeting.

The crowd that day was fairly large for a prayer meeting; it must have numbered nearly five hundred. Karkare and Apte had pushed their way forward and stood on either side of Nathuram, but if he saw them he gave no sign of recognition. There was a stir in the crowd, and they saw Gandhi coming across the lawn and go up the steps.

Nathuram later told his brother Gopal that he was put off by the two girls walking in front of Gandhi. As Gandhi raised his hand to greet the crowd, Nathuram slid forward the safety catch on the Beretta while it was still in his pocket, and then stepped up to him.

> With the pistol in my right hand. I folded my hands and said "Namaste!" [Greetings!] With my left hand I pushed aside the girl who might have come in my line of fire. Then the shots went off, almost on their own. I never knew whether I had fired two rounds or three. Gandhi gave a quick gasp, a sound like "Aaaah!" and fell down, I kept holding my hand high, gripping the pistol tightly, and began to yell "Police... Police!" I wanted everyone to see that this was something premeditated, something deliberate – that I had not acted in a fit of passion. I wanted no one to say that I tried to run away or to get rid of the pistol, but wanted to be caught complete with the pistol. But everything was suddenly still, and for at least half a minute no one came forward.

He realized that they were frightened to come near him while he still held the smoking pistol in his hand and hoped that they would somehow realize that he was not going to resist arrest. He felt almost limp with relief when a man in an Air Force uniform sprang at him and caught his wrist. He released the pistol. Then other people who later testified how they had rushed and overpowered him came crowding all round, screaming abuse and hitting him. He saw the pistol being passed from hand to hand and shouted to a Police Officer, 'You'd better take possession of it and put on the safety catch before they shoot one another!'

By the time Manu Gandhi had picked up the spittoon and the rosary that had fallen from her hands when she had been pushed aside, and turned to look at her great-uncle, he was laying still and the blood was pouring from the bullet wounds in his bare chest.

No one noticed whether Gandhi's face bore a smile as he faced his assailant. But Gurbachan Singh, a Sikh businessman from Panipat who was a devotee of Gandhi and who was only a few steps behind him as he fell, deposed that Gandhi's last words were, 'Hai Rama!' Karkare, on the other hand, who stood within a few feet of Gandhi and saw him as the bullets struck him swore to the author that all Gandhi uttered was a cry of pain, a guttural rasp, 'Aaaah!'

It is, of course, possible that both are wrong, and that what they heard, or say they heard, was conditioned by the one man's veneration for Gandhi and the other man's contempt. Then again it is possible that both are right, and the invocation 'Hai Rama!' uttered with his last breath may have sounded to Karkare like a cry of pain.

While Nathuram was being led away by the police to one side of the building to save him from being lynched by a section of the crowd, many frightened people were making a scramble for the exits.

Following pages 252-273: Nathuram Godse was arrested from Birla House as he did not make any attempt to escape from the scene of crime. He was arrested and taken to the Tuqlak Road police station, where the DSP, Sardar Jaswant Singh filed the First Information Report. A copy of the translation of the report as prepared by S. Jaswant Singh.

Printed by Supdt., Govt. Printing, Punjab—1941.

Stereo, No. H. C. J. D./C.—56.

MURDER REFERENCE
CRIMINAL APPEAL No. —— OF 19 . (Page 1

Abstract Translation of the *Zimni* Reports.

Zimni Report No. 1 prepared by S. Jaswant Singh D. S. P., Tughlak Road Delhi, Police Station, on the 30th day of January 1948.

Para. No.	Name of deponent or Police Officer.	Abstract of statement made.
1	D. S. P. (30.1.1948 at 5.30 pm)	I was at Parliament Street Police station ready to go on official duty by a truck when I received the news of this occurrence. I at once reached Birla House by the truck. In one of the rooms of the Birla House I found Mahatma ji lying in an injured condition. Shri Nand Lal Mehta stated all the facts witnessed by him. His statement was recorded and was sent for preparation of an Initial Report. In the meantime Dasaunda Singh had also joined me.
2	Lala Brij Kishan son of Lala Banarsi Das, Hindu, resident of Narindar Place no. 1, Thana Parliament street New Delhi	Today I accompanied Mahatma ji from his residential room to the prayer ground in Birla House. We started from his residential room at about 5–10. Shrimati Abha Gandhi and Shrimati Manu Gandhi were also accompanying him. He walked by placing hands on their shoulders Sardar Gurbachan Singh contractor

Printed by Supdt., Govt. Printing, Pb.—1943.
Stereo No. H. C. J. D./C. 57.

Abstract Translation of *Zimni* Report No. 1 (*continued*). (Page 3

Para. No.	Name of deponent or Police Officer,	Abstract of statement made.
2	Lala Brij Kishan (contd)	Timarpur and Shri Nand Lal Mehta also accompanied us. Besides, other ladies from Birla House also accompanied. Passing through the garden we went up to the prayer ground by means of the steps. As usual the public stood on both sides and there was nearly three feet wide passage for Mahatma Ji to pass. According to his usual practice he greeted the public with folded hands. About 500 people had assembled in the prayer ground. When he had gone 6 or 7 paces from the steps one man from out of the crowd whose name was afterwards known to be Narayan Vinayak Godse stepped forward and fired three shots at Mahatma Ji from a distance of about 2 or 3 feet which hit him on the belly and chest. Mahatma Ji fell down uttering "Ram, Ram". We gave support

Stereo No. H. C. J. D./C. 57.

Printed by Supdt., Govt. Printing, Pb.—1943.

Abstract Translation of *Zimni* Report No. 1 (*continued*). (Page

Para. No.	Name of deponent or Police Officer.	Abstract of statement made.
2 (concld)	L. Brij Kishan (concld).	to Mahatma ji. The public and the Police men caught hold of the assailant with the pistol on the spot. We all carried Mahatmaji to his residential room in the Birla House where he expired after a few minutes. The culprit wore a khaki bush shirt. He had also received minor injuries at the time he was apprehended.
3.	D.S.P. (6 P.M)	At this time I reached the prayer platform. At a distance of 6 paces from the steps on the platform I found two empty pistol cartridges and two lead bullets and a khaki shoulder pad stained with blood. Rattan Singh constable no. 497, Tughlak Road, posted in the Birla House, was found on watch duty at the spot. I took all the said articles into possession. The signatures of Gurgan Lambardar, resident of Manikka and Rattan Singh,

Printed by Supdt., Govt. Printing, Pb.—1943.

Stereo No. H. C. J. D./C. 57.

Abstract Translation of *Zimni* Report No. 1 (*continued*). (Page

Para. No.	Name of deponent or Police Officer.	Abstract of statement made.
3 (concld)	D. S. P. (concld)	constable no. 491, were secured as witnesses. The empty cartridges and the bullets were made into a parcel which were sealed with the seal of Gugan Lambardar. The description of the cartridges is as under:— 1. One empty cartridge having G. F. L. 1936 inscribed thereon 2. One empty cartridge having G. F. L. 1941 inscribed thereon. The place of occurrence is at a distance 120 paces from the room where Mahtama ji was putting up. A plan of the spot will be got prepared. A few drops of blood are forthcoming on the place of the occurrence.
4	Rattan Singh, constable no. 491 posted in the Birla House	I too was present on the prayer platform on duty. When Mahatma ji along with the girls and other men of the staff reached the platform at about 5-15 P.M. the culprit who was caught at the

Sketch plan of the place where the body was found.

West

South

North

East

sd/- Jaswant Singh D.S.P. N.D.

Printed by Supdt., Govt. Printing, Pb.—1943.

Stereo No. H. C. J. D./C. 57.

Para. No.	Name of deponent or Police Officer.	Abstract of statement made.
4 (concld)	Rattan Singh (concld)	spot all of a sudden fired three pistol shots one after the other. He was caught along with the pistol on the spot by Amar Nath, A.S.I, Dharam Singh Head constable and others. On the spot there lay two empty cartridges, two lead bullets and a blood stained shoulder pad belonging to the culprit. I kept watch on those articles. They have been taken into possession by you. I have signed the Fard. The bullets and the empty cartridges have been made into a parcel.
	D. S. P.	On enquiry Chhotu Ram, son of Todar Mal cleaner, resident of Birla House, said that two empty cartridges, two lead bullets and a blood stained Khaki shoulder pad were found and taken possession of by the Police from a distance of six paces from the steps, from the prayerground

Printed by Supdt., Govt. Printing, Pb.—1943.

Stereo No. H. C. J. D./C. 57.

Para. No.	Name of deponent or Police Officer.	Abstract of statement made.
6	D. S. P (contd)	Gugan Lambardar, resident of Marika, supported the statement of Chhottu Ram.
7	D. S. P. (after 6 P. M)	I reached the residential room of Mahatma ji and found the dead body of Mahatma ji lying there. Lala Brij Kishore Chandiwala and Shri Nand Lal Mehta were present beside the dead body. The Inquest Report was prepared. Three injury marks caused by shots were found on his body—one on the chest, one on the abdomen below the chest and one on the abdomen below injury No. 2. All the three injuries were on the right side of the body. Excepting injury on the chest the bullets causing the other two injuries pierced through the body. Statement of injuries has been prepared. The two Chadars one of white Khaddar and the other of white wool on the dead

Printed by Supdt., Govt. Printing, Pb.—1943.

Stereo No. H. C. J. D./C. 57.

Abstract Translation of *Zimni* Report No. 1 (*continued*). (Page 17)

Para. No.	Name of deponent or Police Officer.	Abstract of statement made.
7 (concld)	D. S. P. (concld)	body of Mahatma ji contain bullet marks. This shows that the shots were fired from a close distance. A small Chadar of Khaddar round the loins of Mahatma ji is also blood stained. Mehta Nand Lal and Brij Kishore said that they were not prepared to give those clothe, at that time because they considered them to be sacred and would make arrangements to retain them permanently, that if they would be needed by the court he would themselves produce them. A guard under the charge of Dharam Singh Head constable no. 1676 has been posted to keep watch on the said room.
7	Dharam Singh, Head constable no. 1676.	Today I was on duty in the Birla House. Lala Amar Nath A.S.I and other officials were present there. About 500 men and women had assembled in

Printed by Supdt., Govt. Printing, Pb.—1943.

Stereo No. H. C. J. D./C. 57.

Abstract Translation of *Zimni* Report No. 1 (*continued*). (Page 15

Para. No.	Name of deponent or Police Officer.	Abstract of statement made.
7 (concld)	Dharam Singh (~~contd~~) (concld)	the platform. At about 5.15 P.M. Mahatmaji came to the prayer-ground along with two girls and other men and women of the staff. Out of the crowd the culprit whose name I have come to know as Nathu Ram alias Narayan ~~Rag~~ Vinyak Godse, resident of Poona, all of a sudden fired three pistol shots at ~~Mahl~~ Mahatmaji. The culprit was caught at the spot with the pistol, with the help of the public. He received minor injuries on the head at the hands of Raghunath Chaukidar and others, in consequence whereof his head began to bleed. Lala Amar Nath A.S.I & I took him to the Tughlack Road Police Station. A separate Fard regarding the pistol has been prepared.

Printed by Supdt., Govt. Printing, Pb.—1943.

Stereo No. H. C. J. D./C. 57.

Abstract Translation of *Zimni* Report No. 1 (*continued*). (Page 17)

Para. No.	Name of deponent or Police Officer.	Abstract of statement made.
	S. Gurbachan Singh contractor, son of Bishan Singh, caste Kaist, resident of Timarpur Delhi	To-day I accompanied Mahatma ji to the prayer ground from his residential room. Both the girls namely Aba Ben Gandhi and Manu Ben Gandhi, Lala Brij Kishore Chandiwala, Mehta Nand Lal ji and some other men and women were also with him. When Gandhi ji reached the prayer ground at a distance of 6 or 7 paces from the steps the culprit whose name was subseq known as Narayan Vinayek Godse resident of Poona fired three pistol shots at him from a distance of 2 or 3 feet. Mahatma ji got wounded and fell down uttering 'Ram, Ram'. We gave him support. The culprit was apprehended on the spot by the Police officials and the public. ~~They~~ He had a pistol in his hand. At the time of his apprehension he also received

Printed by Supdt., Govt. Printing, Pb.—1943.

Stereo No. H. G. J. D./C. 57.

Para. No.	Name of deponent or Police Officer.	Abstract of statement made.
8 (contd)	S. Gurcharan Singh (concld)	minor injuries. The occurrence took place at about 5-15 P.M. We carried Mahatma ji to his residential room and he expired shortly after.
	Shrimati Aba Ben wife of Kanu Gandhi, resident of Rashtriya Shala Rajkot, now resident of Birla House	I have been living with Mahatma ji in Birla House. To-day at about 5-10 Mahatma ji left his residential room for the prayer ground. Shrimati Manu Ben Gandhi, Shri Brij Kishore Chandiwala, Mehta Nand Lal and Sardar Gurbachan Singh accompanied him. Mahatma ji had placed his hands on my and Manu Ben's shoulders Besides the above named persons Shrimati Shusla Mehta and other women of the Birla House were also with him. When he reached near the prayer ground he greeted the people who had assembled there in large number, with folded hands. When he reached at a short distance from the steps,

Stereo No. H. C. J. D./C. 57.

Printed by Supdt., Govt. Printing, Pb.—1948.

Abstract Translation of *Zimni* Report No. 1 (*continued*). (Page 21

Para. No.	Name of deponent or Police Officer.	Abstract of statement made.
8 (contd)	Shrimati Aha Ben (concld)	one man who was caught at the spot and whose name was subsequently known as Narayan Vinayak Godse resident of Poona fired three pistol shots at him from the close distance. Mahatma ji got wounded. We supported him. The culprit was caught on the spot by the Police and the public. Mahatma expired shortly after in his residential room.
	Manu Ben Gandhi daughter of J. Kar Dalal? Gandi, resident of Parmandal Gujrat Kathiawar, now residing in Birla House New Delhi.	~~Manu Ben Gandhi, daughter of J. Kar Dalal? Gandhi~~ At about 5-10 I ~~left~~ started in the company of Mahatma ji from his residential room for the prayer ground. Shrimati Aha Ben Gandhi, Shri Brij Kishore Chandiwala, Mehta Nand Lal and Sardar Gurbachan Singh also accompanied us. Mahatmaji had placed his hands on my and Aha Ben's shoulders. Besides the above named persons Shrimati Sharla Mehta and other women of the Birla House

Printed by Supdt., Govt. Printing, Pb.—1943.

Stereo No. H. G. J. D./C. 57.

Abstract Translation of *Zimni* Report No. 1 (*continued*). (Page 23

Para. No.	Name of deponent or Police Officer.	Abstract of statement made.
8 (concld)	Manu Ben Gandhi (concld)	also accompanied us. When Mahatma ji reached the prayer ground he greeted the people with folded hands. When he reached a short distance away from the steps a man who was caught on the spot and whose name was subsequently known as Narayan Vinayak Godse, resident of Poona fired three pistol shots at him from a close distance. Mahatma ji got wounded. We supported him. The culprit was caught on the spot by the Police and the public. Mahatma ji expired shortly after.

Stereo No. H. C. J. D./C. 57.

Printed by Supdt., Govt. Printing, Pb.—1943.

Abstract Translation of *Zimni* Report No. 1 (*continued*). (Page 25

Para. No.	Name of deponent or Police Officer.	Abstract of statement made.
	~~S. Gurcharan Singh~~ (~~contd~~)	~~minor injuries. The occurrence took place at about 5-15 P.M. We carried Mahatama ji to his residential room and he expired shortly after.~~
9	D. S. P. (7-15 P.M)	At this time I reached the Parliament street. Narayan Vinayak culprit was present there in custody. He had two injuries on ~~his person~~ the head and a scratch mark on the right cheek. Statement of injuries was prepared and made over to the duty officer. Arrangements for sending the doctor were made so that the culprit might be got examined. On enquiry the culprit confessed having killed the Mahatma. He states that he has murdered him because he had caused harm to the Hindu community.
10	D. S. P. (8 P.M)	Amar Nath A.S.I states that he has made over the recovered

Printed by Supdt., Govt. Printing, Pb.—1948.

Stereo No. H. C. J. D./C. 57.

Abstract Translation of *Zimni* Report No. 1 (*continued*). (Page 27

Para. No.	Name of deponent or Police Officer.	Abstract of statement made.
10 (concld)	D.S.P. (concld).	pistol and four bullets to Kabul Singh Muharrir Head constable no. 402 for being kept in the Malkhana.
11	D.S.P. (8-30 P.M)	At this time Amolak Ram, Head constable was asked to make a search for Raghunath Naik now living in Birla House and Shrimati Sarla Mehta daughter of Ratilal Mehta, resident of Birla House, but both of them could not be found
12	D.S.P. (10 P.M)	At this time a sealed parcel containing two empty cartridges and two bullets was made over to Daswanda Singh Sub Inspector for being placed in the Malkhana of the Thana. The blood stained shoulder pad belonging to the culprit was also given to him.

Date of receipt at the Thana = 31—1—1948

Date of despatch from the Thana = 1—2—1948

Date of receipt at the Sadar = 1—2—1948.

Printed by Supdt., Govt. Printing, Punjab—1947
Stereo, No. H. C. J. D/C.—56.

MURDER REFERENCE / CRIMINAL APPEAL No. ——— OF 19 (Page 29)

Abstract Translation of the *Zimni* Reports.

Zimni Report No. 1(a) prepared by Mehta Amar Nath Assistant Sub Inspector Tughlak Road Delhi Police Station, on the 30th day of January 1948.

Para. No.	Name of deponent or Police Officer.	Abstract of statement made.
1.	Assistant Sub Inspector (30.1.1948 at 5.30 P.M.)	In continuation of Zimni Report No. 1 prepared by S. Jaswant Singh D.S.P., I beg to submit as under:— I was in charge of the guard in the Birla House. In the evening there were about 500 men & women on the platform where Mahatma Ji holds his prayers. I was present on duty along with Dharam Singh Head constable and constables. Mahatma Ji came to the prayer ground at about 5.15 P.M. along with two girls on whose shoulders he used to place his hands, and also the other members of his staff. The people assembled near the steps. Rows were formed on both the sides. When Mahatma Ji reached at a distance of 6 or 7 paces from the steps, the culprit who was caught on the spot fired three pistol shots at him. I with the help of the

Printed by Supdt., Govt. Printing, Pb.—1943.

Stereo No. H. C. J. D./C. 57.

Para. No.	Name of deponent or Police Officer.	Abstract of statement made.
(contd)	A.S.I. (contd)	aforesaid Head constables and Dev Raj Singh ~~sear~~ sergeant son of Narain Singh, caste Rajput, employed in R.I.A.F. No. 10, New Delhi, caught the culprit. The sergeant aforesaid snatched the pistol from him. Then the pistol was unloaded. Four live cartridges were recovered from it. The cartridges and the pistol were taken into possession by the Police after preparation of a Fard in respect thereof. The signatures of Dev Raj Singh sergeant, Behari Lal of Ludhiana, Balak Ram Bhatia of Delhi and Gugan Lambardar of Manirka were ~~sig~~ secured on the Fard as witnesses. The pistol was made into a parcel and sealed with the seal of Gugan Lambardar. The description of the pistol is as under:—

Printed by Supdt., Govt. Printing, Pb.—1943.

Stereo No. H. G. J. D./C. 57.

Abstract Translation of *Zimni* Report No. ~~1~~(a) (*continued*). (Page 33)

Para. No.	Name of deponent or Police Officer.	Abstract of statement made.
1 (Contd)	A. S. I. (Contd)	Automatic no. 606824, maker P. Beretta – Cal 9, Corto – M g 1934, Brevettato. Four cartridges bear the inscriptions ~~S.B.P.~~ S. B. P, G.F.L 1941, G. F. L. 1941 and C.A.B.42
2	Assistant Sub Inspector	The person of Nathu Ram culprit was searched. The following articles were recovered 1. White handkerchiefs – 4 2. A small phial containing some oil 3. Leather purses – 2 4. Leather bound note book 5. One Parker Fountain pen 6. Cash Rs 592/4/10 as per detail below: Five hundred rupee notes bearing nos: B/3 028016, B/4 184285 B/14 654765, A/43 480617 & A/13 099821 Eight ten rupee notes bearing nos: Ee/81 275674, Ee/20 365994, Ee/35 905223, F/71 282928, C/52 173040, Ee/28 093071, J/21 326244 & J/27 703583 One five rupee note bearing no. ~~J/65~~ N/43 224746, Five one rupee notes bearing

Printed by Supdt., Govt. Printing, Pb.—1943.

Stereo No. H. C. J. D./C. 57.

Para. No.	Name of deponent or Police Officer.	Abstract of statement made.
2 (concld)	A. S. I. (concld).	nos: J/65 954005A; H/25 347955A, 20/65 030103, H/20 589670A and H/28 619308A, Small coins of the value of Rs2/4/6 Copper coins — 3 Buckle — 1 Iron key — 1 Tooth ~~brush~~ pick and ear pick — 1 A Fard in respect thereof was prepared in the presence of Dev Raj Singh sergeant and Behari Lal Mishra and their signatures were secured thereon.
3	Dev Raj Singh sergeant R.I.A.F no. 10, son of Narain Singh, caste Rajput resident of New Delhi.	To-day I had come to the Birla House to attend Mahatma Ji's prayers. He reached the prayer grounds at about 5.15 P.M along with the members of his staff and the girls. Out of the audience one man whose name is known to be Narayan Vinayak alias Nathuram fired three pistol shots at him. I with the help of the A.S.I & the Head Constable Police caught the culprit on the spot along with

Printed by Supdt., Govt. Printing, Pb.—1948.
Stereo No. H. C. J. D./C. 57.

Abstract Translation of *Zimni* Report No. ~~1~~ (a) (continued). (Page 37

Para. No.	Name of deponent or Police Officer.	Abstract of statement made.
3 (concld)	Dev Raj Singh (concld).	pistol and snatched the pistol from his hand. The pistol was made over to the A.S.I. On its being ~~unloaded~~ opened four cartridges were recovered from inside it. They were taken into possession by the Police by means of a Fard. The A.S.I. made them into a parcel. Mahatma ji's men took him towards the Birla House in an injured condition.
4	A.S.I.	On enquiring Behari Lal, son of Buta Ram, caste Midha; resident of G.T. Road Ludhiana and Malak Ram Bhatia, son of Thakar Das, resident of Bhera, now employed in R.I.A.F. 2010 New Delhi stated as under:— Nathu Ram culprit was arrested in our presence. His person was also searched in our presence. ~~As a result thereof~~ one pistol containing ~~four~~ cartridges

Printed by Supdt., Govt. Printing, Pb.—1943.

Stereo No. H. C. J. D./C. 57.

Para. No.	Name of deponent or Police Officer.	Abstract of statement made.
4 (concld)	A.S.I (concld).	was recovered from him. A Fard bearing our signatures was prepared in respect of the articles recovered on his personal search. His person was searched in our presence.
5.	A.S.I.	At this time a Rugga for registering a case, sent by S. Jaswant Singh, Deputy Supdt. Police from Birla House was received. Accordingly a case under section 302 I.P. Code was registered against the culprit, and there being sufficient proof against him he was arrested under section 302 I.P. Code. He was sent to the Tughluk Road Police Station. His description is as given below:— Nathu Ram son of Vinayak Godse, caste Brahman, resident of Poona, Mohalla Narayan Pith Lakshmi Road. Description:— Tawny complexion, an oblong head,

Printed by Supdt., Govt. Printing, Pb.—1943.

Stereo No. H. C. J. D./C. 57.

Abstract Translation of *Zimni* Report No. ~~1(a)~~ (*continued*). (Page 41

Para. No.	Name of deponent or Police Officer.	Abstract of statement made.
5. (concld)	A. S. I. (concld)	injury mark below the chin, ~~bald~~ a black mole on the neck, at the place below the uppermost button of the shirt, flat face, height about 5 feet 5 inches & aged 36 years.

Date of receipt at the Thana — 31.1.1948

Date of despatch from the Thana — 1.2.1948

Date of receipt at the Sadar — 1.2.1948

Printed by Supdt., Govt. Printing, Punjab—1941.

Stereo, No. H. C. J. D/C.—56.

MURDER REFERENCE
CRIMINAL APPEAL No. ——— OF 19 (Page 43)

Abstract Translation of the *Zimni* Reports.

Zimni Report No. 1 (b) prepared by Late Behari Lal Inspector Police Tughlakd Police Station, on the 30th day of January 1948.

Para. No.	Name of deponent or Police Officer.	Abstract of statement made.
1	Inspector Police (30.1.1948 at 6 P.M.)	The D.S.P. C.I.D. ordered me to go to the Railway station and make a thorough search of the bedding and bag which belonged to the accused and which had been kept by him there, and take the same into possession.
2	Ditto (7.30 P.M)	On reaching the Railway station Delhi I took the Railway Inspector Delhi and on the indication of Nathu Ram accused recovered a bedding and a bag containing clothes & books from the First class waiting ~~room~~ room. They were taken into possession and a Fard in respect thereof was prepared. Chandan Singh, Major C. H. Batten and Babu Ganpat Rai Handa were present there. Four shirts bearing the mark N.V.G. One shirt bears N.W.G., one N.B.G & one V.V. Probably the publishers and authors of the Hindi books

Justice G.D. Khosla: At the unprecedented interest aroused by the case, the Chief Justice of India decided to constitute a bench of three judges to hear the appeal by Godse and his accomplices. The judges were Justice Bhandari, Justice Achhruram and Justice G.D. Khosla.

ELEVEN

...had the audience of that day [in the High Court] been constituted into a jury and entrusted with the task of deciding Godse's appeal, they would have brought in a verdict of 'not guilty'.

— JUSTICE G.D. KHOSLA

It was exactly as Madanlal had said, '*Phir Ayega*!' They had come again, and this time they had struck. The police had been given at least nine days' advance notice and told that one of the principal leaders of the plot was the editor of a Marathi paper in Poona or Bombay which Madanlal had said was called *Hindu Rashtra*. Now that very man had killed Gandhi.

The murder galvanized the authorities into a frenzy of action. Within twenty minutes of it, Bombay's Home Minister, Morarji Desai, who, it will be recalled, had been told by Professor Jain nine days earlier that Madanlal and his accomplices had plotted to kill Gandhi, was on the telephone to Deputy Commissioner Nagarvala, telling him about the murder and ordering him to 'take any necessary further action'.

However, for the time being, any action to arrest the people on the

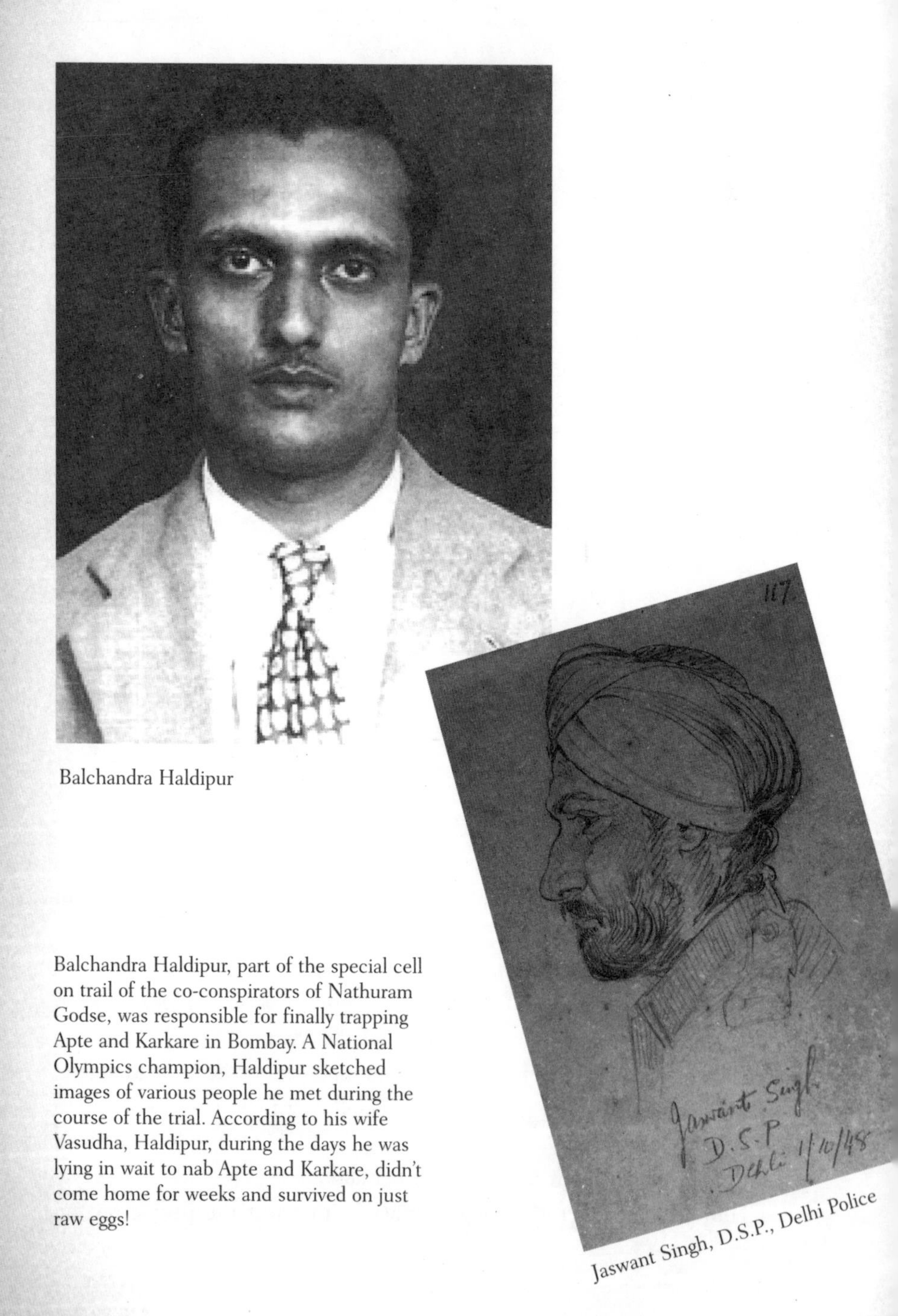

Balchandra Haldipur

Jaswant Singh, D.S.P., Delhi Police

Balchandra Haldipur, part of the special cell on trail of the co-conspirators of Nathuram Godse, was responsible for finally trapping Apte and Karkare in Bombay. A National Olympics champion, Haldipur sketched images of various people he met during the course of the trial. According to his wife Vasudha, Haldipur, during the days he was lying in wait to nab Apte and Karkare, didn't come home for weeks and survived on just raw eggs!

dhusudan Gopal Golwalkar

Javardan Dinkar Lovalekar

Digambar Vinayak Khemkar

police list of suspects had to cede precedence to a fresh problem of law and order set in motion by Gandhi's murder. As soon as it became known that the murderer was a Brahmin, in the towns and villages of central and western India Brahmins were jeered at and stoned, and their houses and places of business burned by gangs of hooligans professing to be outraged by what one of the order had done.

This is a madness peculiar to India, where communal strife means much more than the hostility between two religions. The entire fabric of society is fissured with it, and nowhere is it more deep-seated or more savage than among the different gradations of the Hindu caste structure. Whichever caste or sub-caste or clan Gandhi's killer may have belonged to, there would inevitably have been some people who would have wanted to use the opportunity to get their own back on that caste or sub-caste or clan.

And, if the killer had been a Muslim, it would have given the Hindus and Sikhs a legitimate grievance to rise against the entire Muslim population of India, which in turn would, almost in the natural course of events, have extended to a full-scale war with Pakistan. Lord Mountbatten was perhaps quicker to sense this danger than the Indian leaders. He had reached Birla House within minutes of Gandhi's murder. Alan Campbell-Johnson describes what happened:

> The tension is such that one careless word and rumour will spread like a forest fire. Even on our arrival, [Mountbatten] was greeted by a scaremonger who told him "It was a Moslem who did it." At that moment we still did not know the religion and the name of the assassin, but Mountbatten, appreciating that if he was a Moslem we were lost anyhow and that nothing could then avert the most disastrous civil war, replied in a flash, "You fool, don't you know it was a Hindu!"

Everyone was relieved that it was a Hindu – everyone that is, except the Brahmins, who now suddenly became 'Gandhi-killers'. The anti-Brahmin riots were particularly virulent in the city of Bombay where the Army had to be called in to help the police to restore order. As such, it was not till the next afternoon that Nagarvala was able to take the further action that was ordered by his political superior, and this took the form of a raid on Savarkar's house and the seizure of all his private papers, which consisted of 'some 143 files containing as many as 10,000 letters'.

But that day Savarkar was left a free man. The evidence against him was not strong enough to charge him with being an accomplice in a murder plot. In fact, there was no evidence at all. What was known was the affiliation of the conspirators to the Hindu Mahasabha and their personal veneration for Savarkar. And this, in addition to whatever Morarji Desai may have told Nagarvala (which was based on what Jain had told Morarji), provided the main, if not the only, basis for suspecting Savarkar as the man behind the conspiracy. But even Professor Jain cannot be shown to have mentioned Savarkar's name in his confidential revelations to Morarji Desai. During his cross-examination at the murder trial, Jain admitted, 'I did not give the facts of the case to anyone in writing till 17 February 1948 and [in a] statement I made some ten days later I did not state that Madanlal had told me that Veer Savarkar had sent for him.'

It was not till much later, and when Jain polished up his story, that Savarkar's name first appeared in it. How or why he had failed to mention so vital a piece of information in his first sworn statement was never satisfactorily explained.

Madanlal, on the other hand, is far more emphatic on this point. 'I had never been sent for by Savarkar... I had never had any talk at any time about Savarkar with Jain,' he told the judge at his trial. And, even twenty years later, after he had served his sentence and was a free man again, he still swore[8] that he had not even mentioned Savarkar's name to Jain.

Two other men who served 'life' sentences for Gandhi's murder, Vishnu Karkare and Gopal Godse, who were also questioned on this point after Savarkar had died, were equally insistent, when the author spoke to them, that he had absolutely no connection with the plot to murder Gandhi.

All three thought that it was significant that Dr Jain should not have even mentioned Savarkar's name in his first recorded statement, which, they pointed out, had been made more than three weeks after the murder, and also *after* Savarkar had been 'detained'. From this they inferred that his name had been included later.

Their argument ran as follows. Jain had undergone a term of detention and had acquired a marked aversion for the police. He had irritated the police hierarchy by going over their heads to their political superior, with the result that, at Jain's very first interview with him, Deputy Commissioner Nagarvala had treated him with brusqueness and had even threatened to put him under arrest.

They believed that Jain was seeking to make amends by strengthening the prosecution's case against Savarkar, and supported this contention by citing the discrepancies between Jain's first version of what Madanlal had told him and later versions which had also struck Justice Kapur. According to Justice Kapur, 'Jain first said that Madanlal's statement indicated a conspiracy to murder and later introduced the story of the objective being to create confusion and kidnapping Mahatma Gandhi.' All this, they felt, fitted snugly into Nagarvala's own 'kidnapping' theory.

Oddly enough, even Justice Kapur finds it puzzling that Jain should have gone with his story to a minister instead of to a police officer, and suggests that this may have been because 'he could not have been very fond of the police', being a 'progressive' and a 'leftist'.

But, in fairness to Jain, it must be emphasized that few people in his position would have gone to the police with so sensational a story. On the contrary, it is quite common in India for most citizens who have been witnesses to a road accident or a robbery to disappear from the scene as quickly as possible to avoid becoming involved in the subsequent inquiries and court proceedings. And, if Justice Kapur found Jain's reluctance to approach the police somewhat unusual, another judge, Justice Atma Charan, who tried the Gandhi murder case, has actually commended him for his 'courage and integrity' in making a report at all: 'He rose to the occasion. He shouldered the burden of inevitable consequences and did his duty to society.'

As such, the contention of some of the accused that Dr Jain was dutifully trying to strengthen 'the prosecution's case by bringing in Savarkar's name is hardly tenable. But, even if it were, why were the police so anxious to implicate Savarkar? Was it merely that, having failed in their proper function to arrest Nathuram *before* he killed Gandhi, they were making a bid to save face by raising the bogey of some sensational plot which involved a big leader who, providentially happened to be in bad odour with the government of the day? Or was that government itself, or some powerful group in it, using the police agency to destroy a rival political organization or at least to destroy a fiercely uncompromising opposition stalwart?

Or, again, was the whole thing a manifestation of some form of phobia peculiar to India, religious, racial, linguistic, or provincial, that made Savarkar a natural target for the venom of some section of society?

Whatever it was, Savarkar himself was so conscious of these currents, so convinced that the authorities were determined to take him to court as an accomplice of Nathuram, that when, five days after Gandhi's murder, a police party entered his house he went forward to meet it and asked: 'So you've come to arrest me for Gandhi's murder?'

Savarkar being made an accused in the Gandhi-murder trial may well have been an act of political vendetta. Of course, Badge, on his track record is a slippery character and not to be relied upon, but he was most insistent to me that he had been forced to tell lies, and that his pardon and future stipend by the police department in Bombay depended upon his backing the official version of the case and, in particular that, he never saw Savarkar talking to Apte, and never heard him telling them: '*Yeshaswi houn ya.*'

But if the suspicion that big-name political figures were determined to 'frame' Savarkar was voiced in Delhi's dinner-table conversation at the time, among Savarkar's own followers it was an unassailable belief; something taken for granted but not to be openly talked about.

But many years later on 16 June 1983, the Poona newspaper *Kal* edited by S.R. Date, published a report on the subject, which was later reprinted

Following pages 282-283: Copy of the affidavit submitted by Veer Savarkar to the magistrate in Bombay refuting the Police's theory that he was the mastermind behind the Mahatma's killing.

IN THE COURT OF THE CHIEF PRESIDENCY MAGISTRATE, BOMBAY.

Case No.   of 1948.

R E X. ....Complainant.

v/s.

Vinayak Damodar Savarkar. ...Accused.

Charge:- Ss.302-34-109-120 B and 307 I.P.C. read with Ss.4 & 5 of the Explosive Substances Act and Sec.19(f) Arms Act.

Affidavit of Mr. Vinayak Damodar Savarkar:

I, Vinayak Damodar Savarkar, do hereby swear and state on solemn affirmation as under:-

1. That on 5th February 1948 I was arrested, in my house "Savarkar Sadan" at Dadar, Bombay, by the Bombay -- Police. I am, since then, under detention in the Arthur Road Prison, Bombay.

2. That on the 18th of February 1948 I was served - with an order being Detention Order No.1202 of 1948 and a notice under the same number under Sec.3 of the Bombay Public Security Measures Act, VI of 1947, by the Commissioner of Police, Greater Bombay.

3. As directed in the said notice I made my representation to the Commissioner of Police, Bombay, on 22-2-48.

4. That on 11th March 1948, for the first time, I - was placed before The Chief Presidency Magistrate, Bombay, and in the remand application filed before the said Learned Chief Presidency Magistrate, Bombay, the Bombay Police --- alleged that I was arrested on that day in connection with C.R.Nos.40 and 68 of 1948 of Tughlak Police Station, New Delhi, and prayed the said Learned Chief Presidency Magistrate to remand me to Police custody for 14 days. The said application was granted by the Learned Chief Presidency - Magistrate, Bombay and I was remanded to Police custody. I was then taken to the ~~Arthur Road Prison~~ Arthur Road Prison.

The

The Bombay Police repeated the remand applications from time to time and they were granted. The present remand expires on the 18th of May 1948.

5. That on the 11th of May 1948 I was taken from the Arthur Road Prison, Bombay, to the C.I.D.Office by the -- Bombay Police Officers. I was then made to sit in a chair and Godse and others who are suspected to be concerned in the murder of Mahatma Gandhiji were placed by my sides. We were then all photographed in a group. I disclaim any -- association with them or any of them at any time whatsoever.

6. That I apprehend that the same photograph may possibly be used to concoct evidence against me.

7. That after I was photographed, as stated above, I got an opportunity, for the first time, to see my Advocate Mr. S.V.Deodhar on 14th May 1948. At the interview I got with him on 14.5.1948 I instructed him to file an application before ~~Your Worship~~ the Learned Chief Presidency --- Magistrate, Bombay, placing the above facts before him and further praying the Learned Chief Presidency Magistrate, - Bombay, to issue an order to the Police to produce the said photograph and its negatives and positives in the Court of the Learned Chief Presidency Magistrate, Bombay, for being deposited in the Court pending the trial I am to face in - Delhi as the said photograph may prejudice my defence and the same ought not to have been taken during the pendency of the trial. I have also instructed Mr.S.V.Deodhar, my Advocate to send in a notice to the Commissioner of Police, Bombay, to refrain himself from making any use of the said photograph during the pendency of the trial, as it tends to a contempt of the Court.

Dated this ~~15th~~ 18th May 1948. V. D. Savarkar

Solemnly affirmed before me.

Oscar H. Brown

CHIEF PRESIDENCY MAGISTRATE, BOMBAY.

18/5/48

MAGISTRATE'S COURT BOMBAY

INDIA 1R ONE RUPEE

in a volume published by the Savarkar Memorial Committee on 16 Feb. 89. I quote excerpts from it. It purports to report something that Savarkar's counsel at the trial, L.B. (Annasahen) Bhopatkar, a Poona lawyer, had revealed to his friends after he returned to Poona from Delhi in January 1949, after the Red Fort trial was over, and Savarkar found 'Not Guilty'.

> While in Delhi for the trial, Bhopatkar had been put up in the Hindu Mahasabha office. Bhopatkar had found it a little puzzling that while specific charges had been made against all the other accused, there was no specific charge against his client. He was pondering about his defence strategy when one morning he was told that he was wanted on the telephone, so he went up to the room in which the telephone was kept, picked up the receiver and identified himself. His caller was Dr Bhimrao Ambedkar, who merely said; "Please meet me this evening at the sixth milestone on the Mathura road," but before Bhopatkar could say anything more, put down the receiver.
>
> That evening, when Bhopatkar had himself driven to the place indicated he found Ambedkar already waiting. He motioned to Bhopatkar to get into his car which he, Ambedkar himself, was driving. A few minutes later, he stopped the car and told Bhopatkar: There is no real charge against your client; quite worthless evidence has been concocted. Several members of the cabinet were strongly against it, but to no avail. Even Sardar Patel could not go against these orders. But, take it from me, there just is no case. You will win." Who... Jawaharlal Nehru?... But why?

They had arrested Savarkar even though they did not possess sufficient evidence to do so. To be sure, the mass of papers seized from his house had yielded scores of letters from Nathuram and half a dozen from Apte, but these were disappointingly innocuous. All that they did was to establish the fact that Nathuram and Apte knew Savarkar and held him in great esteem. But this in itself was not enough to satisfy a magistrate that a *prima facie* case existed so that he could issue a warrant.

This, however, was no more than a technicality, and they got over it by arresting him under the Preventive Detention Act – one of the most malignant pieces of legislation with which the British had armed themselves while they ruled India. Even though Indian politicians of all shades of opinion had persistently condemned the British for this Act, the Congress had been in no hurry to repeal it after the British had gone. Under its provisions Savarkar was initially held 'as a detenu'. After that they proceeded to build up evidence against him that would enable them to change his *detention* into arrest, with what would be called 'retrospective effect'.

He was sixty-four years old, and had been ailing for a year or more. He was detained on 5 February 1948, and remained in prison for the whole of the year which the investigation and the trial took. He was adjudged 'not guilty' on 10 February 1949. The man who had undergone twenty-six years of imprisonment or detention under the British for his part in India's struggle for freedom was thus slung back into jail for another year the moment that freedom came.

From Birla House, Nathuram was taken to the Tughlak Road police station for questioning. It seems that the police exercised moderation in their treatment of Nathuram.

He maintained that he alone was responsible for killing Gandhi, and that he had no accomplices, and took great care not to give away any information that might implicate any of the others. But men like Nathuram make bad liars. For one thing, the police had discovered in his pocket a diary in which he had meticulously put down all the sums that he had spent from their common fund. And these included, in addition to 'Rs 9-00 Taxi. Rs 8-00 Dinner', and even 'Rs 2-00 Tongawala', sums given to people such as 'Rs 50-00 Bandopant, Rs 250-00 Gopal', and 'Rs 308-00 Bombay-Delhi Aeroplane', Even if the police had experienced a little difficulty in discovering who Bandopant might be – it was that Nathuram and Apte called Badge – they must have known right from the start that Gopal was the name of Nathuram's brother and that Rs 308-00 was the price of two tickets from Bombay to Delhi, not one.

But it seems that Nathuram, for all his care, had also given his interrogators other pointers. He had told them that between 20 and 30

January he was mostly in Bombay, and that from 24 to 27 January he had stayed at the 'Elphinstone Hotel'.

Accordingly the Delhi Police had asked the Bombay Police to find out from the register of the Elphinstone who else had been staying with Nathuram form 24 to 27 January.

The Elphinstone Hotel is in Hornby Road. On 5 February a couple of Bombay's CID men went there to look over its register of guests. The entries in the register were of no help to them and neither the manager nor any of the hotel servants could remember anyone who might have fitted the description of Nathuram that the Delhi Police had sent out. Or did they mean the Elphinstone Annexe, the manager asked, which was a branch of the Elphinstone on Carnac Road?

The policemen asked the manager to ring up the other hotel and find out.

The Elphinstone Annexe is a small and cheap hotel in a crowded locality, and as its manager, Kashmiri Lal, took the call he could be easily seen and even heard from the open gallery which also served as a passage to some of the rooms on the same floor. As Kashmiri Lal later testified:

> Two passengers [sic] who were putting up in Room No. 5 happened to come out into the gallery. Govinda [one of the room-boys] thereon told me that one of the two passengers looked like one who had stayed in Room No. 6 on 24 January.

One of the two men came over and asked Kashmiri Lal what the excitement was about and Kashmiri Lal brushed him off by telling him that 'it did not concern him'. He then took the register over to the Elphinstone Hotel where the two policemen were waiting for it. By the time he returned, accompanied by the policemen, the two 'passengers' had already left.

They were Apte and Karkare.

In its efforts to dig up facts about who knew what about the conspiracy in advance, the Kapur Commission kept encountering an exasperating tendency among the country's most senior officers to differ from one another in their versions of what one had told the other. Mr Nagarvala's account of what the two police officers from Delhi, Sardar Jaswant Singh and Mr Balkishen, told him differs sharply from what they themselves have to say. Asked by the Kapur Commission whether he thought that a certain paragraph in the report of these two officers, which contained a reference to a paper they had shown him in Bombay, was a fake [sic], Mr Nagarvala replied: 'As far as I am concerned, yes.'

There are similar differences on vital points between Mr Sanjevi, the Police Chief of Delhi, and Mr Rana, the Deputy Inspector General of the CID of the Bombay province; Mr Sanjevi and Mr Nagarvala; and even Mr Nagarvala and his immediate superior, Mr Bharucha, who was the Commissioner of Police for the city of Bombay, and from whom, incredibly, the fact that his department was investigating a report that some people were trying to murder Gandhi was being kept as 'confidential'.

In the main, these differences can be ascribed to the fact that the officers concerned were giving evidence before a commission of inquiry. They were being excessively guarded in their answers, and taking shelter behind what the Kapur Commission calls the 'multi-secitionalsim' of the organization. In the initial stages, the investigation was not the business of just one department under one man who could be held responsible for the way it was run, but of three separate police forces – the Delhi Police, the Bombay Provincial Police, and the Bombay City Police – and cooperation among the three was far from perfect. There were several instances where vital information available on the files of one force was not passed on to another promptly merely because it was not asked for. As Nagarvala told the Kapur Commission: 'The investigation was by the Delhi Police and it was up to them to ask for help.'

To be sure, this is true of departmental procedures all over the world; big organizations must work in compartments, and it is mainly by hindsight that one learns that some piece of information in the possession of one office might have averted a catastrophe if it had been in the possession of another.

But, if Nagarvala had stated the case to show that what the Kapur Commission characterized as a 'bland and legalistic approach' was only to be expected in organizations such as his, ironically enough it was Nagarvala himself who was to be tripped badly by a tricky little departmental fence. In fact, it would be quite correct to say that, if a certain order issued by him had been carried out by the concerned 'section' with no more than routine diligence, it would have averted Gandhi's assassination.

On 24 January Nagarvala had ordered the Poona Police to arrest Badge. Poona is just over a hundred miles from Bombay and, as far as communications go, might be regarded almost as a suburb of Bombay. But 24 January was a Saturday, and it is unlikely that the order was even read in Poona by whoever was to act on it until after the weekend. Badge, as has been narrated earlier, had reached Poona on the night of the twenty-second, and was living at his usual address. His arrest was not effected till the morning of 31 January, seven days after Nagarvala had issued the order for it and, as it happened, twelve hours after Gandhi was shot down.

Badge's arrest turned out to be the sort of lottery-winning stroke of luck that policemen all over the world must dream of; a single break that presents them with a panoramic view of a highly complex criminal plot.

The curious part is that, when he gave that order, Nagarvala had no idea that Badge himself might be implicated in the plot. In fact, the only name he knew at this stage, apart from Madanlal's, was that of Karkare. But what he had gathered from whatever the two Delhi policemen had told him was that, according to Madanlal's statement, all the people in the plot were either from Bombay or Poona, and that they had armed themselves with grenades and explosives.

On the basis of this information, Nagarvala had his records checked for the names of people who were known to traffic in illicit arms and explosives and, perhaps among half a dozen others, had come upon that of Digambar Badge. He thought he would get hold of Badge and see if he could put them on the right track as to how Madanlal and his colleagues could have acquired gun-cotton slabs and hand grenades. As Nagarvala told the Kapur Commission, they wanted Badge only 'as a person dealing in illicit arms who might tell us from where the gun-cotton slab had come'.

As it happened, the Poona Police did not even need to go through too many tiresome formalities to effect Badge's arrest; he was what was called a habitual offender, who could be pulled in any time the police needed him for questioning.

But the request had come from the Bombay City Police, and the Poona District Police, who came under the provincial organization, took their time to carry it out. Later they made the excuse that Badge had been 'hiding in a jungle' for seven days, and at the subsequent inquiries Nagarvala dutifully backed them up. Badge himself says that he had done nothing of the kind, that he had hardly left his home since his return, and in any case never left it at night.

At 5.30 in the morning of 31 January, Badge was awakened by a knocking at the door. Inspector Oak of the Poona District Police had come to arrest him and take him to the police station. Badge went quietly.

At the station the Inspector began by explaining how a man called Madanlal, who had exploded a charge of gun-cotton near Gandhi's prayer meeting in Delhi, was arrested on the spot and was found to have primed hand grenade in his pocket. Then he asked Badge if he could tell them how Madanlal might have got hold of the gun-cotton slab and the grenade.

Badge could. He had supplied both articles himself.

Badge was familiar with police procedure. He had no wish to submit himself to the kind of interrogation that is commonly practised by the police in India. He made a clean breast of everything.

The details came pouring out, and names were mentioned by the dozen. Madanlal being brought to his store by Karkare; the request by Apte and Nathuram for grenades, explosives and revolvers; the trip to Bombay to deliver the *mal* and the rendezvous at the Hindu Mahasabha office. What Apte had to say about his chance meeting with the actress Shanta Modak, whose professional name was Bimba; the name and address of Karkare's friend in Bombay, G.M. Joshi; the several meetings with the two holy

Following pages 290-299: Copy of the crime report as prepared by the Special Branch CID, Bombay, which named all the conspirators.

G. P. Z. P. Poona. 1946. **Special Branch, C.I.D. Bombay.** K B. C. P. 83 a.

C.R.No.40 and 68, of 1948,
CRIME REPORT
Tughluq Rd. Police Stn., New Delhi.

POLICE STATION— 20.1.48 & 30.1.48, Birla House, New Delhi. DIVISION.

First Information Book No. ... of 19 — Secs.4 & 5 of the Explosive Subs.Act., 1878, & Sec.307, 302, 120B, 34, 114, I.P.C. & Sec.19(f) Indian Arms Act. Crime Report No.

Date and Place of Occurrence—

Offence—	5.30 p.m. 30.1.48	Complainant—
Date on which action was taken ...		Places visited by him—
Time at which the Investigating Officer received information of the Offence.	12 m.n. to 12 m.n.	
Time at which he began and concluded his investigation.		

CRIME REPORT NO.4

2.2.48.

Record of Investigation

Accused:- 1 Nathuram Vinayak Godse, arrested at Delhi on 30.1.48.
2. Madan Lal Kashmiri Lal, arrested at Delhi on 20.1.48.
Both in Police custody in Delhi.

Information was received that prior to his departure to Delhi, accd. Nathuram Vinayak Godse and his associates were in Thana, and hence the police party under me proceeded to Thana at 1 a.m. on 2.2.48, and with the assistance of the local police searched the residences of the following persons for absconding accused. Apte and Karkare, and also for documents and other material connected with the case:

1. Vidyasagar Bhagwan Oak.
2. Bhikaji Gangadhar Oak
3. Waman Prabhakar Oak
4. Sadashiv Mohiniraj Khare
5. Ganesh Dattatray Gadre
6. Madhukar Govind Atre
7. Keshav Vishnu Dabke
8. Madhav Narayan Kelkar.
9. Shankar Ramchandra Sahasrabudhe.

The above individuals were arrested and detained by the Thana Police for further interrogation. Nothing of importance was recovered from their residences. They were interrogated at length but no ~~xxxxxxx~~ useful information was learnt

Instructions were also sent to Poona C.I.D. to search the residences of Messrs. W. B. Gogte of the "Hotson Case", and Mr. G. V. Gutti, as they were reported to be fast friends of accd. N. V. Godse.

Interrogation of Kasar, Damle and others continues and also the watches for Apte and Karkare at different places where they are likely to come are continued. The Delhi and Poona Police have been contacted with a view to co-ordinating the information. The former are requested to send accused Madan Lal to Bombay for further enquiries as he was reported to have started on the evil mission along with others in Bombay. The Poona Police reported that they have arrested Badge in Poona on 31.1.48. They were also requested to send down Badge to Bombay as he was one of the conspirators.

Further enquiries regarding the absconding accused continue.

Sd/-

Dy. Commissioner of Police,
S.B., Bombay.

3.2.48.

CRIME REPORT NO. 5.

3.2.48.

Accused: As mentioned in Crime Report No.4 , viz.N.V.Godse, and Madan Lal.
3. Digambar Ramchandra Badge, arrested by Poona Police on 31.1.48.

Further enquiries were made in this case. The Gurkha watchman of Sawarkar Sadan, named Devi Singh Balbir Singh, who had been previously called to this office and interrogated, was put under arrest at about 8 a.m. on 3.2.48, under B.P.S.M.Act, and detained.

It transpired from the statements of Appa Kasar and Damle that this watchman was the first individual that every visitor to Sawarkar Sadan, had to approach before getting admittance. His hours of duty by day generally were not fixed, but he had

been

CRIME REPORT

POLICE STATION— " " DIVISION.

First Information Book No. of 19 Crime Report No.

Date and Place of Occurrence—

Offence—		Complainant—
Date on which action was taken ...		Places visited by him—
Time at which the Investigating Officer received information of the Offence.		
Time at which he began and concluded his investigation.		

Record of Investigation

Crime Report No.5 contd.

been provided with a room to stay on the premises, and was always to be found seated at the entrance gate. He is being further interrogated on the points elicited from Damle and Appa Kasar.

Intimation has been received both from Delhi and Poona Police that the two accused called for, i.e. Madan Lal and Badge, respectively are being sent down to Bombay on 4.2.48 for further enquiries.

Efforts to trace Apte & Karkare continue and the watches at the haunts likely to be visited by them have been maintained.

The Poona Police also reported that as per instructions given to them by me on 30.1.48, at about 10.20 p.m., on the wireless that they carried out the searches of the houses of the following places in Poona:-

1. Hindu Rashtra Press and Office, 14 344-345 Narayan Peth Poona.
2. Hindu Mahasabha Office, Poona.
3. Residence of Nathuram V. Godse, at 786 Sadashiv Peth, Poona City.
4. Residence of N.V.Godse's parents at 282 Shukrawar Peth Poona City.
5. The Udyam Engineering Works at 32, Yerandawane, Poona 4.
6. Residence of N.D.Apte at 22, Budhwar Peth, Poona.
7. Residence of D.R.Badge, at 300 Narayan Peth, Poona.
8. Residence of Nagesh Raghunath Athavle at ~~227~~ 837 Om Narayan Peth, Poona.

9.

9. The residence of Prof. D.S.Joag, 363/9 Narayan Peth, Poona.
10. Residence of Bal Gopal Palsule, at 196/52 Sadashiv Peth, Poona.
11. Residence of Vithal Ramchandra Joag at 740 Sadashiv Peth, Poona.
12. Residence of D.G.Lele, at 527 Sadashiv Peth, Poona.
13. Residence of Nandakumar Kashinath Khanvilkar at 196/56 Sadashiv Peth, Poona.
14. Residence of Ramchandra Krishnaji Ranade, at 196/2 Sadashiv Peth, Poona.
15. Residence of Madhusudan Tukaram Kulkarni at 568 Narayan Peth, Poona.

From the house search of accused N.V.Godse, about two lbs. of a sticky substance resembling gelignite was seized, vide Punchanama dated 31.1.48.

From the house search of D.R. Badge, the following ammunition was recovered:-

1. 20 small cartridges.
2. 12 revolver cartridges
3. 5 .32 bore revolver cartridges
4. 2 big cartridges.
5. 1 empty cartridge case.
6. 2 spent bullets.

vide Punchanama dated 31.1.48. Some letters and correspondence were attached from the house search of V.R.Joag. The Poona Police arrested the following individuals:-

1. D. R. Badge.
2. Prof. D. S. Joag.
3. Madhusudan Tukaram Kulkarni.
4. Nagesh Raghunath Athavle
5. Dattatraya Vinayak Godse.
6. Dr. D.G.Lele.
7. Vithal Ramchandra Joag.
8. Bal Gopal Palsule.

On my further directions one Hari Bhaskar Bhide and Jayant Shridhar Tilak were also put under arrest by the Poona Police. The former's residence could not be searched as it had already been burnt by hooligans. The latter's residence was searched but nothing of importance was traced.

In the enquiries that were continued at Poona by the Poona Police for the absconding accused Apte, the Poona Police received information that a flame thrower belonging to Apte had been deposited with one Shivlal Manekchand Shah residing at Sarang Building behind Modern High School, Jungli Maharaj

Rd.,

G. P. Z. P. Poona, 1946. B. C. P. 68 c.

CRIME REPORT

POLICE STATION— " " DIVISION.

First Information Book No. of 19 Crime Report No.

Date and Place of Occurrence—

Offence—		Complainant—
Date on which action was taken ...		Places visited by him—
Time at which the Investigating Officer received information of the Offence.		
Time at which he began and concluded his investigation.		

Record of Investigation

Crime Report No.5 Contd.

Rd., Poona. The information was verified by Dy.S.P. Deulkar of the Poona C.I.D. and the flame thrower was taken charge of from his residence, vide punchanama dated 1.2.48.

One Bhalchandra Dattatraya Kher who was employed in the Hindu Rashtra Press of accd. N.V. Godse was questioned about Nathuram Godse and N.D. Apte, and according to him both of them had left Poona on or about 16th Jan.48 when he resumed duty in the press and since then he has not seen or heard of them. His statement was recorded by Dy.S.P. Deulkar on 1.2.48.

One Vishwanath Ramchandra Dixit Patwardhan who was connected with accd. Badge in the trafficking of arms and ammunition, was interrogated by the Poona Police and his residence was searched but nothing of importance was found therein.

Shivlal Maneckchand Shah from whom the flame-thrower was recovered was arrested under the B.P.S.M. Act, and has been detained.

The Poona Police recorded the statements of Shivlal ManeckchandShah, his wife Prabhavati Shivlal Shah, his mother Jeevbai Maneckchand Shah and Maneckchand

Maneckchand Ramchandra Shah on 2.2.48 in connection with the flame-thrower which was recovered from their house on 1.2.48. They all stated that the gunny bag containing the flame-thrower was depostted with them by accd. N.D.Apte, who is now absconding. Their statements xxx were recorded by Dy. S.P. Deulkar.

The Poona C.I.D. reported that according to my instructions they have searched the houses of Messrs. V. G. Gogte and G.V. Gutti, close associates of N.V. Godse, but nothing of importance was found.

Received a copy of statement of accused N.V.Godse from Delhi, and it is being verified.

The efforts to trace the absconding accused, viz. Apte and Karkare, continue.

Further enquiriesx continue.

Dy.Commissioner of Police,
S.B., Bombay.

4.2.48.

CRIME REPORT NO.6.

4 . 2 . 1948
and
5. 2. 1948.

Accused:-1.N.V. Godse.)Arrested by the Delhi
2.Madan Lal Kashmirilal.)Police on 30.1.48 and 20.1.48 respectively.

3.D.R. Badge............ Arrested by the Poona Police on 31.1.48.

Enquiries in this case continued. On 4.2.48 accused Madan Lal was flown to Bombay under the escort of Delhi Police from Delhi. He was taken over at the Santa Cruz Aerodrome at about 5.45.p.m. from Dy.S.P. Mehta Chhabildas who was in charge of the escorting party. Madan Lal's interrogation started immediately after his arrival in Bombay. In the course of interrogation he stated that besides him there were six others who had taken part in the first attempt on the life of Mahatmaji at Birla House on 20.1.48. He described them as

G. P. Z. P. Poona, 1946. B. C. P. 68 a.

CRIME REPORT

POLICE STATION— " " DIVISION.

First Information Book No. of 19 Crime Report No.

Date and Place of Occurrence—

Offence—		Complainant—
Date on which action was taken ...		Places visited by him—
Time at which the Investigating Officer received information of the Offence.		
Time at which he began and concluded his investigation.		

Record of Investigation

Crime Report No. 6 contd.

as follows:-

1. Godse - who was already arrested by Delhi Police.
2. No. 1's partner of Hindu Rashtra paper.
3. A. Sikh Maratha of Poona.
4. Servant of the Sikh Maratha.
5. Kirkare of Ahmednagar.
6. A Punjabi speaking Maratha.

Whilst Madan Lal was being interrogated in the evening, Sub-Inspr. Joshi of Poona brought down accused D.R. Badge to the C.I.D. Office from Poona. Badge was questioned about his complicity in the incident on 20.1.48. He denied all knowledge of it. He was, therefore, confronted with accused Madan Lal who identified him as the Sikh Maratha referred to by him. This confronting with Madan Lal and the severe searching interrogation that followed thereafter led to Badge's making a clean breast of the whole conspiracy and the persons concerned. The attempt made on Gandhiji's life on 20.1.48 was in pursuance of this conspiracy. His interrogation continued.

<u>5.2.48.</u>

The interrogation of accused D.R. Badge also revealed information regarding the collection of arms and ammunition in Poona. He stated that he had given some arms and ammunition to one Ram Jaywant Deshmukh residing at Shanwar Peth, Poona. He agreed to point him out.

Accused D.R.Badge therefore was sent with my staff to Poona on 5.2.48 at 12.30.a.m. and I followed them and reached Poona at about 9.a.m. I took the assistance of the Poona Police for further enquiries there. Accd. D.R.Badge took the Police party to House No.191, Shanwar Peth, Poona, which Badge pointed out as the residence of Ram Jaywant Deshmukh. One Padmakar Venkatesh Deshpande was found in the room. He was questioned about the whereabouts of R.J. Deshmukh. He offered to point out one R.J. Deshmukh. S.I. D'Souza and S.I. Pradhan of the Bombay C.I.D. were sent with him and he pointed out R.J. Deshmukh in the house of one Anant Ambadas Kulkarni at Sadashiv Peth. R.J. Deshmukh was brought back to his place at house No.191 Shanwar Peth, Poona. This place was searched in the presence of Punchas and one empty pistol magazine was taken charge of, vide punchanama dtd. 5.2.48. The said Deshmukh stated that he had three more places. He took the police to house No.486 Shanwar Peth, Poona, which is a godown owned by him. The godown was searched in the presence of punchas when the following articles were attached:-

1. 162 rifle cartridges bearing No. 4101.
2. One 9 mm. spent bullet.
3. Two packages empty, of .303 bullets.
4. One empty box of 12 bore cartridges.
5. One empty tin of revolver bullets.
6. One ring of a handgrenade.
7. Two air-tight containers containing phosphorus sticks.
8. One package of yellowish powder.
9. 1 Chocolate coloured sticky substance.
10. 1 mortar and pestle smeared with yellowish powder.

A punchanama was made regarding the search.

The said R.J. Deshmukh also pointed out another house No.307, Narayan Peth, Poona, which stood on his name, but was let to one Sheshrao and one Nayak. These two persons were not there in the room. The lock of the room was opened by Deshmukh. The same was searched in the presence of punchas. Some papers

G. P. E. P. Poona, 1945. R. C. P. 68 a.

CRIME REPORT

POLICE STATION— " DIVISION.

First Information Book No. of 19 Crime Report No.

Date and Place of Occurrence—

Offence—		Complainant—
Date on which action was taken ...		Places visited by him—
Time at which the Investigating Officer received information of the Offence.		
Time at which he began and concluded his investigation.		

Record of Investigation

Crime Report No. 6 contd.

papers were taken charge of, vide punchanama dated 5.2.48.

R.J. Deshmukh again took the Police to house No. 693 Budhwar Peth, Poona, in which one V.G. Paranjpe was residing. This house was searched in the presence of panchas and some steel armours were seized, vide Punchanama dtd. 5.2.48.

All these places were searched under my directions with a view to recover explosive substances which Badge had given to R.J. Deshmukh. As Badge stated that Anant Ambadas Kulkarni with whom Deshmukh was found and Padmakar Venkatesh Deshpande who was found in the room of Deshmukh, were his companions and were likely to be aware of the subversive activities of the said Deshmukh. They were therefore taken to the Poona C.I.D. Office for interrogation. During the course of enquiry it was revealed that one Nagesh Raghunath Athavle and one Vishwanath Ramchandra Dixit Patwardhan were in the custody of the Poona Police and were close associates of Apte who is concerned in the conspiracy of the murder of Mahatmaji.

Accused Badge in his statement had stated that Gopal, the younger brother of accd. Nathuram Godse, was also concerned in this conspiracy . Enquiries were therefore made for him at Poona and it was learnt that he was residing at Kirkee and had gone to Kamset. Inspr. Korgaonkar, D.I. Pinto and D.I. Sawant were therefore deputed to make enquiries about him at Kamset near Lonavla. They traced him at Village Uksan near Kamset and brought him to Poona. The said Gopal Vinayak Godse on being questioned about his place of residence took the Police to his room at Kirkee. This room was searched in the presence of punchas and a pair of trousers and two photos of Sawarkar were taken charge of, vide punchanama dated 5.2.48.

While at Poona, one Bashrat Kondiba Chintamane who was a servant of Digambar Ramchandra Badge, was arrested by the Poona Police.

The following persons were arrested at Poona at 8.30.p.m. as they were suspected to have been concerned in the conspiracy and were brought down to Bombay:-

1. Gopal Vinayak Godse.
2. Ram Jaywant Deshmukh.
3. Bashrat Kondiba Chintamane.
4. Anant Ambadas Kulkarni.
5. Padmakar Venkatesh Deshpande.
6. Vishwanath Ramchandra Dixit @ Patwardhan.
7. Nagesh Raghunath Athavle.

The last two were in the custody of the Poona Police, having been detained under the B.P.S.M. Act.

Enquiries in progress.

Dy.Commr.of Police,S.B.,
Bombay.

6.2.1948.

CRIME REPORT No.7.

6. 2. 1948.

Accused:-					
1. N.V. Godse............	arrested by	Delhi	Police	on	30.1.48
2. Madan Lal Kashmiri Lal.	"	"	"	"	20.1.48
3. D.R. Badge............	"	Poona	"		31.1.48
4. Gopal Vinayak Godse....	"	Bombay	"		5.2.48
5. Nagesh Raghunath Athavle.	"	Poona	"		5.2.48
6. Anant Ambadas Kulkarni..	"	Poona	"		5.2.48
7. Padmakar Venkatesh Deshpande.	"	Poona	"		5.2.48
8. Vishwanath Ramchandra Dixit Patwardhan..................	"	Poona	"		5.2.48
9. Ram Jaywant Deshmukh.........	"	Poona	"		5.2.48
10. Dashrat Kondiba Chintamane...	"	Poona	"		5.2.48
11. Shankar Kistayya............	"	Bombay	"		6.2.48

I returned to Bombay from Poona along with the accused mentioned above, except Nos. 1 and 2, and my staff, at about 2.a.m. on 6.2.48. In Bombay the interrogation of accd. Madan Lal was continued at great length. During the course of brothers of the Bhuleshwar temple; the efforts to get hold of a more powerful revolver, the long taxi-ride, Apte's romance with Manorama Salvi, and the names and addresses of the people who had paid money to Nathuram and Apte in Bombay.

And then the activities in Delhi: the meeting with Gopal Godse, who had brought his own revolver; the reconnaissance survey of the Birla House grounds; the target practice in the woods at the back of the Birla temple; the final briefing in the room at the Marina Hotel; the full story, as far as he knew it, of what happened at Birla House; and the stashing away of the unused explosives in the grounds of the Hindu Mahasabha Bhavan in Delhi.

Nagarvala asked for Badge to be sent to Bombay so that he could arrange to have him 'confront' Madanlal, who was being flown over from Delhi. Apparently, even at this confrontation, Madanlal did not give away much more information than he already had. But, by then, Nagarvala himself had a long interview with Badge and must have realized his potential as an 'approver' or state witness, who knew enough about the plot to make it easy for him to arrest the remaining members of the conspiracy and even to prove the charges against them in a court of law.

Badge was altogether in the dark about what the others had been doing since the evening of 20 January, and thus was not able to enlighten the police as to who might have supplied the Beretta. But he gave them the names of all those who had gathered in the Marina Hotel room on the afternoon of the twentieth: Nathuram, Apte, Karkare, Madanlal, Gopal, Shankar and himself.

On 5 February, Nagarvala drove to Poona to see if he could find Apte and Gopal Godse as well as Shankar Kistayya who, Badge had told him, had gone on 'leave' to see his mother but was due back on that day. But Apte, his neighbours told Nagarvala's men had not been seen in Poona for more than

Facing page: Arrested on 31 January in Poona, Digambhar Badge was the first conspirator to be arrested. Familiar with the police procedures he had no wish to submit himself to the interrogation. Quite easily he gave out all the details and became the police approver. Copy of the pardon passed on by Atma Charan, Judge of the Special court hearing the Gandhi murder trial.

RE: 'THE MAHATMA GANDHI MURDER CASE'

ORDER:

Whereas Digambar R Badge, Proprietor, Shashtra-Bhandar, Poona, appears to have been directly or indirectly concerned in or privy to the offences punishable u/ss 109,114,120B & 302 of the I.P.C. and the offences connected therewith in the Mahatma Gandhi Murder Case;

Whereas Digambar R Badge, Proprietor, Shashtra-Bhandar, Poona, is willing to make a full and true disclosure of the whole circumstances within his knowledge relating to the above offences and to every other person concerned, whether as principal or abettor, in the commission thereof on condition a pardon is tendered to him;

I, Atma Charan, I.C.S., Judge, Special Court, Red-Fort, Delhi, with a view to obtaining full details of the facts of the case before me, hereby tender a pardon to DIGAMBAR R BADGE on condition of his making a full and true disclosure of the whole circumstances within his knowledge relating to the offences and to every other person concerned, whether as principal or abettor, in the commission thereof.

June 21,1948.
Red-Fort, Delhi.

I.C.S.
Judge, Special Court.

two weeks, and they discovered that Shankar had still not returned. But Gopal was in his house. He was arrested and taken to Bombay.

As it happened, Shankar, who had gone to Sholapur for a few days to see his mother, returned to Poona within a couple of hours after the police party which had come to arrest him had gone away. When he was told that his master, Badge, had been arrested and taken to Bombay, he decided to go to Bombay in search of him. As he later told the judge who tried him: 'At Bombay I did not know where to go. I thought of Dixitji Maharaj and went to his house. I met one of his servants who took me to the CID building. I met Mr Nagarvala there. Somebody said something to Mr Nagarvala. He thereupon gave me a slap.'

Among other things that Gopal blurted out under what he has described as 'inescapable procedural harassment' was the fact that he had entrusted his revolver to a friend for safekeeping. On 8 February the Bombay Police brought Gopal to Poona for a 'confrontation' with that friend, Pandurang Godbole. They stopped their car a little distance from his house and two policemen in plain clothes accompanied Gopal to the door.

When Godbole had come to know that it was Gopal's brother Nathuram who had killed Gandhi, he was seized by a fit of panic at the thought that he was keeping Gopal's revolver. He mentioned his fear to a friend, Gopal Kale, and Kale had offered to get rid of the revolver for him.

So when Gopal Godse, accompanied by the plain-clothes men, came to reclaim his revolver, Godbole, after first trying to make out that he had thrown it away, told them that he had given it to Kale. Upon this, they bundled Godbole into the car and drove to Kale's house. But Kale, true to his word, actually had thrown the revolver away 'on the right side of the road opposite the main gate of the Feruguson College'.

Gopal's revolver was never found. Both Godbole and Kale were arrested and taken for questioning. They were kept in custody for six weeks.

Of the seven men whose names Badge had given Nagarvala, five were already in the hands of the police, in addition to Savarkar, whose name Badge may not have mentioned. Now only Apte and Karkare remained.

It was Karkare who caused Nagarvala special worry. He was sharp-witted and unpredictable, a man who had knocked around and learned to fend for himself, who was used to a low-key life and able to merge into his background. Already he had been in hiding for nearly a month. How were they going to nab Karkare before he finally slipped into Goa, which in those days was a Portugese colony and a convenient hiding-ground for criminals from India.

About Apte, Nagarvala had a detective's hunch that he would show up in Bombay itself. If he lived up to the image that Badge had painted of him, he was bound to get in touch with Manorama Salvi, and that would be like walking into the CID headquarters, because Manorama's father's flat was a Police Department flat, and his telephone an extension on the general police exchange. Nagarvala gave orders for the flat to be kept under surveillance and for the telephone to be tapped.

And only then did he discover that both men were together and already in Bombay, or at least they had been in Bombay till the previous afternoon. Within minutes of his return from Poona, two shamefaced CID men brought the register of the Elphinstone Annexe for his inspection. They also told him that the man who was believed to be Nathuram's companion, and who had given his name as Narainrao D., and another man who might be Karkare had been staying at the Elphinstone Annexe since 3 February and had checked out only minutes before they had gone to the hotel to nab them.

Nagarvala cursed. Now the only thing to do was to wait and see if the tapped telephone would produce results. Much depended on how desperately Apte wanted to see his beloved. And, even then, would Karkare still be with him?

'Friends and comrades, the light has gone out of our lives and there is darkness everywhere ... our beloved leader, Bapu as we called him, the Father of the Nation, is no more.'

— Jawaharlal Nehru announcing the news on 30 January 1948

Photograph by Henri Cartier-Bresson

DELHI EDITION

The Hind

LARGEST CIRCULATION IN NORTHERN

VOL. XXV. No. 34 NEW DELHI: SA

MAHATMA G BY ASSASS

SHOTS FIRED AT PO BLANK RANGE

Mahatma Gandhi died on Friday shortly after 5 p.m. He was shot at three times at point-blank range by Nathuram (Narayan) Vinayak Godse, believed to be the Secretary of the Hindu Mahasabha, Poona.

Gandhiji was walking to the prayer ground as usual with his arms resting on the shoulders of his grand-daughter and grand-daughter-in-law, when the tragedy occurred. Just as he climbed the steps leading to the platform from where he used to address his prayer gathering and was returning the greetings of the crowd with folded hands, a man dressed in khaki tunic suddenly stepped out in front of him and, whipping out a revolver, fired three shots at him at point-blank range. One bullet hit Gandhiji in the chest and two in the abdomen.

Gandhiji at once fell down and was carried almost unconscious into the House. There were still signs of life when he was being carried, but his eyes were closed. The moment shots were fired

THE

(By Our S

The weapo sailant use is matic pistol, a sound of 9 discharging filling. It is u police took p three rounds rest were in

Regd. No. [illegible]

...stan Times

...WESTERN AND CENTRAL INDIA

JANUARY 31, 1948. — PRICE TWO AN[illegible]

...NDHI KILLE[D]

...N'S BULLET

...JT

...N

...dent)

...ji's as-
...is assai-
... It fires
...pable of
...out re-
...when the
... weapon
...and the

THE LIGHT HAS GONE FROM OUT OF OUR LIVES

—NEHRU

"The light has gone out of our lives and there is darkness everywhere." In these words, in a voice quivering with emotion, Pandit Nehru, Prime Minister, broadcast to the nation, to the world, last night.

"The best prayer that we could offer Gandhiji and his memory is to take a pledge to dedicate ourselves to truth and to the cause for which this great countryman of ours lived and for which he has died," said Pandit Nehru adding: "We must hold together and all our petty troubles, difficulties and conflicts must be ended in the face of this great disaster."

Pandit Nehru said: "Friends and comrades, the light has gone out of our lives and there is darkness everywhere. I do not know what to tell you and how to say it. Our beloved leader, Bapu as we called him, the Father of the Nation, is no more. Perhaps I am wrong to say that. Nevertheless, we will not see him again as we have seen him for these many years. We will not run to him for advice and seek solace from him and that is a terrible blow not to me only but to the millions and millions in this country, and it is a little difficult to soften the blow by another advice that I or anyone else can give you.

"The light has gone out, I said, and yet I was wrong. For the light that shone in this country was no ordinary light. The light that has illumined this country for these many years will illumine this country for many more years and a thousand years later, that light will still be seen in this country and

... weak but rather that we should in strength and in unity, face all the troubles that are in front of us. We must hold together and all our petty troubles and difficulties and conflicts must be ended in the face of this great disaster.

A great disaster is a symbol to us to remember all the big things of life and forget the small thing, of which we have thought too much. In his death he has reminded us of the big things of life, that living truth, and if we remember that, then it will be well with India."

Cremation Today

Giving the programme for today, Pandit Nehru said: "It was proposed by some friends that Mahatmaji's body should be embalmed for a few days to enable millions of people to pay their last homage to him. But it was his wish, repeatedly expressed, that no such thing should happen, that this should not be done, that he was entirely opposed to any embalm-...

Last Goodwill Gesture

(By Our Special Correspondent)

Sergeant D. R. Singh of the Royal Indian Air Force, who was the first to tackle the assassin and disarm him, gave me the following account of the tragedy:—

"Gandhiji was going to the dais for his prayer meeting. Today he was a little late. I was standing among the spectators when the assailant stepped forward and pulled a pistol from his pocket.

"Gandhiji was going to say something when the assailant started firing at point-blank range of no more than a few feet.

"Gandhiji folded his hands in a last gesture of farewell and fell on the ground.

"I pounced upon the assailant and snatched the pistol from his hand. People started beating the assailant. I wanted to shoot him myself, but the assailant was immediately taken into custody by the police."

Route Of Funeral Procession

The mortal remains of the Father of the Nation will leave Birla House at 11-30 a.m. today and follow the route below to the river Jumna:

Albuquerque Road, Queensway, Kingsway, Memorial Arch, Hardinge Avenue, Muttra Road, Power House Road.

The Prime Minister appeals to the ...

The bullets fired at point-blank range were fatal. Gurbachan Singh, a Sikh businessman from Panipat who was only a few steps behind Gandhi as he fell, deposed that his last words were 'Hai Rama!' On the contrary, Vishnu Karkare, who

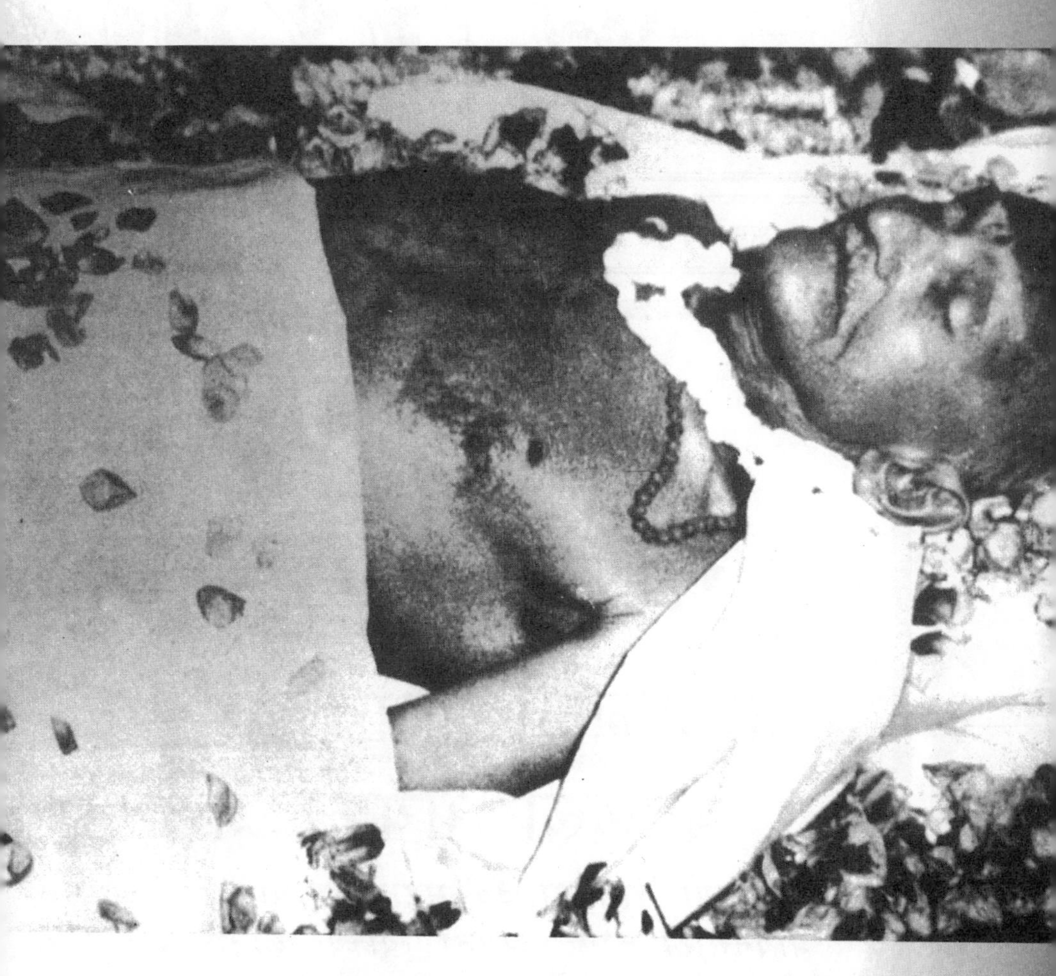

too stood within a few feet of him and saw him as the bullets struck him swore that all Gandhi uttered was a cry of pain, a guttural rasp, 'Aaah!' Visible on the left side of his chest is the bullet wound.

The Daily "LOKASATTA" BOMBAY SATURDAY 31 JANUARY 1948.

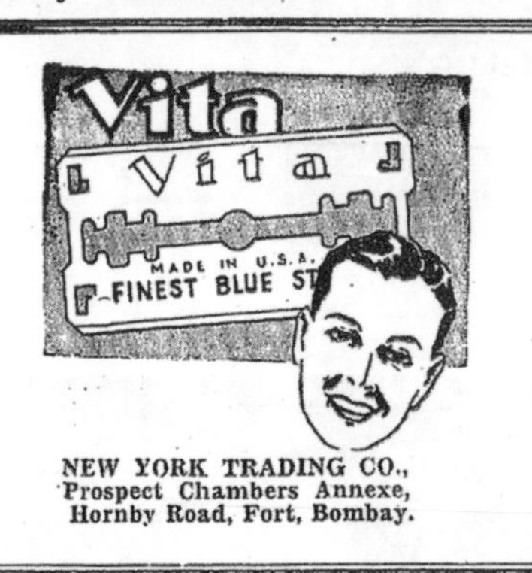

संपादक :

वर्ष १ : अंक १६]

मुंबई, शनिवार

हिंदुस्थानावर अ

माथेफिरूच्या गो

संध्याकाळीं प्रार्थनेच्या स्थळीं घडलेला भयंकर प्रकार

नवी दिल्ली, ता. ३०--महात्मा गांधीं आज संध्याकाळी प्रार्थनेसाठी चालले असतां त्यांच्या छातींमध्यें चारवेळां गोळ्या झाडल्यामुळें ते कोसळून खाली पडले व थोड्याच अवधींत मरण पावले.

महात्मा गांधीवर झाडण्यांत आलेल्या चार गोळ्यांपैकी एक गोळी त्यांना पोटांत लागून ते खालीं कोसळले व

ITY EDITION Regd. No. B 5222. PHONE NO. 35105, 35132,36352.

ष्णु पर्वते

३१ जानेवारी १९४८ [किंमत १ आणा.

काश कोसळलें!

ँ गांधीजींचा मृत्यु

जन्म

ह्या महान् विभूतीचा जन्म पोरबंदर येथें भाद्रपद वद्य द्वादशी संवत् १९२५ (२ ऑक्टोबर १८६९) या दिवशीं झाला. त्यांचा जन्म ज्या घरांत झाला तें घर सुद्धां एका विशिष्ट तऱ्हेनें वसलेलें आहे. एका बाजूस श्रीकृष्णाचें व दुसऱ्या बाजूस श्रीरामाचें मंदिर अशी दोन मंदिरें आज सुद्धां त्यांच्या घराजवळ सांपडतील.

त्यांचे वडील हे पोरबंदर संस्थानांत त्यावेळेस दिवाण होते आणि त्यांचा करारीपणा आणि न्यायबुध्दि ह्याबद्दची त्यांची कीर्ति सर्व काठेवाडांत दुमदुमत होती.

शाळेंतील जीवन

शाळेंत असतांना स्वतःच्या बुध्दिमत्तेबद्दल अभिमान वाटण्यासारखें असें श्री. मोहनदास करमचंद यांनीं कांहीं विशेष केलें नाहीं. परंतु घरीं आणि शाळेमध्यें सर्व वातावरण धार्मिक वृत्तीचें असल्यामुळें त्यांचें सर्व जीवन नीतिप्रधान विचारांनीं भारलेलें होतें.

The country was in mourning and people rushed to the Birla House for their last *darshan* of the Mahatma. Bapu was no more to guide them, to show them the way of life. Seen here is Mahatma Gandhi's body being taken out of the Birla House in the presence of Pandit Nehru and Sardar Patel. People from all religions and faiths flocked to be a part of the Mahatma's last journey. Seen here in the picture above, are people digging earth from the spot where Gandhi was shot dead.

LARGEST NET SALES of any Daily Newspaper Printed in Northern

The Times

NO. 27. VOL. CX BOMBAY: SATURD

MAHATMA GANDHI A

MA

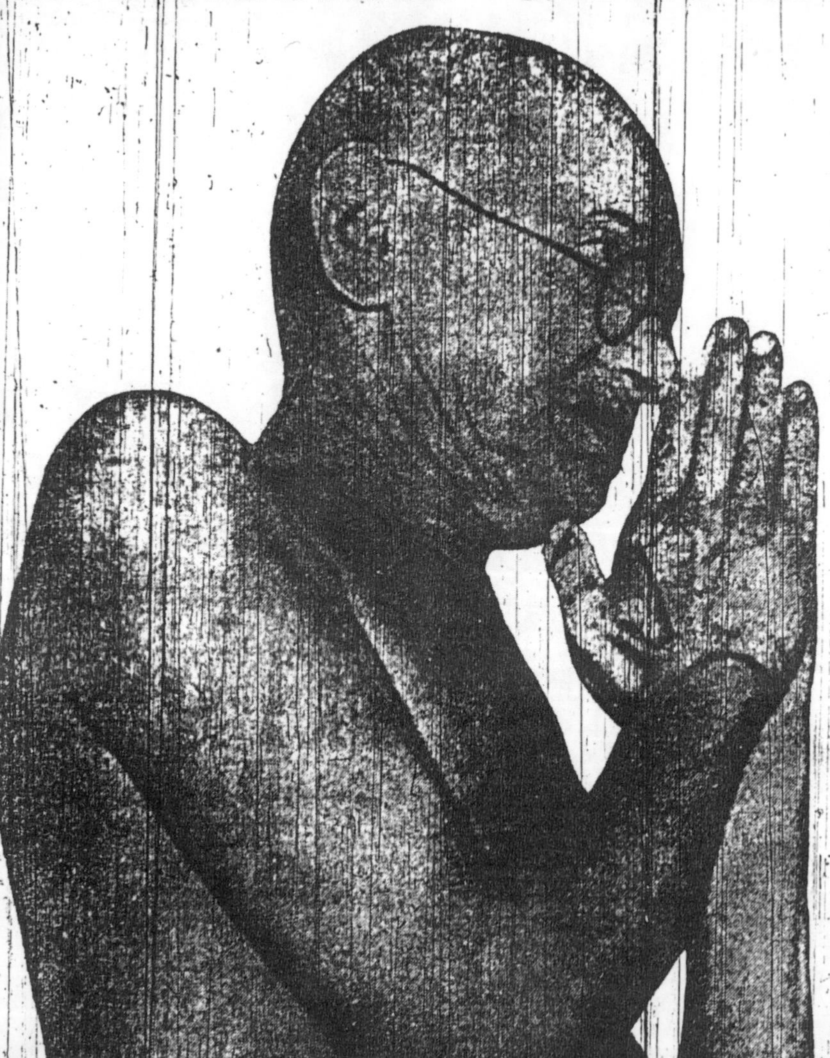

Out

FUN

MAHA
IN
Whil
as sh
f the c
Three
House. I

Th
He is stat
pronounc

cremat
"Ma
force." T
the Depu
ly inform

Pandit
Patel and
ed to Birla

The M
Governor-G
and Genera
Chief of th
Jam Saheb
rived imme

An A. P
was presen
was assassi

The cor
was anxiou
Gandhi to a
ing at five
dhi was de
emerged ou
ed by his c

tral or Western India. REGD. No. B111

of India

ISHED 1838

ARY 31, 1948. PRICE TWO ANNAS DO NOT PAY MORE

ASSINATED AT DELHI

HA FROM POONA FIRES POINT-BLANK RANGE

On Way To Prayer Meeting

, TODAY AT JUMNA GHAT: OUNTRY-WIDE GRIEF

From Our Special Representative

NEW DELHI, Jan. 30.

ANDHI WAS ASSASSINATED ON FRIDAY EVEN-

way to the prayer meeting, the Father of the Nation mes at point-blank range by a man who sprang out ion.

truck the Mahatma, and he was immediately taken to Birla way at 5-40—35 minutes after the crime.

sassin is Nathuram Vinayak Godse, a 36-year-old Maratha Hindu from Poona. irly well-known Marathi literature and his writings are reported to show his feelings. He had arrived in Delhi on Thursday evening.

andhi's funeral procession will leave Birla House tomorrow at 11 a.m. The place according to Vedic rites at Jumna Ghat about 4 p.m.

dhi's death shocked Delhi and the whole of India with "the impact of atomic -General, Lord Mountbatten, the Prime Minister, Pandit Jawaharlal Nehru, ister, Sardar Vallabhbhai Patel, and other Cabinet Ministers were immediate- agedy.

d Sardar ters rush-

tary to the H. Currie, nander-in- y, and the also ar- a House. ondent who ma Gandhi

bout 500 Mahatma ayer meet- atma Gan- utes. He se support- Aya Gan-

carried back to the room where Mahatma Gandhi had died. The lights were dimmed. The crowds silently melted away.

Members of Mahatma Gandhi's *ashram* and other intimate associates will sit beside his body throughout the night and chant hymns.

The news of Mahatma Gandhi's death flashed throughout the city in a few minutes. Business houses, shops, restaurants and cinema houses were immediately closed. A marriage procession, proceeding along Connaught Place, halted and dispersed silently. Traffic in the city came to a standstill. Men, women and children who were on their evening walk in Connaught Circus were

ARRANGEMENTS FOR FUNERAL

Running Commentary By A.I.R.

NEW DELHI, January 30:

The funeral procession of Mahatma Gandhi will start from Birla House at 11 a.m. tomorrow, pass through a number of localities reaching

IRREPARABLE LOSS TO MANKIND

The King's Message

LONDON, January 30.

HIS Majesty the King has sent the following message to the Governor-General of India, Lord Mountbatten:

"The Queen and I are deeply shocked by the news of the death of Mr. Gandhi. Will you please convey to the people of India our sincere sympathy in the irreparable loss which they, and indeed mankind, have suffered."—Reuter.

Delhi Takes Swift Security Steps

ARMY CHIEFS ASKED TO STAND BY

NEW DELHI, January 30.

WITHIN five hours of Mahatma Gandhi falling a victim to an assassin's bullet, security measures were speedily put into force by the Government of India throughout the country, and commanding officers in army units were ordered to be prepared to assist the civil authorities.—A.P.I.

DISTURBANCES IN BOMBAY

Curfew Imposed On

The morning of 31 January saw Delhi being emptied of its citizens. The news had spread like a shock wave and almost a million people had come out to line the route of Gandhi's funeral procession.

Paying tribute to the Father of the Nation: An overwhelmed crowd watches as the Mahatma's pyre is lit up.

Complying with Gandhi's wish that his remains be immersed in the rivers of India, his ashes were collected in twenty urns and later sent to different regions of the country.

GANDHI IS KILLED BY A HINDU; INDIA SHAKEN, WORLD MOURNS; 15 DIE IN RIOTING IN BOMBAY

MOHANDAS K. GANDHI

The New York Times

THREE SHOTS FIRED

Slayer Is Seized, Beaten After Felling Victim on Way to Prayer

DOMINION IS BEWILDERED

Nehru Appeals to the Nation to Keep Peace—U. S. Consul Assisted in Capture

By ROBERT TRUMBULL
Special to The New York Times.

NEW DELHI, India, Jan. 30—Mohandas K. Gandhi was killed by an assassin's bullet today. The assassin was a Hindu who fired three shots from a pistol at a range of three feet.

The 78-year-old Gandhi, who was the one person who held discordant elements together and kept some sort of unity in this turbulent land, was shot down at 5:15 P. M. as he was proceeding through the Birla House gardens to the pergola from which he was to deliver his daily prayer meeting message.

The assassin was immediately seized.

He later identified himself as Nathuram Vinayak Godse, 36, a Hindu of the Mahratta tribes in Poona. This has been a center of resistance to Gandhi's ideology.

Mr. Gandhi died twenty-five minutes later. His death left all India stunned and bewildered as to the direction that this newly independent nation would take without its "Mahatma" (Great Teacher).

The loss of Mr. Gandhi brings this country of 300,000,000 abruptly to a crossroads. Mingled with the sadness in this capital tonight was an undercurrent of fear and uncertainty, for now the strongest influence for peace in India that this generation has known is gone.

[Communal riots quickly swept Bombay when news of Mr. Gandhi's death was received. The Associated Press reported that fifteen persons were killed and more than fifty injured before an uneasy peace was estab-

All Britain Honors Gandhi; Truman Deplores Tragedy

By HERBERT L. MATTHEWS
Special to The New York Times.

LONDON, Jan. 30—Mohandas K. Gandhi, in death, has won the unanimous tribute of Britons—something he never hoped for or expected during his life. Nowhere outside of India has the shock of his assassination contained the feelings and emotions evident here today because Britain and Mr. Gandhi have been linked for good or evil over the last forty years.

In a special broadcast to the British people tonight the Prime Minister said:

"The voice which pleaded for peace and brotherhood has been silenced, but I am certain that his spirit will continue to animate his fellow countrymen and will plead for peace and concord."

[President Truman and Secretary Marshall expressed their

U. S. WARNS CITIZENS IN PALESTINE FIGHT

Consulate General Says They Face Loss of Passports and All Protective Rights

By SAM POPE BREWER
Special to The New York Times.

JERUSALEM, Jan. 30 — United

The Times London report of Mahatma Gandhi's assassination.

TWELVE

I do not desire that any mercy should be shown to me.

— NATHURAM GODSE

The news of Gandhi's death had spread like a shock wave, almost by its own power, and even before the All India Radio had broadcast it in a special bulletin a crowd had gathered at Birla House.

Darkness had fallen. No one noticed two men, muffled in grey shawls, slip out of the service gate. They did not have to walk far to find a tonga. It took them to Old Delhi railway station.

That night they slept on the platform among the refugees.

The next morning they saw Delhi as a city that was being emptied of its citizens. Out of its population of two million, at least a million had gone to line the route of Gandhi's funeral procession, 'a crowd far too great for either the police or the military to check,' as Alan Campbell-Johnson describes it. Apte and Karkare, whether they wanted to or not, became a part of that tide of humanity and witnessed Gandhi's body being taken past.

Actually they had hoped to call on one or two influential political leaders in Delhi whom they believed to subscribe to their thinking. Before them they would claim responsibility for Gandhi's assassination and demand money and assistance to go and live in some foreign country. But, even if there were any such people in Delhi, that day they were not approachable. All doors were closed. Even if, as they resolutely insisted for the rest of their days, Apte and Karkare never felt the slightest regret for what they had done, it is impossible that on that day they could not have been overwhelmed by the sheer enormity of their deed, and made conscious of how great Gandhi was, how puny they themselves were.

It was long past noon when they slunk back to the railway station, and even the vast station building wore a hushed and empty look. Knowing that the Bombay trains would be watched, they bought tickets for Allahabad by the Express which was due to leave at 3.30.

It is a comment on the lifelong habits of the two men who, even now, could have derived some small measure of comfort from being together, that Apte travelled second class and Karkare third.

Even before their train pulled out, the Secretary of the Hindu Mahasabha had received a telegram from Bombay which said: 'ARRIVING DELHI ARRANGE FOR DEFENCE N.D. APTE.'

Manorama had dutifully sent off the agreed telegram as soon as she had heard that something 'had happened to Nathuram'. But it seems that Apte had already realized that it was not going to be of much use as an alibi.

They reached Bombay on 2 February and went to the Sea Green (North) Hotel. All the rooms were full, and the best that the Manager, Mr Satyavan Rele, could do for them was to give them a bed each in two separate rooms which they would have to share with other occupants, and for which they would have to pay in advance. They accepted the beds, and the next morning moved to the Elphinstone Annexe Hotel where they managed to get a room to themselves. That same day they went and saw Karkare's friend G.M. Joshi in Thana. Joshi later told the police that, when he asked his visitors where they had been since he last saw them, Apte told him: 'It won't do us any good to tell you, and it would be too dangerous for you to know.'

Joshi seems to have been satisfied with the answer, and had no more questions to ask. At least that is the impression he gave the police.

When they had bolted from the Elphinstone Annexe, Apte and Karkare had jumped into a taxi and driven to the Arya Pathikashram at Sandhurst Bridge where, Apte confidently told Karkare, he could easily get a room because he knew the Manager, G.P. Dube. He left Karkare in the taxi with the luggage and went in to see Dube. But this time Dube had no room for Apte and, if anything, he went out of his way to be rude. Noticing that Apte was wearing a dhoti Dube sneeringly asked him 'why he had changed his dress from English style to Indian.' Apte had meekly answered, 'Such things happen.' Later Dube revealed that he could easily have given Apte a room but was put off by his 'dirty clothes and dishevelled appearance as if he had no change and wash for three days'.

When Apte returned to the taxi, looking crestfallen, Karkare for the first time felt that they were like hunted animals whom nothing could save.

They had themselves dropped at the Victoria Station, took a train to Thana and again turned up at Mr G.M. Joshi's house in Navpada, this time with their luggage.

No one can believe that even now Joshi was unaware that his two visitors were deeply involved in Gandhi's murder and were hiding from the police. Nonetheless, he stuck by them. They were desperately in need of a base while they decided on their next course of action, and Joshi's relationship with Karkare and Apte was such that he could never have turned them out of his house. Indeed, it is possible that it was he who now went to see a few friends on their behalf and brought a man called M.G. Ghaisas to see them.

Ghaisas came on the morning of the seventh, had a long talk with Apte and Karkare, and went to Poona to see what the situation was like there and to bring them news of their families. He returned on the morning of the ninth, and what he had to say must have persuaded Apte and Karkare that they could visit Poona without much risk. That same afternoon they caught a train to Poona.

Now they were on home ground – a great bustling city which had always been regarded as the headquarters of the Hindu Sanghatan movement, and where they had dozens of close friends. It was the ideal place to get lost in. Their friends hid them in their houses, commiserated with them, gave them food, and even brought some of Apte's clothes from his house.

If Karkare is to be believed, it was only after they were back in their own environment that they were both gnawed by a problem of conscience. Nathuram, Madanlal, Gopal, Badge, and even the solitary camp-follower Shankar had been arrested; so had Savarkar and dozens of others who had no direct connection with the crime. It somehow did not seem right that they themselves should still be free and go on incriminating more and more of their friends who were helping them. And still less did it seem right that they should try to escape.

Karkare told the author that he believed they could quite easily have crossed into the Hyderabad state which was barely a hundred miles away and which, in those days, was as good as 'foreign' territory. What was more, in Hyderabad he had dozens of friends who subscribed to their thinking on the Hindu revival movement and whom he had helped with money as well as weapons in their struggle to hold out against the marauding gangs of Kassim Rizvi.

'Then, again, we might have been able to flee to Goa,' Karkare added. 'But, even though we talked about all this often enough, we knew we were not going to do it.'

In his book, *Gandhi hatya ani Mee* (The Gandhi Assassination and I) Gopal Godse, too, speaks of the same sort of reluctance to escape. A day or two after Gandhi's murder, while Gopal was burning some letters, he heard a knock on the door. A Punjabi friend whom he calls Ramnath was standing outside.

'So it was your brother,' Ramnath said.

'Yes.'

'Listen. I think that you should vanish. I'll give you a letter to a friend in Delhi. He'll look after you and then you go and live among the refugees. You speak Punjabi well in any case. No one'll find you out if you're careful.'

And then Ramnath had offered him Rs 150 in case Gopal didn't have the money to go to Delhi.

But Gopal turned down the offer – not, he says, because he thought it was impractical, but because he just did not want to run away.

Apte and Karkare now found themselves in a similar situation. It is possible that they were incapable of rational thinking anyway, or were afflicted by a fit of bravado. They decided to return to Bombay instead.

On the morning of 11 February, they were back in Joshi's house, and acutely aware that the game of hide-and-seek was up.

Any hour, any minute, they expected to hear the sirens in the street or see a group of casual passers-by suddenly coming to a halt and deploying themselves all round the house. The suspense had the effect of making them desperate. They endured it for two days and then, as if drawn by a spell to meet trouble halfway, they decided to go and live in a hotel in Bombay. The date was 13 February, the day a Friday.

Apte boldly walked into the foyer of Pyrke's Apollo Hotel behind the Regal Cinema and demanded a room. The Apollo was one of several hotels in Bombay at which he and Manorama Salvi had stayed earlier as 'Mr and Mrs N.D. Apte.' The reception clerk, Candido Pinto, offered him room No. 29 on the second floor. Apte agreed to take it, went out and returned with Karkare and their luggage. He signed the register as 'N Kashinath' and put Karkare's name down as 'R Bishnu'. This was their act of surrender. Throughout that day and during much of the night, they waited for the sound of stealthy footsteps, a loud banging on their door.

No one came for them and towards the morning, they got a little sleep.

To use the telephone at Pyrke's Apollo guests have to go down to the reception desk. Soon after ten o'clock on the morning of the fourteenth, Apte and Karkare came down the steps and Apte made a telephone call. After that both went out.

Used as a 'love nest' on many occasions by Narayan Apte, he along with Karkare checked in Pyrke's Apollo Hotel, Bombay on 13 February. Inspector Haldipur arrested them from there on 14 February 1948.

At eleven a police party under inspector B.A. Haldipur came looking for the occupants of room No. 29. Pinto told Haldipur that both 'Mr Kashinath' and 'Mr Bishnu' had gone out.

The inspector sat down to wait. He had to wait a long time. Apte had asked Manorama to meet him at the hotel at six in the evening, and it was not till 5.30 that he returned. Haldipur saw a taxi stop at the door and glanced inquiringly at Pinto. Pinto gave him a nod.

Haldipur arrested Apte and sent him off under escort to the CID headquarters, and himself, decided to wait in the hope that Karkare would show up. Karkare, who had again gone to Thana and seen Joshi, came in at 8.25.

The register of retiring-rooms at Old Delhi railway station showed that Nathuram had held two tickets from Gwalior to Delhi, and with this information in hand the police, even with their 'soft' interrogation, seem to have made him admit that the pistol had been given by Dr Parchure of Gwalior. Armed with this information, Deputy superintendent N.Y. Duelkar of the Bombay CID arrived in Gwalior on 14 February to secure Parchure's arrest.

He discovered that Parchure was already under arrest, and that he was being held as a maximum-security prisoner in a dark cell in the ancient fort of Gwalior in which the Mogul emperors used to incarcerate *their* maximum-security prisoners.

The substance of the accusation against Parchure seems to have been that, when he heard that Gandhi had been assassinated, he had 'distributed sweets'. The distribution of sweets, in India, has the same sort of significance as standing a round of drinks would have in Europe, a gesture of celebration. If Parchure was indeed so stupid as to 'celebrate' Gandhi's death, he was by no means alone in doing so. There are crackpots everywhere, and even men like Gandhi have their detractors. The fact remains that in several towns, and particularly in some of the refugee camps, Gandhi's murder had been similarly celebrated. Parchure later denied that he had distributed sweets when Gandhi died, but admitted that he had said

The register of retiring-room at Old Delhi railway station showed that Godse had held two tickets from Gwalior to Delhi. This information helped the police to nail Sadashiv Parchure who had arranged the murder weapon. The picture shows the retiring-room as it is today.

plenty of things that were sure to raise the ire of the newly formed local Congress ministry.

In Gwalior, the Congress and the Hindu Mahasabha were rival parties of matching strength, and Parchure for one firmly believed that it was the government at Delhi that had dragooned the Maharaja of Gwalior into handing over power to the Congress instead of to his party. For their part, Congressmen in Gwalior hated Parchure with the true vehemence of suburban politicians. So when, following Gandhi's murder, there were communal disturbances in Gwalior, they seized the chance of locking up Parchure and his lieutenants under the Maintenance of Public Order Ordinance.

It was a reversal of fortune reminiscent of Mogul days. Parchure had been riding on the crest of a wave and gambling for the highest stakes. Only a couple of weeks earlier, he had confidently expected to be called in to head Gwalior's first-ever democratic government. Now he was in prison.

Gwalior at this lime was neither a princely state nor a part of India but something in-between. The maharaja's powers had passed to a Congress ministry, but the legislative formalities to merge Gwalior into the Indian Union had still not been completed. This meant that the police in India were still required by law to seek the extradition of criminals who might have escaped into Gwalior territory.

But neither the Bombay Police nor the Gwalior Police seem to have bothered unduly about this fine print in the procedure. Deulkar came and interrogated Parchure who, within two days, seems to have been persuaded to make a full confession. By this time Deulkar's superior, Deputy Inspector-General U.G. Rana, had also arrived in Gwalior. They both demanded that Parchure, who was to be charged as a member of the conspiracy to murder Gandhi, should be transferred to the 'Dominion Police'. This was done on 17 February, 'without completing the extradition proceedings'.

This unseemly hurry might have cost the police dearly. Later, they tried to make out that they did not need to have Parchure extradited in any case on the grounds that, even though he was born in Gwalior, he happened to be a citizen of 'the dominion of India'. To support this contention, they produced Parchure's genealogical tree showing that his ancestors had lived in India, that his father had passed the matriculation examination of the Bombay University in 1879, and that his family had paid local taxes in the Bombay province as far back as 1855.

On 17 February, Nagarvala received a telephone call from Delhi telling him that he had been appointed as the superintendent on special duty to conduct the investigation into Gandhi's murder. The appointment was clearly a mark of special approbation; for a police officer, it was nothing less than the chance of a lifetime to prove his professional abilities.

By this time, all the principal suspects were in his hands. The only three wanted men who were still 'absconding' were very much on the edge of things. They were G.S. Dandvate, who had sold the Beretta to Nathuram; Gangadhar Jadhav, a lieutenant of Parchure's; and S.D. Sharma, the man who had given Badge a .32 revolver in exchange for Nathuram's .22 pistol.

To judge by the evidence of four of the men who figured in this case – Madanlal, Gopal, Karkare and Badge – the process of building up a case of this nature is largely a matter of extorting confessions from the persons already in police hands, and then setting about trying to unearth evidence to sustain these confessions. For instance, if a suspect revealed that he had taken a meal in a certain restaurant, the police then went to that restaurant and as often as not managed to discover some waiter, or at least another customer, who could swear to having seen the man in the restaurant. If there are flashes of inspiration, or feats of intellectual deduction, at best they only supplement this process of investigation through third-degree.

Of course, the evidence of convicted men must not be relied upon too heavily in passing judgement upon the methods employed by the keepers of the law, even if the keepers of the law themselves sought to make out that

Facing page: Jamshed Dorab Nagarvala, or 'Jimmy' to his friends was Bombay's Deputy Commissioner in charge of the Intelligence Branch. It was Nagarvala who always believed that there was no conspiracy to kill Gandhi but the failed attempt of 20 January was also carried out to kidnap him. After the assassination, he was appointed Superintendent of the Delhi Police, which was investigating the murder.

No.16/9/48-Police

Government of India,

Ministry of Home Affairs,

New Delhi, the 19th February 1948.

NOTIFICATION

Mr.J.D.Nagarvala, I.P., Deputy Commissioner of Police, Bombay City, is appointed as Superintendent of Police, Delhi, in addition to his own duties, with effect from the 31st January 1948.

Sd/- U.K.Ghoshal

Deputy Secretary to the Govt.of India

No.16/9/48-Police

Copy forwarded for information to -

(1) Chief Commissioner, Delhi

(2) Accountant General, Central Revenues

(3) Govt of Bombay

(4) Mr.J.D.Nagarvala

Assistant Secretary to the Govt. of India

one out of the same set of criminals, Badge, was incapable of falsehoods and made him their star witness. Truth, as a Sanskrit proverb states, has many sides. But the fact remains that whatever methods they used, the police had obtained the full confessions or, as they are officially termed, 'statements' of all the accused persons in their custody except Savarkar. Shankar Kistayya, ostensibly of his own volition, guided them to the spot in the grounds of the Mahasabha Bhavan in Delhi where he, at Badge's bidding, had buried the unused grenades and explosives after their first attempt to kill Gandhi had failed; and Apte, equally willingly, showed them the tree which Nathuram had used for target practice in Delhi and even led his captors to Gwalior and the enclosure at the side of Parchure's house to show the door against which they had tried out the Beretta before buying it.

Both the tree trunk and the door panel were made exhibits in the case.

Thus, bit by bit, what was revealed in the 'statements' was painstakingly rebuilt by prodigious effort into cases that the most adroit of defence lawyers could not dent.

The exception was Savarkar.

The mass of papers seized from his house had revealed nothing that could remotely be connected with Gandhi's murder and, of course, even under arrest Savarkar was too big a personality to be subjected to the standard methods of 'dragging out' information.

However, Nagarvala had convinced himself that Savarkar was the organizer of the plot to kill Gandhi and was desperate to be proved right. It is also possible that the entire police organization believed, rightly or wrongly, that 'someone up there' would be highly gratified if Savarkar could be implicated.

In his book on the assassination, Gopal Godse writes of the difficulty he experienced in trying to convince his interrogators that he had not visited Savarkar on his way to Delhi. By the time he was able to do so 'no pan of my body was free from bruises'.

His problem was that he really had no idea where Savarkar's house was and thus could not, even through terror of pain, evade the beatings by admitting whatever they wanted him to because, 'even a false admission would have instantly been followed by other questions. How had I gone to the house, who else was there, what did we talk about, at what time? It was just not possible for me to weave a credible story.'

The one man among the captives who looked likely to co-operate with the police in helping them to establish Savarkar's involvement was Digambar Badge, and he actually was as good as two separate witnesses because, even in police custody, Shankar still remained wholly dependent upon Badge and could be relied upon to say whatever Badge told him to.

But in this the police were wrong and Badge was far from cooperative. In his testimony at the trial, he asserted that he 'regarded Savarkar as a Devta' (incarnation of God), and twenty-seven years later he still professes to hold Savarkar in the same veneration.[9]

It is difficult to see Badge as a man who sets much store by conventional norms of veracity, and still less as the sort of person who would remain blindly loyal to a cause or person, but perhaps he did venerate Savarkar with the sort of unquestioning devotion that only the most uncultivated of people are capable of developing towards their heroes. Indeed, the bulk of Gandhi's own following was made up of such people. Whatever it was, Badge insisted to the author that even though he had blurted out the full story of the plot as far as he knew it, without much persuasion, he had put up a valiant struggle against being made to testify against Savarkar. And even Gopal Godse. who has no reason to regard Badge with friendliness, mentions how the police found him 'extremely difficult' over this issue. 'But then,' Gopal concludes, 'the interrogators possessed the ability to make even a dumb man articulate.'

In the end Badge gave in. He agreed to say on oath that he saw Nathuram and Apte with Savarkar and that Savarkar, within Badge's hearing, had blessed their venture with the words, '*Yeshaswi noun ya*'.** After that Badge's troubles ceased. Even while in custody, he lived as a sort of favoured guest of the Police Department. He was plied with meat, eggs, sweets, cigarettes and liqour, and put on a stipend. Shankar also came in for preferential treatment.

Poor Shankar must have been more bewildered than ever. Almost without knowing what was happening, he had found himself facing a life sentence. He was incapable of taking in the situation. The things he came out with in the sworn statement that he made in the court make one wonder whether they were hallucinations or sobering glimpses of the inner workings of police methods. He says:

> Nagarvala used to meet Badge and ask: "Have you instructed Shankar?" and to the Jailer he said, "If he instructs Shankar give Badge liquor." Badge was instructing me as to what to say. I had told Badge, "When I do not know anything why should I say all this?"
>
> Badge answered that he had to say all this because it was the only way to make sure that he would be acquitted. He used to coach Shankar assiduously and make him repeat all that he was told to say.

Shankar goes on:

> One night Nagarvala came and ... asked Badge, "Have you given Shankar enough practice?" [and then] asked me in Hindustani what I had to say. I committed 5-6 mistakes.

Apparently, when Shankar revealed all this to the court-appointed counsel who had to defend him and the Jailer somehow came to know of it, he got angry with him and berated him and 'Badge slapped me before the Jailer.'

At least that was the sort of language Shankar could understand. After that he made no difficulties and learned his role diligently. And at the end of his statement, after making a plea that he knew nothing and had no connection with the case, Shankar, as though seeking proof of good behaviour, ends with the admission: 'Whatever Badge has instructed me to say I have said.'

The trial opened in Delhi in the searing heat of midsummer. It was held not in a common courtroom but in a spacious hall in Delhi's Mogul stronghold, the Red Fort.

And, if the courtroom was something out of the ordinary, so was the court itself; it was specially constituted by an order of the government and empowered, by another order, to exercise a special power that Delhi courts had not hitherto possessed – that of tendering a full pardon to an accused in a murder case.

The purpose of this cumbersome legislative provision was to make it possible for the trial judge to pardon Badge in advance, and this he promptly did. From then on Badge, from being an accused, became 'the Approver'.

And, almost in line with the 'special' nature of everything else, even the accused persons were housed in barracks within the Red Fort which, by another government notification, was declared to be 'a prison'.

Eight men were charged with murder, conspiracy to commit murder, and other charges connected with violations of the Explosive Substances Act. They were Nathuram Godse, Narayan Apte, Vishnu Karkare, Madanlal Pahwa, Gopal Godse, Vinayak Savarkar, Dattatray Parchure and Shankar Kistayya.

Nathuram admitted that he had killed Gandhi, but the others pleaded 'not guilty' to all the charges. The trial went on for nearly eight months while the summer turned to winter. On 10 February the judge, Atma Charan, delivered his judgement. Only Savarkar was acquitted. Of the remaining seven, Nathuram and Apte were sentenced to death, and the others given sentences of imprisonment for life.

Shankar, Gopal Godse says, looked dazed. He found it altogether impossible to comprehend how the man for whom he had done whatever he was accused of doing – Badge – had got off, while he himself was to spend his life in jail. Gopal Godse also mentions that, much to everyone's surprise, the only man who burst into violent sobs when he heard the judgement was Badge.

The convicted men were sent to the Central Jail in Ambala to serve their sentences. From there all, including Nathuram, filed appeals in the

Punjab High Court against this judgement. Nathuram's appeal was not against his own sentence, but against the charge of conspiracy for which the others had been convicted. Four months later, the High Court pronounced its judgement. Parchure and Shankar were both 'given the benefit of doubt' and acquitted, but the sentences of the other were confirmed.

November 15 was fixed as the day for the hanging. On the day before, Nathuram and Apte were allowed to be visited by relatives and close friends. Apte, who was allowed only half an hour to see his wife, found that she was weeping bitterly; he had to admonish her: 'You have the rest of your life to weep; but we have only half an hour to talk about practical things.'

She stopped weeping and listened.

The relatives had brought them things to eat, with which they supplemented their last meals. After dinner, the other three prisoners, Gopal, Madanlal and Karkare, were allowed to go and sit in the condemned cell and keep them company. Together they recited the second, the eleventh and the eighteenth cantos of the Gita.

By that time it was ten o'clock; time for the others to go back to their cells.

But at dawn the next morning they again went to the condemned cells and read more verses from the Gita. After that, Nathuram and Apte had their baths. Gopal asked his brother: '*Anna* [elder brother] are you going to shave?'

Nathuram rubbed his hand over his chin. 'I shaved last night. It's not as though I'm going to a party.'

As a last courtesy, the prison warders brought in coffee for Nathuram and tea for the others, and they all drank together. But now the others had to leave. The condemned men had to be 'prepared' for the hanging. The black robes in which they were to be dressed were brought in by the guards.

Nathuram and Apte came out of their cells, wearing black and each carrying in his hands a map of undivided India, the saffron flag of the Hindu movement, and a copy of the Gita. This was the first time they had been allowed out of their maximum-security cells so early in the morning, and

Apte drew Nathuram's attention to the clear cold morning sunlight of the Punjab winter.

'Yes, like the sun in Simla,' Nathuram commented.

As they walked towards the hanging shed, they both shouted: '*Akhand Bharat Amar Rahe*!' ('Long live undivided India!')

They were guided towards the single gallows that had been erected for them, with two loops neatly arranged to slip over their heads, suspended from the same beam. They went towards it, singing a Sanskrit verse in unison which had the refrain: 'Even as we die, we salute you, our land of birth.'

They were cremated with Hindu rites in the open ground outside the prison wall. And in order that no sort of monument may ever come on the place of cremation, in time-honoured Mogul style, the entire field was ploughed and planted with grass. Also, even though, according to ritual, their ashes were immersed in a nearby river, the Ghaggar, it was all done under a strict cloak of secrecy so that no one should ever discover the actual spot where the ashes were thrown.

Following pages: 'While the whole nation mourned Gandhi's untimely death, the police took up the investigation of by far the most dastardly crime they had ever had occasion to handle. As the enquiries proceeded, it transpired that Nathuram Godse was not the only person concerned in the murder. His act of shooting Gandhiji was the culmination of a widespread and carefully laid conspiracy in which several persons were involved and declared the case ripe for trial.' Justice G.D. Khosla
Seen in the picture are Vishnu Karkare (extreme right, leaning over the dock); Narayan Apte (second from right); Nathuram Godse (sitting third from right) and Digambhar Badge (sitting in the second row, extreme left).

Charged with murder, conspiracy to commit murder and offences punishable under the Arms Act, the trail started on 22 June 1948, before Atma Charan, a senior member of the judicial branch of the Indian Civil Service. Held inside the Red Fort, Delhi the court was open to the public and the Press. Arguments of counsel lasted a whole month and the court pronounced judgement on 10 February, 1949. Seen in the picture is Judge Atma Charan.

Seen in the picture above are (sitting in the dock): Vishnu Karkare (first from right), Narayan Apte (second from right), Nathuram Godse (extreme left); second row: Gopal Godse (first from left); and in the third row: Veer Savarkar (second from left).
Following pages 342-345: The highlight of the appeal for mercy was the statement delivered by Nathuram Godse in his defence. He spoke for hours about the facts, the motives that had prompted him to take the Mahatma's life. Excerpts from his statement.

PART V.

CLIMAX OF ANTI-NATIONAL APPEASEMENT.

112. The day on which I decided to remove Gandhiji from the political stage, it was clear to me that personally I shall be lost to everything that could be mine. I am not a moneyed person but I did have a place of honour and respect amongst those known as middle class society. I have been in the public life of my Province and the service that I have been able to render so far has given me a place of honour and respect amongst my people. Ideas of culture and civilisation are not strange to me. I had in my view before me some schemes of constructive work to be taken in hand in my future life and I felt I had enough strength and enthusiasm to undertake them and carry them out successfully. I have maintained robust health and I do not suffer from any bodily defect and I am not addicted to any vice. Although I myself am not a much-learned man, I have a great regard and admiration for the learned.

114. About the year 1932 late Dr. Hedgewar of Nagpur founded the Rashtriya Swayam Sevak Sangha in Maharashtra also. His oration greatly impressed me and I joined the Sangha as a volunteer thereof. I am one of those volunteers of Maharashtra who joined the Sangha in its initial stage. I also worked for a few years on the intellectual side in the Province of Maharashtra. Having worked for the uplift of the Hindus I felt it necessary to take part in the political activities of the country for the protection of the just rights of Hindus. I therefore left the Sangha and joined the Hindu Mahasabha.

... part in public life. By nature I am not a person of violent temperament. The approver Badge in his deposition at Page 225 has stated that I took out a knife to stab Mr. Bhopatkar. This statement is totally false Mr. Bhopatkar is at present leading the lawyers defending the accused. Had I made any such assault as described by the approver could he have come forward to render us assistance in our defence ? If that alleged incident were true, I should have least thought of taking the help of Mr. Bhopatkar.

117. Those, who personally know me, take me as a person of quiet temperament. But when the top-rank leaders of the Congress with the consent of Gandhiji divided and tore the country—which we consider as a deity of worship—my mind became full with the thoughts of direful anger.

I wish to make it clear that I am not an enemy of the Congress. I have always regarded that body as the premier institution which has worked for the political uplift of the country. I had and have my differences with its leaders. This will be clearly seen from my letter addressed to Veer Savarkar on 28th February 1938 (RX. D/30) which is in my hand and signed by me and I admit its contents.

118. There was no enmity between Gahdhiji and myself on any personal grounds. To those who speak of Gandhiji's honest motive in supporting the Pakistan, I have only to say that I had nothing but the purest interest of our nation at my heart in taking the extreme step against the person of Gandhiji, who was the most responsible and answerable person for the terrible events culminating in the creation of Pakistan. I could foresee the result of my action against the life of Gandhiji and did very well realise that the moment the people came to know about it they would change their view about me inspite of the circumstances. My status and honour in the society and the sympathies which the people entertained for me will be smashed completely. I fully realised that I would be looked upon as the most despicable fellow in the society.

30

119. I had a very good idea about fiery attacks that would be launched against me in the Press. But I never thought that I could be cowed down by the fire poured against me by the Press. For had the Indian Press impartially criticised the anti-national policy carried on by Gandhiji and had they impressed upon the people that the interest of the nation was far greater than the whim of any individual howsoever great he may be, Gandhiji and his followers could never have dared concede Pakistan to the Muslims as easily as has been done. The Press had displayed such weakness and submission to the High Command of the Congress that if allowed the mistakes of leaders pass away freely and unnoticed and made vivisection easy by their policy. The fear about such Press—weak and subservient as it was could not therefore dislodge me from my resolve.

40

122. Every day that dawned brought forth the news about thousands of Hindus being massacred, Sikhs numbering 15,000 having been shot dead, hundreds of women torn of their clothes being made naked and taken into procession and that Hindu women were being sold in the market places like cattle. Thousands and thousands of Hindus had to run away for their lives and they had lost everything of theirs. A long line of refugees extending over the length of 40 miles was moving towards the Indian Union. How was this terrible happening being counter-acted by the Union Government? O! by throwing bread to the refugees from the air. !!

30

124. When all these happenings were taking place in Pakistan, Gandhiji did not even by a single word protest and censure the Pakistan Government or the Muslims concerned. The Muslim atrocities resorted to in Pakistan to root out the Hindu culture and the Hindu society have been entirely due to the teachings of Gandhiji and his behaviour. If the Indian politics had been handled in a practical manner there would never have been the terrible human slaughter as has taken place—a thing without any precedent in History.

60

125. The most noticeable and important thing is that Gandhiji never cared for the opinion of the people so far as Muslims were concerned. His theme of non-violence had now been deeply soaked in human blood and it was impossible for people to entertain any idea in favour of Pakistan. So long as there is a theocratic State and Government by the side of Indian Union, the peace and tranquility of the Union shall ever remain in danger. But inspite of all these facts, Gandhiji had taken in his hand the task of a propaganda which 10 even the staunchest adherent of the Muslim League would scarcely have been able to do for stopping the spread of unfavourable opinion about Pakistan in the minds of the people.

126. About this very time he resorted to his last fast unto death. Every condition given by him for giving up the fast is in favour of Muslims and against the Hindus.

Gandhiji himself has said about these 55 crores that it is always very difficult to make any Government to alter its decisions. But the Government have altered and changed their original decision of withholding the paymet of Rs. 55 crores to Pakistan and the reason for doing so was his fast unto death. (Gandhiji's sermon at Prayer-meeting held on or about the 21st of January 1948). The decision to withhold the payment of Rs. 55 crores to Pakistan was taken up by our Government which claims to be the people's Government. But this decision of the people's Government was reversed to suit the tune 40 of Gandhiji's fast. It was evident to my mind that the force of public opinion was nothing but a trifle when compared with the leanings of Gandhiji favourable to Pakistan.

135. Briefly speaking, I thought to myself and foresaw that I 40 shall be totally ruined and the only thing that I could expect from the people would be nothing but hatred and that I shall have lost all my honour even more valuable than my life, if I were to kill Gandhiji. But at the same time I felt that the Indian politics in the absence of Gandhiji would surely be practical, able to retaliate, and would be powerful with armed forces No doubt my own future would be totally ruined but the nation would be saved from the inroads of Pakistan. People may even call me and dub me as devoid of any sense or foolish, but the nation would be free to follow the course founded on reason which I consider to be necessary for sound nation- 50 building. After having fully considered the question, I took the final decision in the matter but I did not speak about it to any one whatsoever. I took courage in my both hands and I did fire the shots at Gandhiji on 30th January 1948 on the prayer-grounds in Birla House.

136. There now remains hardly anything for me to say. If devotion to one's country amounts to a sin, I admit I have committed that sin. If it is meritorious, I humbly claim the merit thereof. I fully and confidently believe that if there be any other Court of justice beyond the one founded by the mortals, my act will not be taken as unjust. If after the death there be no such place to reach or 60

to go to, there is nothing to be said. I have resorted to the action I did purely for the benefit of the humanity. I do say that my shots were fired at the person whose policy and action had brought rack and ruin and destruction to lacs of Hindus.

137. Really speaking, my life also came to an end simultaneously with the shot fired by me at Gandhiji. Since then I have been passing my days as if in trance and meditation. Whatever I have seen and observed during this time has given me complete satisfaction.

139. I am prepared to concede that Gandhiji did undergo sufferings for the sake of the nation. He did bring about an awakening in the minds of the people. He also did nothing for personal gain but it pains me to say that he was not honest enough to acknowledge the defeat and failure of the principle of non-violence on all sides. I have read the lives of other intelligent and powerful Indian patriots who have made sacrifices even greater than those done by Gandhiji. I have even seen personally some of them. But whatever that may be, I shall bow in respect to the service done by Gandhiji to the country, and to Gandhiji himself for the said service, and before I fired the shots I actually wished him and bowed to him in reverence. But I do maintain that even this servant of the country had no right to vivisect the country--the image of our worship—by deceiving the people. But he did it all the same. There was no legal machinery by which such an offender could be brought to book and it was therefore that I resorted to the firing of shots at Gandhiji as that was the only meet thing to do.

140. Had this act not been done by me, of course it would have been better for me. But circumstances were beyond my control. So strong was the impulse of my mind that I felt that this man should not be allowed to meet a natural death so that the world may know that he had to pay the penalty of his life for his unjust, anti-national and dangerous favouritism towards a fanatical section of the country. I decided to put an end to this matter and to further massacre of lacs of Hindus for no fault of theirs. May God now pardon him for his egoistic nature which proved to be too disastrous for the beloved sons of this Holy Land.

148. I have now finished but before I sit down I most sincerely and respectfully express my gratitude to Your Honour for the patient hearing given, courtesy shown and facilities given to me. Similarly I express my gratitude to my legal advisers and counsel for their legal help in this great trial. I have no ill-will towards the Police officers concerned with this case. I sincerely thank them for the kindness and the treatment given by them to me. Similarly, I also thank the Jail authorities for the good treatment given by them.

149. It is a fact that in the presence of a crowd numbering 300 to 400 people I did fire shots at Gandhiji in open daylight. I did not make any attempt to run away; in fact. I never entertained any idea of running away. I did not try to shoot myself. It was never my intention to do so for it was my ardent desire to give vent to my thoughts in an open Court.

150. My confidence about the moral side of my action has not been shaken even by the criticism levelled against it on all sides. I have no doubt honest writers of history will weigh my act and find the true value thereof on some day in future.

50 NATHURAM V. GODSE—

He is found 'guilty' under section 120-B of the Indian Penal Code read with section 302 of the Code, under section 19 (*c*) of the Indian ...

... with section 6 of the Act and (6) to death under section 302 of the Indian Penal Code—he is to be hanged by the neck till he is dead: the sentences of imprisonment shall run concurrently.

* * *

NARAYAN D. APTE—

He is found 'guilty' under section 120-B of the Indian Penal Code read with section 302 of the Code, under section 19 (*c*) of the ...

... Substances Act read with section 6 of the Act and (6) to death under section 109 of the Indian Penal Code read with section 302 of the Code—he is to be hanged by the neck till he is dead: the sentences of imprisonment shall run concurrently. 40

* * *

VISHNU R. KARKARE—

He is found 'guilty' under section 120-B of the Indian Penal Code read with section 302 of the Code, under section 114 of the Indian ...

... Act read with section 6 of the Act and (5) to transportation for life under section 109 of the Indian Penal Code read with section 302 of the Code: the sentences of imprisonment shall run concurrently and concurrent with the sentence of transportation for life.

* * *

MADANLAL K. PAHWA—

He is found 'guilty' under section 120-B of the Indian Penal Code read with section 302 of the Code, under section 5 of the Explosive ...

... Penal Code read with section 302 of the Code: the sentences of imprisonment shall run concurrently and concurrent with the sentence of transportation for life.

* * *

SHANKAR KISTAYYA—

He is found 'guilty' under section 120-B of the Indian Penal Code read with section 302 of the Code, under section 5 of the Explosive ...

... of Criminal Procedure: the sentences of imprisonment shall run concurrently and concurrent with the sentence of transportation for life.

* * *

GOPAL V. GODSE—

He is found 'guilty' under section 120-B of the Indian Penal Code read with section 302 of the Code, under section 5 of the Explosive Sub-life under section 109 of the Indian Penal Code read with section 302 of the Code : the sentences of imprisonment shall run concurrently and concurrent with the sentence of transportation for life.

* * *

DATTATRAYA S. PARCHURE—

He is found 'guilty' under section 120-B of the Indian Penal Code read with section 302 of the Code and under section 109 of the Indian Penal Code read with section 302 of the Code, is convicted thereunder and is sentenced to transportation for life under section 109 of the Indian Penal Code read with section 302 of the Code.

He is found 'not guilty' of the remaining offences as specified in the charge, and is acquitted thereunder.

* * *

VINAYAK D. SAVARKAR—

He is found 'not guilty' of the offences as specified in the charge, and is acquitted thereunder : he is in custody, and be released forthwith unless required otherwise.

I may bring to the notice of the Central Government the slackness of the Police in the investigation of the case during the period between 20th January, 1948 and 30th January, 1948. The Delhi Police had obtained a detailed statement from Madalal K. Pahwa soon after his arrest on 20th January, 1948. The Bombay Police had also been reported the statement of Dr. J. C. Jain that he had made to the Hon'ble Mr. Morarji Desai on 21st January, 1948. The Delhi Police and the Bombay Police had contacted each other soon after these two statements had been made. Yet the Police miserably failed to derive any advantage from these two statements. Had the slightest keenness been shown in the investigation of the case at that stage the tragedy probably could have been averted.

All arms, ammunition and explosives and the articles connected therewith brought on the record of the case are confiscated to the Crown under section 517 of the Code of Criminal Procedure. Exs. 14, 28, 29 and 30 are the shells of the hand grenades that had been distributed at the Marina Hotel on 20th January, 1948. Ex. 39 is the automatic pistol with which Mahatma Gandhi was shot dead on 30th January, 1948. Exs. 9, 10 and 55 are the empty cartridge-cases of the cartridges that had been fired at Mahatma Gandhi on 30th January, 1948. Exs. 11 and 12 are the spent-bullets that had passed right through the body of Mahatma Gandhi on 30th January, 1948. No action in regard thereto be taken without first consulting the Central Government. They may perhaps be required for the National Museum

RED FORT, DELHI :
February 10, 1949.

ATMA CHARAN,
I.C.S.,
Judge, Special Court.

The final order: The death sentence and life imprisonment. Excerpts from Judge Atma Charan's final judgement in the trial at Red Fort.

IN THE HIGH COURT OF JUDICATURE FOR THE PROVINCE OF EAST PUNJAB AT SIMLA.

CRIMINAL APPELLATE SIDE

CRIMINAL APPEAL NO. 66 of 1949.

PRESENT:-

MR. JUSTICE BHANDARI,
MR. JUSTICE ACHHRU RAM,
AND
MR. JUSTICE KHOSLA.

Appeal from the order of Atma Charan, Esquire, Judge, Special Court, Red Fort, Delhi, dated the 10th February, 1949 convicting the appellant.

Nathu Ram V. Godse, ... Convict-Appellant,

Versus

Rax, ... Respondent.

Charge:- Under Section 120-B of the Indian Penal Code read with Section 302 of the Code, under Section 19(c) of the Indian Arms Act or in the alternative under Section 114 of the Indian Penal Code read with Section 19(c) of the Indian Arms Act, under Section 19(f) of the Indian Arms Act, under Section 5 of the Explosive Substances Act or in the alternative under Section 5 of the Explosive Substances Act read with Section 6 of the Act, under Section 4(b) of the Explosive Substances Act read with Section 6 of the Act, under Section 3 of the Explosive Substances Act read with Section 6 of the Act, under Section 115 of the Indian Penal Code read with Section 302 of the Code and under Section 302 of the Indian Penal Code.

The judgement given by the appeal court. Excerpts from the final statement of Justice G.D. Khosla.

I concur with the conclusions arrived at by my learned brothers Bhandari and Achhru Ram JJ. I would accept the appeals of Dattatraya S.Parchure and Shankar Kistayya and set aside their convictions upon all the charges. I would dismiss all the remaining appeals and uphold the convictions and sentences awarded to Nathuram V.Godse, Narayan D.Apte, Gopal V.Godse, Madanlal Pahwa and Vishnu R.Karkare. I wish, however, to dissociate myself from the recommendation for mercy made by my learned brother Achhru Ram J. in favour of Madanlal Pahwa. Pahwa took a very prominent part in the plan of conspiracy as originally conceived. The success of the original plan depended to a great measure on the number of persons in the conspiracy, each one of whom was assigned a specific role. Madanlal did not hesitate to play the part assigned to him and he did this with full consciousness of the consequences that might have followed. The fact that the plan of the 20th January miscarried does not, in my opinion, extenuate Pahwa's guilt. I am not, therefore, prepared to recommend that the sentence awarded to him should be commuted.

Sd/- G.D.Khosla,

Judge.

21st June 1949.

Words: 1,65,962.

Fees: 311-4-0

NOTES

1 In 1949, Akbar Khan became the Chief of the General Staff of the Pakistani Army, and in 1950 he was imprisoned for organizing a military coup.

2 Mountbatten did entreat Gandhi to tack on the Rs 55 crores payment to Pakistan as a condition for ending his fast. He told this to Larry Collins and Dominic Lapierre (Vide their "*Mountbatten and the Partition of India*) 'I shall make no bones about it. I am the man who suggested the Rs 55 Crores to Gandhi. He hadn't even heard about it.'

3 Digambar Badge, who, for the help he rendered the police as The Approver in the Gandhi murder trial, was given a lifetime pension and a tiny official flat in the compound of Bombay's CID Headquarters, still runs a one-man business making 'permitted' weapons. The two products he is most proud of are a belt made of thin steel which doubles as a sword, and the *waghnak* or tiger's claw, which can be hidden in a man's fist and used to rip open an enemy's stomach. He sold me a *waghnak* for the left hand. 'Because you are a writer', he explained, 'you can pretend to go on writing with the right hand and strike with your left.'

4 Alas, only too true. In 1976 or 77, I tried to track her down, and found she lived as a poor relation with her brother, a medical practioner in a small township called Sonai, about 20 miles from Ahmednagar, and earned a pittance as a saleswoman in the local chemist's shop. When I and a friend entered the shop she just ran away and hid herself. Her brother Dr Salvi, who tried to reassure her that I meant no harm, did not succeed in breaking her resolve not to come out again. Manorama was just as much a victim of the Gandhi-murder conspiracy as the principal conspirators. I found out from Godse's family that her child from Apte... I think a girl... did not survive childhood, and may have been yet another casualty of the deed, subjected to horrifying social ostraicism and invective.

5 In the last week of August 1974. I saw Badge several times and, in particular, questioned him about the veracity of his testimony against Savarkar. I quote his answer

from my notes: 'I never heard Savarkar say "*Yeshaswi houn ya*!" In fact, when we passed through Bombay on our way to Delhi Savarkar did not even see them [Nalhuram and Apte].'

6 This was how I saw him, on my way to the office, on the morning of 30 January. M. M.

7 The confession bristled with inconsistencies and glaring procedural flaws. It was as though in their zeal to make their case against Parchure absolutely watertight, the police had overreached themselves. The deplorable part in this affair is that a magistrate who is said to be a tool of justice had been roped in to assist in the exercise. Ironically, the extra bracing sought to be given to the 'Confession' to make it stick in a court of law which necessitated blatantly self-incriminatory statements being put into the mouth of the confessor, gave it a 'doctored' look; it was all too well-engineered to ring true, and ultimately had the contrary effect, of vitiating the very strong circumstantial evidence against Dr Parchure. For instance this part: 'I mentioned to my brother Krishnarao Parchure that two gentlemen had come to me with a plot to kill Gandhi at Delhi, and that I had arranged a pistol for them.' It screamed of artifice designed to establish that Parchure had provided the pistol to his visitors in the full knowledge that it was going to be used to murder Gandhi.

At the Red Fort trial, Parchure's lawyer, P.L. Inamdar, had a wonderful time discrediting the confession. He charged that the magistrate who had taken it down, Mr R.B. Atal, had violated professional norms in that he had not recorded the confession in the prison cell in the Gwalior Fort but had worked on it in his own house and under the guidance of Deputy Superintendent Deulkar. Pouncing on Atal's own sworn testimony that he had spent 'Not more than three hours in Parchure's cell' to record it, Inamdar proceeded to establish that it was just not possible to record a statement of such length while still observing the requirements of judicial procedure within less than five hours!

But these arguments, and the glaring inconsistances in the body of the confession itself, don't seem to have persuaded the trial judge, Atma Charan, into dismissing the confession as not being admissible as evidence. Parchure was given a life sentence. It was later, during the hearing of the appeal in the Punjab High Court that all three sitting Judges agreed with Inamdar that Parchure's confession was not admissible as evidence. Indeed one of the judges, Justice Achroo Ram, scoffed: 'Who will believe it. Think of a magistrate who says all this? It is an absurd exaggeration.' In the High Court, Parchure was let off, given the benefit of doubt.

8 To the author. By then, of course, Savarkar was dead.

9 As he told the author.

INDEX

ABOUT THE AUTHOR

Manohar Malgonkar was born in 1913 in a royal family, which had its roots in Goa. After graduating from Bombay University, he served in the Maratha Light Infantry. A big game hunter, civil servant, mine owner and farmer, he also stood for Parliament in the early seventies. Most of this activity was during momentous times of Indian history – the build up to independence and its aftermath – often the setting for his works.

The socio-historical milieu of those times forms the backdrop of his works, which are usually full of action and adventure, reflective, in some way, of his own life. His works spans all genres from novels to biographies to history books.

Some of them are *Distant Drum*, *Combat of Shadows*, *The Princes*, *A Bend in the Ganges*, *The Devil's Wind*, *The Garland Keepers*, *Bombay Beware*, *Inside Goa*, *The Sea Hawk: Life and Battles of Kanhoji Angrey*, *Chhatrapatis of Kolhapur* and *Dropping Names*.

After retirement, Manohar Malgonkar settled on his farm at Barbusa near Belgaum.

An assassin for the world, Pandit Nathuram Vinayak Godse who was given capital punishment by the special court hearing the trial, is nothing less than a 'martyr' for his family and friends. A person completely devoted to his ideology and cause, he is still revered by people who see reason behind his killing of the Mahatma.